Domestic Violence and Abuse

Recent Titles in the
CONTEMPORARY WORLD ISSUES
Series

Abortion in the United States: A Reference Handbook, Second Edition
Dorothy E. McBride and Jennifer L. Keys

The Youth Unemployment Crisis: A Reference Handbook
Christine G. Villegas

Transgender: A Reference Handbook
Aaron Devor and Ardel Haefele-Thomas

Eating Disorders in America: A Reference Handbook
David E. Newton

Natural Disasters: A Reference Handbook
David E. Newton

Immigration Reform: A Reference Handbook
Michael C. LeMay

Vegetarianism and Veganism: A Reference Handbook
David E. Newton

The American Congress: A Reference Handbook
Sara L. Hagedorn and Michael C. LeMay

Disability: A Reference Handbook
Michael Rembis

Gender Inequality: A Reference Handbook
David E. Newton

Media, Journalism, and "Fake News": A Reference Handbook
Amy M. Damico

Birth Control: A Reference Handbook
David E. Newton

Bullying: A Reference Handbook
Jessie Klein

Books in the **Contemporary World Issues** series address vital issues in today's society such as genetic engineering, pollution, and biodiversity. Written by professional writers, scholars, and nonacademic experts, these books are authoritative, clearly written, up-to-date, and objective. They provide a good starting point for research by high school and college students, scholars, and general readers as well as by legislators, businesspeople, activists, and others.

Each book, carefully organized and easy to use, contains an overview of the subject, a detailed chronology, biographical sketches, facts and data and/or documents and other primary source material, a forum of authoritative perspective essays, annotated lists of print and nonprint resources, and an index.

Readers of books in the Contemporary World Issues series will find the information they need in order to have a better understanding of the social, political, environmental, and economic issues facing the world today.

Domestic Violence and Abuse

A REFERENCE HANDBOOK

Laura L. Finley

ABC-CLIO®

An Imprint of ABC-CLIO, LLC
Santa Barbara, California • Denver, Colorado

Copyright © 2020 by ABC-CLIO, LLC

Library of Congress Cataloging in Publication Control Number: 2019917125

ISBN: 978-1-4408-5883-3 (print)
        978-1-4408-5884-0 (ebook)

24 23 22 21 20   1 2 3 4 5

This book is also available as an eBook.

ABC-CLIO
An Imprint of ABC-CLIO, LLC

ABC-CLIO, LLC
147 Castilian Drive
Santa Barbara, California 93117
www.abc-clio.com

This book is printed on acid-free paper ∞

Manufactured in the United States of America

This book is dedicated to my amazing daughter, Anya Finley. Just fifteen at the time of this writing, Anya has been volunteering with domestic violence services since she was four. I am so very proud of this talented young woman and delighted to be her mother. I am also thrilled to be able to include her personal perspective in this book. As always, I dedicate any royalties of this volume to No More Tears for its continued invaluable services for victims of domestic violence.

Contents

Preface, xv

Acknowledgments, xix

1   **BACKGROUND AND HISTORY, 3**

A Global Overview, 3

Risk of Victimization, 10

Understanding Abusers, 14

Insights from Criminology Theory, 17

Effect on Victims, 19

Criminal Justice Interventions, 21

Services for Victims, 23

Prevention Programs, 25

History of Efforts to End Domestic Violence
in the United States, 26

Current Issues, 34

References, 40

2   PROBLEMS, CONTROVERSIES, AND SOLUTIONS, 51

Introduction, 51

Do Athletes Commit More Sexual Assault and
Domestic Violence? 51

Are Men Abused as Frequently as Women? 56

Which Groups Are Disproportionally Victimized
and Why? 58

What Happens When Abuse Occurs within
Progressive Groups or Organizations? 60

Should Domestic Violence Be Automatic Grounds
for Asylum or Refugee Status? 65

Should Children Be Removed from
Abusive Homes? 69

What Is the Connection between Pet Abuse
and Domestic Violence? 72

Is Arming Victims of Domestic Violence an
Appropriate Intervention to Stop Abuse? 74

Should Domestic Violence Offenders Be Allowed
to Own Firearms? 78

What Role Does Mass Media Play in Domestic
Violence? 80

Are Restraining Orders a Good Way to Protect
Victims? 83

Do Mandatory Arrest Policies in Domestic
Violence Cases Work? 86

Is a Feminist Perspective the Best Approach to
Domestic Violence Advocacy? 89

What Is the Role of Health-Care Professionals in
Domestic Violence Cases? 92

Is the Shelter Model of Domestic Violence Services the Best Way to Help Victims? 95

What Role Can Self-Defense Classes Play in Efforts to Prevent Sexual or Domestic Violence? 97

How Accurate Is Battered Woman Syndrome? 98

How Effective Are Batterer Intervention Programs? 100

References, 104

3   PERSPECTIVES, 117

Introduction, 117

Why I Am an Advocate against Domestic Violence in the Bahamas: We Must Continue to Strive
Camille Smith, 117

Moving On from Dating Violence
Amanda Pagano, 120

Rolling with the Punches
Amy Daumit, 123

Abuse from a Male Survivor's Perspective
Dustin LeBrun and Erin Moloney, 125

Why I Volunteer with Victims of Domestic Violence
Anya Finley, 128

Abuse Is Everywhere, But We Can Stop It
Somy Ali, 129

A Counselor's Perspective
Alison Morris, 139

How Abuse Can Turn You into Something You're Not and How to Reclaim Yourself
Rebecca Smith, 140

4   PROFILES, 147

People, 147

Jimmie Briggs, 147

Sarah Deer, 149

Salma Hayek, 150

Francine Hughes, 153

Jackson Katz, 155

Nicole Kidman, 156

Michael Kimmel, 159

Paul Kivel, 162

Nicholas Kristof and Sheryl WuDunn, 164

Erin Pizzey, 166

Tony Porter, 168

Lynn Rosenthal, 172

Susan Schechter, 174

Sir Patrick Stewart, 177

Murray Straus, 179

Lenore Walker, 181

Reese Witherspoon, 183

Organizations, 186

Avon Foundation for Women, 186

Break the Cycle, 189

Futures without Violence, 189

INCITE! Women, Gender Non-Conforming, and Trans People of Color against Violence, 192

National Network to End Domestic Violence (NNEDV), 194

NO MORE, 197

No More Tears, 200

Rape, Abuse, and Incest National Network (RAINN), 201

U.S. Department of Justice Office on Violence Against Women (OVW), 203

References, 206

5   DATA AND DOCUMENTS, 215

Data, 215

Table 5.1. Lifetime Prevalence of Contact Sexual Violence, Physical Violence, or Stalking Victimization by an Intimate Partner, 2015, 216

Figure 5.1. Lifetime Prevalence of Sexual Violence Victimization (Percentage), 2015, 217

Figure 5.2. Lifetime Prevalence of Psychological Aggression by an Intimate Partner, 2015, 217

Table 5.2. Violent Victimization Resulting in Injury and Medical Treatment, by Victim–Offender Relationship, 2003–2012, 218

Figure 5.3. Composition of Victim–Offender Relationships in Domestic Violence Victimizations, by Victim's Sex, 2003–2012, 219

Table 5.3. Rate of Violent Victimization, by Victim Characteristics and Victim–Offender Relationship, 2003–2012, 219

Documents, 220

The Jessica Gonzales Case (2011), 220

Reauthorization of the Violence Against Women Act (2013), 226

United Nations Convention on the Elimination of All Forms of Discrimination against Women (CEDAW) (1979), 234

United States v. Hayes (2009), 247

United States v. Castleman (2014), 250

Voisine v. United States (2016), 252

6   RESOURCES, 257

Reports, Studies, and Articles, 257

Journals and Magazines, 263

Books, 263

Curricula, Manuals, and Handbooks, 275

Documentaries, 278

Short Videos, 280

State and National Coalitions, 282

Organizations, 289

7   CHRONOLOGY, 315

Glossary, 333
Index, 341
About the Author, 349

Preface

Domestic violence is one of the world's worst human rights problems, affecting an estimated one-third of all women and between one-quarter and one-third of all women in the United States. It is a significant source of all violent crime and particularly violent crime against women. Abuse obviously affects victims and their families, but it also affects everyone in a society. Domestic violence costs the country billions annually, through direct costs such as medical bills and policing to less-direct costs such as lost productivity. Children who grow up in abusive homes are more likely to become abusers or victims as adults, perpetuating the cycle of abuse. Further, abuse in a dating relationship is the most common type of violence experienced by youth. At its worst, domestic violence is deadly, with an estimated 1,400 women and men in the United States killed each year by abusers. It is also one of the leading causes of death for police officers and it accounts for more than 50 percent of mass shootings in the United States.

Abuse of one's partner was legally allowable through much of human history, as women were considered possessions. Although activists attempted to draw attention to the issue as early as the 1800s, and Puritans in Massachusetts Bay and Plymouth actually did enact laws prohibiting spousal abuse, it wasn't until the Women's Rights Movement, or what is often called the second wave of feminism, that domestic violence became a topic of significant public attention. Women often had little choice but to stay with abusers since there was a dearth of resources, and police did not always respond. Several high-profile cases drew attention to the dangers of domestic violence in the 1970s and 1980s, helping to usher in certain reforms. Activists pushed for a better police response to domestic violence and for resources for victims.

Activists' efforts resulted in laws prohibiting abuse as well as the development of shelters and other help services for victims. Progress was not quick enough, however, as there was no federal legislation addressing domestic violence until the passage of the Violence Against Women Act in 1994, which has helped assist victims and train police to better respond to domestic violence calls. States enacted laws criminalizing abuse and providing for restraining orders or orders of protection, for example, but it was not until 1993 that the last state finally prohibited marital rape. Yet while abuse is taken more seriously than it has been in the past, much remains unknown about abuse, its impact, and how best to prevent it. Key questions are still unresolved in regard to who is an abuser and why, what are the primary risk factors for victimization, the dynamics of abusive relationships, and the most effective resources for victims. For instance, is it better to enact mandatory arrest policies, or is it better for victims to decide whether they want their abuser to be arrested? Should victims be able to sue abusers and sexual assailants? Is abuse of men as common as of women? Why are some groups of people, such as high-profile athletes, military, and police, overrepresented as batterers? Which approaches are best to help heal victims and to change the behavior of abusers? What works with child witnesses to break the cycle of abuse? Decades of attention has not eliminated the problem, which begs the question, why? This reference book, then, is intended to provide such a resource and to correct the many myths and misconceptions about abuse.

This book provides the most current and thorough review of various elements of domestic violence. It includes a useful chronology of important events and incidents related to abuse, a glossary of relevant definitions, an overview of the scope and extent of abuse, and data and documents highlighting specific facets of abuse. Material herein describes who is most likely to be a victim of domestic violence and why, the forms of abuse, statistics relevant to the frequency of abuse, offender characteristics, the unique characteristics of dating violence, how abuse affects children, the physical and behavioral effects of abuse, the costs of abuse to society at large, and what has and has not worked to date to curtail domestic violence. The book also presents the most relevant criminological theories designed to explain abuse. In addition, the book includes a review of the most pressing controversies in the field, including, but not limited to, the use of self-defense, removing guns from offenders, mandatory arrest policies, and whether athletes are more prone to commit domestic violence.

Likewise, included in this reference book are profiles of individuals and organizations that have played a significant role in understanding and addressing abuse. These include scholars, activists, and celebrities as well as national organizations and foundations that fund domestic violence work. Further, the book includes personal stories from domestic violence victims, advocates, and activists with an array of backgrounds. In addition, the book includes informative graphs and charts as well as several primary source documents. Finally, the book includes a list of useful resources, including books, websites, documentaries, and organizations.

In sum, this timely and important reference book is intended to help advocates, activists, students, educators, and policymakers better understand domestic violence and thus create more effective interventions.

Acknowledgments

I wish to thank Catherine Lafuente and Robin Tutt at ABC-CLIO for allowing me to write this book and for their invaluable assistance throughout the process. Special thanks to Robin for assisting with the data in Chapter 5 and to Catherine for connecting me to individuals who wrote perspectives in Chapter 3. Many thanks to all those who contributed important and thought-provoking perspectives. Camille Smith, Amanda Pagano, Amy Daumit, Rebecca Smith, Erin Moloney and Dustin LeBrun, and Anya Finley are a powerful group of survivors, advocates, and activists, many of whose stories of terror and triumph will leave readers inspired.

I'm also very grateful to Francesca Begala and my dear friend Matthew Johnson for research assistance and to my students at Barry University who contributed to this book as researchers. The following students assisted with this book:

> Erislandy Rives, Briana Noda, Brianna Mercado, Jailene Pulgaron, Maria Manzanares, Natalie Bertran, Christian Ruiz, Tyler Jackson, Dainely Fabregas, Kassandra Guererro, Craig Campbell, Tonya Turner, Gabrielle Estevez, Shania Rodrigues, Saeed Alderai, Genesys Cruz, Jasmine Wilder, Jarlyn Alvarez, Nicaury Lora, Hamad Alderai, Gabrielle Edwards, Princess Labissiere, Toenell Millwood, Kameera Rampersad, Alexandea Hunt, Nicholas Sanelli, Reinier Amarante, Stephan Doliska, Dominic Capron, Dayana Oliva, Jessenia Medina, and Samantha Baden.

Domestic Violence and Abuse

1 Background and History

A Global Overview

Domestic violence is one of the most pressing social issues, not just in the United States but also across the globe. Also referred to as intimate partner violence (IPV), according to the U.S. Department of Justice, domestic violence includes

> felony or misdemeanor crimes of violence committed by a current or former spouse or intimate partner of the victim, by a person with whom the victim shares a child in common, by a person who is cohabiting with or has cohabited with the victim as a spouse or intimate partner, by a person similarly situated to a spouse of the victim under the domestic or family violence laws of the jurisdiction receiving grant monies, or by any other person against an adult or youth victim who is protected from that person's acts under the domestic or family violence laws of the jurisdiction (USDOJ, 2018)

The National Coalition Against Domestic Violence (NCADV) defines it as "the willful intimidation, physical assault, battery, sexual assault, and/or other abusive behavior as part of a systematic pattern of power and control perpetrated by one intimate partner against another. It includes physical violence,

---

Argentinians protest gender violence in Buenos Aries on June 3, 2019. (Carol Smiljan/NurPhoto via Getty Images)

sexual violence, psychological violence, and emotional abuse. The frequency and severity of domestic violence can vary dramatically; however, the one constant component of domestic violence is one partner's consistent efforts to maintain power and control over the other" (NCADV, n.d.). A 2005 World Health Organization study involving interviews with 24,000 women in ten countries (Bangladesh, Brazil, Ethiopia, Japan, Namibia, Peru, Samoa, Serbia and Montenegro, Thailand, and the United Republic of Tanzania) found high rates of abuse, with 20 percent of women in Japan and more than 70 percent of women in rural parts of Ethiopia enduring some form of it. In sum, it estimated that 20–50 percent of the world's women endured some form of domestic violence. Similarly, a 2005 report by Amnesty International found that an estimated 70 percent of women in the Russian Federation had experienced abuse (Russia: One Woman an Hour Being Killed through Domestic Violence, 2005).

This type of abuse takes many forms, including verbal, emotional, financial, spiritual, physical, and sexual. While anyone can be the victim of domestic violence, there are certain demographic characteristics that make someone at greater risk for experiencing abuse. As Heise (1989) noted, "This is not random violence; the risk factor is being female" (p. 13). In the United States, it is estimated that 85 percent of victims are female. Scholars, activists, and advocates generally attribute this overrepresentation of women as victims to global gender inequality. Rates of domestic violence are highest in countries that are patriarchal, that is, male dominated and male identified. In fact, renowned feminist scholar bell hooks argues that the term "domestic" makes "abuse" sound like it is an intimate and private matter and recommends that it be renamed "patriarchal violence" (Heavner, 2017).

The oppression of women begins even before birth. In some countries, although they are illegal, sex-selective abortions are common. This is sometimes called "gendercide." An estimated 117 million girls are "missing" around the globe as a result of either abortions or being murdered as infants because female babies are undervalued. This is particularly a problem in Asia and is the result of a preference for sons and population restrictions. Gendercide is also very common in India and Pakistan. In their book *Half the Sky*, Nicholas Kristof and Sheryl WuDunn (2009) describe cases in which midwives are paid to snap the necks of infant girls and dispose of their bodies. Kristof and WuDunn (2009) note that more girls have been killed from abortion and infanticide in the past fifty years than all the men who have been killed on battlefields. Women globally suffer during childbirth due to inadequate prenatal care or, in some cases, none at all.

Research also shows that, around the globe, families are less likely to provide adequate medical care, vaccinations, and nutrition to girls and that they are more likely to be physically and emotionally abusive. Girls are more likely to be sexually victimized, by both family members and strangers, and are disproportionally victims of sex trafficking. Inadequate access to education limits females' opportunities, and procedures like female genital mutilation are dangerous and even deadly. It is estimated that every ten seconds, a female somewhere is enduring the painful process of circumcision (UNICEF, 2008). Women of reproductive age, and sometimes even younger, are forced into marriage and are vulnerable to marital rape, acid attacks, so-called honor killings, and dowry abuse. So-called honor attacks are most common in the Middle East and in South and Southeast Asia. It is estimated that some 5,000 women die in such killings each year, but because many are not reported or are reported as accidents, that number is likely a significant underestimate. Likewise, many women suffer serious injury and lifetime disfigurement when a loved one, often a boyfriend or a spouse or his family, throws acid on them. The first documented acid attack was in Bangladesh in 1967, and because this type of assault is also significantly underreported, it is unclear precisely how many acid attacks occur annually despite laws in some countries that prohibit buying or having certain acids.

In places where there is violent conflict or civil wars, rape is often used as a tool of control. For example, in Darfur, the Janjaweed militias gang-raped women and then mutilated them, often by cutting off their ears, to mark them as victims. Most women did not report the offense, and those who did were often punished for "fornication" because they had sex before marriage. To have any chance that the perpetrator would be convicted, the women were required to present four eyewitnesses, which was nearly impossible. Similar abuses were reported in Liberia, where an estimated 90 percent of girls over the age of three were sexually assaulted during that country's civil war, and in the Democratic Republic of the Congo, which was considered for some time to be the "rape capital" of the world. Kristof and WuDunn (2009) note that the militias "discovered that the most cost-effective way to terrorize civilian populations is to conduct rapes of stunning brutality. Frequently the Congolese militias rape women with sticks or knives or bayonets, or else they fire their guns into the women's vaginas" (p. 84). Many victims of such brutal rapes develop painful and sometimes deadly fistulas, or a tear in their bodies that leaves them leaking urine and feces. Kristof and WuDunn (2009) commented, "Mass rape is as effective as slaughtering people, yet it doesn't leave corpses that lead to human rights prosecutions. And rape tends to undermine the victim groups' tribal structures, because leaders lose authority when they can't protect the women. In short, rape becomes a tool of war in conservative societies precisely because female sexuality is so sacred. Codes of sexual honor, in which women are valued based on their chastity, ostensibly protect women, but in fact they create an environment in which women are systemically dishonored" (p. 83).

Gender wage gaps across the globe also make women less likely to be financially independent and, as such, more vulnerable to controlling abusers. According to Ariana Hegewisch and Heidi Hartmann of the Institute for Women's Policy Research (2019), in 2018, men earned almost eighteen percent more than women for the same work. This gap is even larger for women of color. The World Economic Forum (2018) concluded that in 2018 the world was on average only 68 percent toward gender parity. Victims often suffer from financial abuse and are controlled by abusers such that their work histories may be sporadic, at best, and their earning potential significantly affected (McLean & Bocinski, 2017). As such, victims of domestic violence are more likely to live in poverty and to be homeless.

A lack of representation of women in politics in most countries also means that males are typically making laws and enacting policies about women's bodies. Only thirty countries have gender quotas that specify a particular percentage of women that must be seated in parliament, typically 30 percent. The world average was 23.8 percent women in parliaments as of September 2018 (Radu, 2018).

Although women are in danger of abuse and assault across the globe, some places are worse than others. In 2018, the Thompson Reuters Foundation surveyed 550 experts on women's issues and determined that India is the most dangerous country in the world in which to be a woman. This is due to the sexual violence, sexual and human trafficking, domestic forced labor, forced marriage and child marriage, physical violence, acid attacks, and female genital mutilation. At number ten on the list of most dangerous countries was the United States, the only Western country to be included. This ranking was largely attributed to the attention paid by the #MeToo movement to the prevalence of sexual harassment and assault in the United States (Dewan, 2018).

In the most severe cases, domestic violence can be deadly. Global research has found that an estimated 40–70 percent of the homicides of women are the result of domestic violence. In Russia, nearly one woman per hour is killed by an abuser (Russia: One Woman an Hour Being Killed through Domestic Violence, 2005). In South Africa, a woman is killed every six hours by a husband or boyfriend (Amnesty International, 2005).

In Guatemala, two women are murdered each day by current or former partners. In Europe, domestic violence causes more deaths than cancer and traffic accidents combined (Chemaly, 2012). A 2018 UN study found that, across the globe, home is the most deadly place for a woman. On average, 137 women are killed every day by a partner or family member. Females are far more likely than are males to be killed by someone close to them, although overall homicide rates for males remain higher. This is because men's violence is against both men and women. The study also found that women in Africa are at greatest risk (BBC, 2018). In the United States, an estimated 1,300–1,400 people are killed annually by abusers. Far more Americans—generally women—have been killed by their partners than in the wars in Iraq and Afghanistan combined. American women are twice as likely to suffer from domestic violence as from breast cancer (Chemaly, 2012). In all, domestic violence kills more women worldwide than civil wars (Parker, 2014).

Over time, advocates and researchers have identified a list of characteristics that tend to predict lethality in a domestic violence situation. Research has found, for instance, that women were ten times more likely to be killed by an abuser if he had previously choked them. The Johns Hopkins School of Nursing prepared a checklist of sixteen questions to assess lethality. It is designed to help police officers and domestic violence shelter staff determine how dangerous a given case may be. The checklist is used in Ohio and Maryland, where authorities say that fatalities dropped 30 percent as a result. The questions include the following:

1. Has he/she ever used a weapon against you/threatened you with a weapon?
2. Has he/she ever threatened to kill you or your children?
3. Do you think he/she might try to kill you?
4. Does he/she have a gun or can he/she get one easily?

5. Has he/she ever tried to choke you?

6. Is he/she violent or constantly jealous or does he/she control most of your daily activities?

7. Does he/she follow or spy on you or leave threatening messages?

8. Have you left him/her or separated after living together or being married?

9. Is he/she unemployed?

10. Has he/she ever tried to kill himself/herself?

11. Do you have a child/children together?

12. Do you have a child that he/she knows is not his/hers?

13. Has he/she been physical toward the child(ren) in a way that concerns you?

14. Does he/she have an alcohol/substance abuse problem?

15. Has he/she interfered with a 911 call?

16. Is there anything else that worries you about your safety? (CBS News, 2014)

The Battered Women's Justice Project has also developed a checklist for lethality, and Jacqueline Campbell of Johns Hopkins University was a leader in developing the Danger Assessment, a tool for assessing lethality. Interestingly, studies have shown that the decrease in domestic violence homicides has been greater for males than for females (Campbell, 2005). One factor that has repeatedly been shown to increase the risk of serious injury or fatality is the presence of a firearm in a domestic violence situation. The American Judge's Association states, "If the abuser has access to a firearm, it is far more likely that homicide will indeed be the result. Research shows that family and intimate partner assaults involving firearms are 12 times more likely to result in death than those that do not involve firearms. Approximately two-thirds of the intimate partner homicides in this country are committed using guns" (Faith Trust

Institute, 2013). More than half of female domestic violence homicide victims are killed by a firearm.

Risk of Victimization

Although gender is the primary risk factor for experiencing abuse, other demographic characteristics increase the likelihood that someone will be a victim. Rates of abuse are similar in same-sex relationships, and it is often more severe, especially for gay men and bisexual women (HRC Staff, 2017). Lesbian, Gay, Bisexual, Transgender, and Queer (LGBTQ) victims face additional barriers in getting free from abusers, as they may not be "out" to their family, friends, or coworkers and police often do not respond appropriately to domestic violence calls involving LGBTQ individuals (HRC Staff, 2017).

Women of color, and especially Native American women, are at greater risk than are Caucasian women, and women of lower socioeconomic status are overrepresented as well. Black women are almost three times more likely to be killed by an abuser, and while they are only 8 percent of the population, they are 29 percent of those who are victimized. Domestic violence is one of the leading causes of death for black women aged eighteen to thirty-five (Jones, 2014). According to a Department of Justice study in 2010, 55.5 percent of American Indian and Alaska Native women had experienced physical abuse by a partner, 48.8 percent had been stalked, 66.4 percent had experienced psychological abuse, and 56.1 percent had experienced sexual violence (Rosay, 2010).

Immigrants are also uniquely vulnerable, although data does not show a particular country or region of origin that is the most represented. These victims face many challenges getting free from abusers, as many know limited, if any, English, are not familiar with resources to help, and lack support systems. Many distrust police and fear deportation, especially in the anti-immigrant climate that has been a hallmark of the presidential administration of Donald Trump in the United States.

Pregnant women also suffer from abuse, especially if the woman is young and the pregnancy is unintended. Often abusers force victims into sexual contact. A 2010 study of fifty-three women at four domestic violence shelters showed that 66 percent of them were forced into sexual intercourse by the perpetrator (de Bocanegra, Rpstovtseva, Khera, & Godhwani, 2010). In addition to outright sexual assault, victims often feel pressure to acquiesce to their partner's advances, fearing that saying "no" will result in further violence to themselves or their children. This may result in unintended pregnancies. Further, abusers often control victims' reproductive choices. This has been referred to as reproductive control or reproductive coercion. Abusers may prohibit victims from using contraceptives or sabotage them. As a result, there is a significant correlation between domestic violence and abortion (Cote & Lapierre, 2014).

Teens experience dating violence at rates even higher than those for domestic violence, and abuse in a dating relationship is the most common form of violence experienced by youth in the United States. According to the nonprofit organization Love Is Respect (2017), 1.5 million teens experience physical abuse from a dating partner annually, and one-third of teen-dating relationships are abusive. College students are particularly vulnerable to dating violence, with an estimated 43 percent of college women experiencing some form of abuse by a dating partner.

Elder abuse is a significant problem as well, by both partners and caregivers. According to the World Health Organization (2018), one in six people aged sixty or above experienced some form of abuse in the previous year. Vulnerable persons, such as those with mental and physical disabilities, are disproportionately victimized, too.

Children are often considered the silent victims, as they may see and hear the abuse or otherwise be aware that it is happening. More than fifteen million children in the United States grow up in homes where there is abuse. In about half of domestic violence cases, child abuse is also occurring. Studies have shown that 60 percent of children in the United States experience one or more adverse child experiences, resulting in trauma and both short- and long-term consequences. According to the Office on Women's Health, preschool-aged children may exhibit behavioral regressions, such as bed-wetting, thumb-sucking, increased crying, and whining. They may also have difficulty falling or staying asleep and show signs of terror, such as stuttering or hiding, as well as exhibit severe separation anxiety. School-aged children often struggle academically and may miss more days than children from homes without abuse. They tend to have fewer friends and to get into trouble more. Teens often act out, including getting involved in fights and skipping school. They are also at increased risk for engaging in other dangerous behaviors, such as using drugs and alcohol and having unprotected sex. Teens who witness abuse are more likely to get into legal trouble, especially boys. Girls are more likely to suffer from depression and to engage in self-cutting and have eating disorders. In the long term, child witnesses are more likely to continue the cycle of abuse, as either abusers or victims. They experience a host of mental and physical health issues at greater rates than those who did not grow up with abuse, including depression, anxiety, diabetes, obesity, and heart disease (Effects of Domestic Violence on Children, 2019).

Although it seems counterintuitive, in many places around the globe, women believe that domestic violence is acceptable. For instance, a study of women in a village in India found 62 percent pledging support for abuse (Kristof & WuDunn, 2009). This was also generally true in the United States until the 1960s, when attitudes began to shift. Yet there are still many myths and misconceptions about abuse that undermine efforts to curtail it and to effectively assist victims and hold batterers accountable. Studies in the 1990s found that the public holds vastly different definitions and understandings of what constitutes domestic violence (Johnson, Sigler, & Crowley, 1994; Klein & Tobin, 1997). Johnson and Sigler (2000) followed a cohort of Alabama residents from 1986 to 1997 to see if their beliefs about abuse changed. While they found that by the end of the study most respondents deemed all physical acts of violence as abuse, some 20 percent still believed that an occasional hitting with a belt or stick was acceptable. Other studies are mixed in terms of acceptance of abuse. Stark and McEvoy (1970) found that only 20 percent of those polled approved of a man slapping his spouse, while Whitehurst (1971, in Dibble & Straus, 1980) found that 62 percent of male college students and businessmen believed that "sometimes" spousal violence is appropriate, such as in response to an extramarital affair. Dibble and Straus (1980), using data from the 1975 national survey regarding family violence, found that 28 percent of their respondents agreed that slapping a spouse was "necessary," "normal," or "good." Sigler (1989) found that 11 percent of respondents still believed that hitting a spouse was only sometimes wrong. In the earlier studies, respondents tended to attribute abuse to stress and the abuser's personality (Davis & Carlson, 1981). While many studies find that the public doesn't necessarily blame women for being victimized, people do believe that women should be accountable for leaving abusers (Davis & Carlson, 1981; Ewing & Aubrey, 1987; Kalmuss, 1979).

A December 2002 study funded by the National Institute of Justice involving telephone interviews with 1,200 adults in six locations across New York State found that older respondents were less likely to deem physical assaults as domestic violence, while women and those who knew victims were more likely to use inclusive definitions of abuse. The most frequent response as to why abuse occurs was that it is the result of work or financial stress (37 percent). Twenty-five percent of respondents believed that women secretly want to be abused, and another 20 percent were unsure about whether that is true. A very high percentage, 63 percent, believed that women could find a way to leave an abusive relationship if they really want to, suggesting that most of the public underestimates the complexity of abusive situations and the serious challenges to leaving abusers.

Outside the United States, as of February 2018, more than 1 billion women live in countries that still do not have laws prohibiting domestic sexual violence, and some 1.4 billion have no protection against domestic economic violence. The latter involves controlling a woman's access to money, education, or employment as a form of control. While 76 percent of the 141 countries included in the World Bank's study have some type of prohibition against domestic violence in general, specific forms may still be allowable by law. Two-thirds of countries do not extend domestic violence protections to unmarried couples (The World Bank, 2018). China enacted its first domestic violence law in 2016 and Kyrgyzstan in 2017, for instance. In contrast, some countries have created very progressive domestic violence laws in recent years. For example, a New Zealand law created in 2018 allows victims to have ten paid days off of work and requires that employers offer victims flexible work schedules and other supports (Erickson, 2018).

Understanding Abusers

Although there is a growing body of literature that helps understand victim characteristics and behaviors, data is far less expansive when it comes to understanding the behavior of abusers. There do seem to be several important risk factors for batterers, however. According to the CDC (2018a), there are individual, relationship, community, and societal factors. Individual risk factors include low self-esteem, low income, low verbal IQ, low academic achievement, young age, aggressive or delinquent behavior as a youth, heavy alcohol and drug use, depression and suicidal ideation, anger and hostility, lack of nonviolent problem-solving skills, antisocial personality traits and conduct problems, poor behavioral control/impulsiveness, borderline personality traits, prior history of being physically abusive, having few friends and being isolated from people, unemployment, emotional dependence and insecurity, belief in strict gender roles, desire for power and control in relationships, hostility toward women, attitudes accepting of IPV, being a victim of physical or psychological abuse, witnessing abuse as a child, experiencing poor parenting as a child, being physically disciplined as a child, and unplanned pregnancies. Relationship factors include marital conflict, jealousy and possessiveness, marital instability (separation and divorce), dominance and control of the relationship by one partner, economic stress, unhealthy family relationships and interactions, association with antisocial and aggressive peers, parents with less than a high school education, and social isolation or lack of social support. At the community level, risk factors include poverty and associated factors (i.e., unemployment, homelessness), low social capital (lack of positive institutions and relationships), poor neighborhood support and cohesion, weak community sanctions against IPV, and high alcohol outlet density. Finally, societal risk factors include traditional gender norms and gender inequality; cultural norms that support aggression toward others; societal income inequality; and weak health, educational, economic, and social policies or laws. Other studies have found additional risk factors for abuse. Pet abuse has been found to be a significant predictor of domestic violence, and batterers who abuse animals have been found to be more physically violent than those who do not (Animal Legal Defense Fund, n.d.). A 2017 study showed that 89 percent of women who had companion animals during an abusive relationship reported that their animals were threatened, harmed, or killed by their abusive partner (Animal Legal Defense Fund, n.d.).

There is also some data to indicate that certain groups of men are overrepresented as abusers. Athletes in certain sports, current and former military members, fraternity members, and police are all more often accused of domestic violence than are males who are not in these groups. It is important to note, however, that these individuals are not necessarily more likely to be convicted of abuse, which may mean they are falsely accused in some cases. It could also mean that they are given leniency by various social institutions such that they may have perpetrated abuse but not be held accountable for it.

Jeff Benedict is one of the leading scholars on domestic violence and athletes. He has written several books focused on college athletes and professional basketball and football players. High-profile incidents involving athletes lend credence to the claim that there is something about the male social bonding, the encouragement of aggression, and the societal power and influence these individuals have that may make them more prone to committing abuse. One of the first of such incidents was in 1994, when former NFL superstar O. J. Simpson was accused of murdering his former wife, Nicole Brown, and her friend, Ronald Goldman. Throughout the investigation and subsequent trial, it was revealed that Nicole had called 911 several times for domestic violence. Simpson was eventually acquitted of the murders. On February 14, 2014, TMZ released a video showing NFL player Ray Rice of the Baltimore Ravens punching his fiancée in an elevator. Rice was suspended for two games and indicted for aggravated assault. He accepted a plea deal to attend a pretrial intervention program. The incident did prompt the NFL to adopt new policies about domestic violence, including training and education requirements.

Military members may be more prone to abuse because of the hypermasculine bonding and aggression that is encouraged. Another factor, however, and one that may also be true of athletes, is brain injuries. Traumatic brain injury is caused by external physical force to the brain, typically due to particularly violent or repeated blows to the head. In addition, many veterans suffer from post-traumatic stress disorder (PTSD), which has also been identified as a risk factor for abuse.

Jackson Katz, Michael Kimmel, Jeff Benedict, and others have noted that fraternities and collegiate athletes are likely overrepresented as sexual assailants and abusers due to the propensity in these groups to engage in misogynistic talk, the frequent presence of alcohol at social events, and their understanding of how to "do" gender.

Yet it is important to note that males are also victims of abuse. Data on the frequency that males are victimized by females is somewhat mixed. Many assert that female self-defense is mistaken for aggression, thus inflating the number of female abusers. What is also clear is that while abuse in general is underreported, males are even less likely to report domestic violence than are females. Female abusers use many of the same tactics as do males but also some that tend to be different. The most common type involves simple assault and the throwing of objects, with weapons' use quite rare for female abusers.

Insights from Criminology Theory

Criminological theory has been applied to explain domestic violence, although there remains no one theory that is the perfect "fit." Some theories focus on biological, genetic, or personality factors. Some assert that abusers tend to have personalities similar to borderline personality disorder, which includes specific characteristics like a tendency to blame others, shame-based rage, attachment anxiety, and sustained outbursts. Some studies have also documented that males with more testosterone commit more acts of violence, in general, so this may be, in part, a cause of abuse. Psychological approaches also point to antisocial personality disorder and narcissistic personality disorder, while still others point attachment disorders as children as a significant factor (Arabi, 2018). Yet there are many concerns about these theories, including the methods used to identify a personality disorder and a lack of clear link to abusive behavior. Domestic violence advocates have been critical of explanations that focus on personality or mental health, as they believe that absolves abusers from taking accountability for their actions.

Other theories are more focused on choice. That is, they assert that individuals make the decision to abuse their partners. According to such theories, often referred to as rational choice or neoclassical, individuals are rational thinkers who weigh out the costs and benefits of committing acts of crime or violence. As such, individuals can supposedly be deterred from committing abuse if the sanctions they will face are harsh enough that they will make a different choice. Most domestic violence advocates emphasize that batterers choose to perpetrate abuse as a way of obtaining and maintaining power and control over victims. They note that, historically and even currently, the chance that an abuser will be arrested, convicted, and punished is pretty slim; thus, they have no incentive to choose different behaviors. Research shows that less than 2 percent of perpetrators ever spend time in jail or prison (Hamby, 2014). Yet still these theories fail to consider what motivates someone in the first place, and they do not do much to address the social and cultural factors that are important to explaining abuse.

Sociological theories emphasize that cultural norms and characteristics shape the likelihood that someone will be an abuser. Such theories focus on family, neighborhood, and societal factors to explain crime in general, although they were not historically applied to domestic violence. A growing body of literature, such as the Adverse Child Experiences Studies, is documenting that family, community, and school exposure to various forms of violence puts people at risk for several forms of delinquent or criminal behavior. Such sociological theories also note the important influence of media depictions of abuse that may normalize it and make it seem acceptable, if not even glamorous. For instance, the popular book and film series *Twilight*, by Stephenie Meyers, features what many see as an abusive relationship that is heavily romanticized. Similarly, the blockbuster *50 Shades of Grey* series focuses on what can only be described as an abusive relationship but makes it seem as though it is sexy. Scholar and media critic Jean Kilbourne has shown how advertisements have long glorified abuse to move products.

Feminist theories, which emerged in the later 1960s, were some of the first to specifically address domestic violence and spawned a wave of theorizing about how abusers learn and are encouraged to commit violence against partners. Most of these emphasize gender role norms and patriarchy. According to scholars like R. W. Connell (1987), men in the United States are often taught that they must behave in a very rigid, hypermasculine fashion, what she calls hegemonic masculinity. Others refer to this narrow definition of gender role norms as "toxic masculinity." Studies have found a significant association between adherence to hegemonic masculinity and frequency of abuse (Lisco, Leone, Gallagher, & Parrott, 2015). Much work remains, however, in terms of isolating those factors that best explain abuse and in crafting appropriate remedies.

Understanding the dynamics of abuse and the barriers victims face in leaving abusers can also be helpful in creating effective reduction strategies. Historical research shows that people used to connect staying with an abuser to lack of intelligence, which has since been obviously debunked. Many also felt that alcohol use was the problem, so activists involved with the Temperance Movement asserted that if men just stopped drinking alcohol they would not be abusive. In the 1930s and 1940s, most explanations emphasized the alleged masochism of victims. In more recent times, however, more complex explanations related to the many barriers victims face when trying to leave abusers have emerged. Among the most important is the fact that victims fear for their safety when leaving. This fear is very legitimate, given that 75 percent of domestic violence homicides occur as the victim is trying to leave the relationship. Concerns about children, love for abusers, lack of support systems, poor advice from faith leaders, and many more factors make it challenging for victims to leave.

Effect on Victims

Also essential is to understand the short- and long-term effects of abuse—on victims and their families and as a cost to society. Victims suffer a host of mental and physical consequences, including, but not limited to, increased risk of depression, ulcers, hypertension, skin disorders, chronic fatigue, back ailments, migraines, reproductive problems, reduced self-esteem, substance abuse issues, and PTSD. Because they do not necessarily want their abuse to be identified or to disclose that it is occurring, many victims delay or refuse to seek treatment for other medical issues like asthma and diabetes. Because victims may not tell others about the abuse, most major medical bodies recommend that physicians screen all patients for possible abuse. Asking screening questions can result in either a disclosure or the identification of probable abuse and can therefore put victims into contact with needed resources (Morse, Lafleur, Fogarty, Mittal, & Cerulli, 2012).

Family members also suffer from seeing loved ones deal with abuse and not knowing what to do to help. In extreme cases, family members and even coworkers and friends are harmed or killed by abusers. In the United States, domestic violence is the number one source of mass shootings. Shooters killed a partner or family member in 54 percent of shootings in which four or more people were killed between January 2009 and December 2016, with 40 percent of the fatalities being children (Zarya, 2017). The costs to society are difficult to tabulate, but efforts have been made to assess the way domestic violence directly and indirectly harms everyone. Domestic violence is the most common cause of injury for women aged fifteen to forty-four in the United States. As such, victims use emergency health-care services far more frequently—eight times—than do nonvictims (Bonomi, Anderson, Rivara, & Thompson, 2009). Women who have been abused may suffer from a variety of health consequences. They are 70 percent more likely to have heart disease, 80 percent more likely to have a stroke, and 60 percent more likely to develop asthma during their lifetime. They are three times more likely to suffer from depression, are four times more likely to commit suicide, and suffer from PTSD at six times the rate of nonvictims. Women experiencing physical abuse are also three times more likely to report having a sexually transmitted infection than nonabused women (Chelala, 2016). The CDC (Centers for Disease Control and Prevention) has estimated that the average cost per female victim is $103,767 and per male victim is $23,414 and that the total economic cost in the United States exceeds $3.6 trillion (CDC, 2018b). Studies have found that these are not just short-term costs; rather, the increased health-care costs for victims can persist for as long as fifteen years after the abuse (Pearl, 2013). Further, according to a 2005 survey, some 64 percent of domestic violence victims say the abuse has impacted their work. It is estimated that victims lose eight million paid days of work annually. Homicide by an intimate partner is the second leading cause of death for women in the workplace (Chemaly, 2012).

Criminal Justice Interventions

Since the 1970s, criminal justice interventions for domestic violence have been among the most frequently proposed and implemented. Women's rights activists were critical of the lack of response by police and prosecutors and so made enhancing legislation and its enforcement a top priority. A major shift in practice occurred in the mid-1980s as a result of a study called the Minneapolis Domestic Violence Experiment (MDVE). It was the first scientific, controlled study assessing the effects of arrest on domestic violence. During an eighteen-month period in 1981–1982, researchers Lawrence Sherman and Richard Berk tested three different practices by the Minneapolis Police Departments—arrest, separation, and mediation—to see which would be most effective and reducing repeat episodes. Sherman and Berk found that arrest was most effective at reducing repeat incidents of abuse, ushering in an era in which many police agencies began introducing mandatory arrest policies for domestic violence. While mandatory arrest was initially applauded, many limitations have emerged over time, and in fact the results of MDVE have never been replicated. Critics note that mandatory arrest often results in

victims being arrested alongside abusers and can be disempowering to victims who perhaps prefer for various reasons
that their abuser not be involved with the criminal justice system. Studies with police have found that many believe they
should be allowed greater discretion in domestic violence cases
(Blount, Yegfidis, & Maheux, 1992; Sinden & Stephens, 1999;
Toon & Hart, 2005).

The courts have not always been understanding of the dynamics of abuse. One of the biggest problems is that prosecutors fail to bring charges. Some research says that fewer than
10 percent of arrests result in prosecution. Although not advised, police and prosecutors still ask victims if they want to
press charges. Many say "no," as they fear retaliation or do not
want that kind of involvement with the system. Because of
these challenges, some advocate no-drop policies for domestic
violence. No-drop policies, in general, deny victims the right to
withdraw complaints after charges have been filed. The idea is
that if there is enough evidence, which might include reports,
medical records, interviews with witnesses, and photos, victims
do not need to participate in the court. Research has shown that
convictions reduce domestic violence recidivism (Ventura &
Davis, 2005).

Restraining orders or orders of protection are also recommended criminal justice interventions, albeit not without limitations. All fifty states allow protection orders, but the process
is intimidating and not foolproof. Many protection orders are
violated without legal consequence, and in some cases, obtaining a restraining order actually exacerbates the abuse. The
Supreme Court has also issued a judgment that enforcement
of a restraining order is not constitutionally required. Jessica
Gonzales obtained a temporary restraining order in 1999 that
restricted her husband, Simon, from coming to their home and
required that he be at least 100 yards from it at all times. When
Simon continued to harass Jessica and their three daughters,
she appeared before the court and had the temporary restraining order made permanent on June 4, 1999. Yet, less than three

weeks later, Simon took the girls without permission, and over the next ten hours, Jessica contacted the Castle Rock police multiple times, to no avail. In the wee hours of the morning, Simon drove his vehicle to the police station and opened fire. Officers returned fire, leaving Simon dead. The three girls were also found dead in the vehicle, although it was unclear whether Simon killed them or if it was the crossfire that resulted in their deaths. Jessica filed suit against the Castle Rock police for negligence of their duty, and eventually the case was heard before the Supreme Court. In 2005 the Court ruled that Colorado law specified that officers "should" but not "must" enforce restraining orders, essentially invalidating the power of this tool for victims. Jessica continued to work with counsel and appeared with them before the Inter-American Commission on Human Rights (IACHR), which in 2011 determined that the failure to enforce the restraining order was a violation of her human rights. In its report to the United States, the IACHR denounced the United States for inadequate training of police and policies to keep victims safe.

Services for Victims

Other efforts have focused on more inclusive measures that address not only accountability for abusers but also services for victims. One of the most significant efforts in this area was the passage of the Violence Against Women Act (VAWA), initially in 1994 and then reauthorized several times. Championed by then Senator Joe Biden, it was first signed into law by President Bill Clinton as part of an omnibus crime bill. VAWA was the first federal legislation to address domestic violence, sexual assault, and stalking. Despite the name, VAWA provisions also apply to male victims. VAWA created the federal Office on Violence Against Women, which is housed in the Department of Justice and administers grants to cities, municipalities, and organizations working to end domestic violence. The 2000 reauthorization of VAWA created additional legal services for victims and expanded coverage to victims of dating violence and stalking. It also provided special visa protections for victims of sexual trafficking. The 2005 reauthorization improved protections for immigrant victims, addressed unfair evictions for victims, and authorized funding for linguistically and culturally appropriate services for victims. American Indian victims were also included for the first time in the 2013 reauthorization. Yet VAWA is not without its critics. Some have expressed concern that it lacks a civil remedy for victims, which was initially part of the legislation but was declared unconstitutional. Others note that the wording of who can be victimized creates a "boyfriend" loophole, exempting many abusers from accountability.

Since the 1970s, the creation of domestic violence shelters has been another preferred alternative for helping victims. Yet still there is not nearly enough space to accommodate the need, in the United States as well as outside of it. Some 10–40 percent of people seeking help from a domestic violence shelter are turned away, largely because the space is full but also because these shelters do not provide all the services that victims need. Some research suggests that for every victim who calls a crisis line or enters a shelter, ten others are enduring similar situations without seeking that help. Shelters also tend to operate on very restrictive budgets and within a bureaucratic list of services that is increasingly required by funders. This has become a concern among advocates and activists, who believe that such restrictions result in limited assistance, "red tape" for victims to navigate, and a lack of wholistic responses that would fully allow victims to achieve safety and independence. As such, some groups like INCITE! have disavowed nonprofit status in order to retain a more grassroots, community approach to abuse.

Many individuals who are profiled in this book have played an important role in raising awareness about abuse and creating programs to address it. Scholars like Lenore Walker, Jeff Benedict, and Jackson Katz have provided strong academic foundations, while activists like Eve Ensler and Gloria Steinem, along with many celebrities, have elevated such platforms. Politicians like Joe Biden and Hillary Clinton have made gender equality, in general, and domestic violence, specifically, part of their platforms. Likewise, grassroots activists and small non-profit groups have played a significant role in raising awareness about abuse and lobbying for new policies and laws. Among the many of these are foundations like Avon and Mary Kay, as well as organizations like the NCADV, the National Network to End Domestic Violence (NNEDV), Break the Cycle, Futures without Violence, and Love Is Not Abuse.

Prevention Programs

Prevention programs, relatively new in the United States, have shown promise to change attitudes and beliefs about domestic and dating violence. Generally, prevention efforts are divided into three types. Primary prevention refers to efforts to prevent a phenomenon from ever occurring. Secondary prevention seeks to disrupt incidents before the abuse escalates, while tertiary efforts focus on assisting those who have been abused. Many primary prevention programs are aimed at bystanders, as in most cases, at least one person will see or hear something, and if those individuals are equipped to disrupt the situation, it can prevent an incident. Many great organizations have created primary prevention initiatives and curricula, including Mentors in Violence Prevention, the Safe Dates curriculum, and Prevention Institute.

Several school-based curricula have been developed to prevent dating violence. A program called Safe Dates involves both school and community components. The school program involves a ten-week curriculum, a theater production performed by peers, and a poster contest. Training for service providers involved with crisis lines, support groups, and resources for parents are included in the community portion. Safe Dates is intended to change norms related to partner violence, reduce gender role stereotyping, and improve conflict management skills. The wider school and community components are intended to change beliefs about the need for help, educate youth about available resources, and encourage help-seeking behavior. One evaluation of Safe Dates conducted in rural North Carolina found that participants reported significantly less psychological abuse perpetration and violence perpetration compared to those in a control group. A follow-up found 25 percent less psychological abuse perpetration, 60 percent less sexual abuse perpetration, and 60 percent violence perpetration against a current dating partner. No significant change was found in help-seeking behavior (Foshee, Bauman, Arriaga, Helms, Koch, & Linder, 1998).

History of Efforts to End Domestic Violence in the United States

Although it was clearly prevalent, little has been written about domestic violence before the 1970s. Yet a review of legislation and other documents shows that abuse was common and, in most cases, perfectly legal, until the 1970s. Further, laws and practices favored men in every realm. The first laws on marriage, formulated by Romulus of Rome, specified that men owned their wives as possessions and that women were to obey them at all times. In 300 BC, Constantine the Great, emperor of Rome, had his wife burned to death because he decided she was of no use to him. He did so with impunity. Women in medieval Europe were considered inferior to men, even subhuman, and the Roman Catholic Church allowed husbands to beat their wives if they needed "correction." Many documents even referred to beating wives as chivalrous behavior.

Historian Elizabeth Pleck (1987) has written that there were two surges of reform prior to the battered women's movement: one between 1640 and 1680 in colonial Massachusetts and another in larger urban areas between 1874 and 1890. Puritans in Massachusetts Bay enacted the first law prohibiting spousal abuse in the American colonies in 1641. The final push started in 1962 and led to the battered women's movement of the 1970s. The early efforts were generally squashed due to the prevalence of stereotypical notions about the ideal family and women's subservience, men's superiority, and keeping affairs private. Until the second wave of feminist activism, there was little accountability for abusers because there were few laws and little political will to address family affairs. Laws supported men's right to control and discipline their wives, as in the now-infamous "rule of thumb" that allowed a man to beat his wife with an object no larger than that width (Gordon, 1988). Some argue that law never actually existed, but the concept did indeed. That said, most communities did have laws that limited the violence against wives and children (Pleck, 1987). Divorce was strongly discouraged, and no shelters or orphanages existed, so Puritans thought that, when the situation was acute, public shaming could correct it. The Temperance Movement of the 1800s did draw attention to domestic violence, although it emphasized prohibiting alcohol as the solution.

The early nineteenth century saw no significant reforms in terms of family violence, and women were pretty solidly resigned to the private spheres. Women's magazines and advice manuals told women the home was where they belonged, and men were to control social, political, and economic matters. These thoughts, however, were largely about white women. In the mid-century, a movement began to carve out a more public space for women, although again largely for white women. Elizabeth Cady Stanton, Susan B. Anthony, and others who are considered part of the first wave of feminism spoke out about the cultural norms that condoned abuse. Yet while they did so, many came from a context of women's moralism and maternalism; thus, much of the anti-domestic violence efforts were tied with some of the conservative Temperance Movement.

The time period between 1874 and 1890 saw another wave of concern about domestic violence and, even more so, child abuse. Many women helped organize various social service agencies and advocated for changes like the juvenile justice system. The Society for the Prevention of Cruelty to Children was formed, yet no specific domestic violence shelters were available.

The twentieth century built on the previous Progressive Era's emphasis on state protection. Freudian psychology, however, emphasized that women were hysterical, which reinforced women's inferiority and tended to see domestic violence as a function of mental illness or deficiency. As the Great Depression waned in the 1930s, many disregarded abuse, attributing it to men's unemployment and struggle to deal with hardship as breadwinners (Gordon, 1988).

Pleck (1987) maintains that it was the publication of an article by five physicians in the *Journal of the American Medical Association* about "Battered Women's Syndrome" in 1962 that was the catalyst for the Battered Women's Movement that coincided with the second wave of feminist activism. Feminist-consciousness-raising circles starting in 1970 brought much-needed attention to the issue, along with a critique of the separate sphere.

This second wave of feminism grappled with the cult of domesticity, with more radical feminists rejecting it nearly completely and more conservatives believing there was still a place for gender differences as long as women had equal opportunity. Prior to the 1970s, theoretical explanations of domestic violence saw it as being the result of relationship dysfunction caused by defective personalities. Such a view blamed women and privatized abuse. Feminists in the 1970s struggled with the degree to which the law should be involved in domestic violence cases. Liberal feminists felt that partnering with the state was essential to keep women safe, while radical feminists believed that the "male" state was simply replacing one form of male control with another oppressor (Schechter, 1980). Radical feminists emphasized consciousness raising. The idea behind it was that women were also raised in a society where men dominated and thus were not truly aware of the ways that were oppressed, because they took this behavior as normal. The idea was that what women "know" is from a male perspective that is presented as truth, thereby prohibiting women from identifying male violence as a tool for reinforcing male domination and societal patriarchy (Houston, 2014). Consciousness raising, then, involved opportunities for women to listen to one another and for lived experiences with male violence to be shared.

Eventually, the liberal side prevailed in debates about how to handle domestic violence, and the emphasis was on ensuring better police response to domestic violence (Stansell, 2010). Even more contentious was support for mandatory criminal intervention, a debate that continues to resonate today. Some feminists, for instance, argue that such intervention can do more harm than good, especially for poor women and women of color (Coker, 2000). The contemporary domestic violence movement has, in many ways, given up a good portion of its feminist principles or, least, followed a liberal feminist emphasis on legal and political rights rather than broader societal change. Both the criminal justice approach and the shelter model are often not feminist or at least not in a critical sense. Many critical feminists today seek to reclaim the radical emphasis.

Lawsuits against police in the 1970s and 1980s resulted in changes in how police responded in domestic violence cases. *Scott v. Hart* (1979) required police to respond to domestic violence cases and to receive additional training on the issue. Despite these battles, movement did occur. Haven House in Pasadena, California, was the first shelter to receive government funding in 1972. Shelters like this and the others that followed in the era were modeled as homes and emphasized that the personal was, at the same time, political. By 1980, forty-four states had laws requiring automatic arrest in domestic violence cases, a vast improvement over ignoring the offense but still controversial.

Additional public attention to the issue generated some funding opportunities. This, too, was and is an issue of contention among feminists. Some believe that whatever sources help address the issue are acceptable, while others disavow those that reinforce the power of the state.

For certain the 1970s saw an increased visibility of the problem of domestic violence. The United Nations declared 1975 as the International Women's Year, and President Gerald Ford established the National Commission on the Observance of International Women's Year. One year later, *Ms.* magazine became the first national magazine to use an image of a battered woman on its cover. In 1978 the U.S. Civil Rights Commission held hearings about domestic violence. President Jimmy Carter established the Office on Domestic Violence in 1979, although it was closed by President Ronald Reagan in 1981. Although there was backlash against the movement in the 1970s, it amplified under the conservative Reagan era.

Activism on domestic violence did not end with the end of the decade, though. Consistent with a more conservative ideology, the primary focus during the 1980s was the criminal justice response. The MDVE, described earlier, seemed to provide support for greater law enforcement intervention. A 1985 lawsuit by Tracey Thurman against the city of Torrington police for failing to protect her from her husband's violence also demonstrated the need for improvement in the criminal justice system. Mandatory arrest became the preferred response.

Many in the movement decry the 1980s for minimizing the feminist perspective on domestic violence. Due to funding, largely, the shelters that opened were often run by Young Men's Christian Association, religious groups, and civic organizations rather than by feminists. Indeed, to obtain funding, shelters had to essentially disavow a radical feminist view. Critics contend that this minimizing of the feminist perspective in favor of a medicalized, individualized view of abuse has created a shelter model that is professionalized and bureaucratic rather than grassroots notion of people helping people.

Another criticism of the second wave of feminism, and one that became even more acute in the 1980s, was that it was predominately about and for white women. The images that were publicly visible were those of battered white women.

> The white battered woman identity, the white-focused empowerment continuum and the white-dominated legal practice are the elements that construct a legal discourse. This legal discourse renders women of color invisible, and subjects victims of domestic violence who are not white to further abuse within a system purporting to exist to help them. Legal discourse includes language written in statutes and spoken in courtrooms, visual images and iconography, and the behavior of those involved with the system. (Morrison, 2006, pp. 1075–1076)

Evelyn White sought to call attention to the plight of African American women with the publication of her book *Chain, Chain, Change: For Black Women Dealing with Physical and Emotional Abuse* in 1985. It was the first book to focus on African American victims.

Yet the 1980s did see some notable improvements. The first National Day of Unity was held in October 1980 and later became Domestic Violence Month. The U.S. attorney general established a task force on domestic violence in 1984. Surgeon General C. Everett Koop called domestic violence a major health problem in 1985.

The 1990s is a pivotal era in terms of federal legislation about domestic violence. VAWA was enacted in 1994 to provide funding for training police and for victim services. In 1997, the anti-stalking law was passed, the first federal legislation to address that issue. The decade also saw one of the most high-profile domestic violence cases.

In 1994, the case of former NFL star O. J. Simpson garnered national attention after the deaths of his ex-wife Nicole Brown Simpson and her friend Ronald Goldman, followed by the trial of Simpson for their murders. The trial revealed that Simpson had abused his former wife and, although he was acquitted, the case prompted additional public dialogue about domestic violence and inspired changes in the legal system's response to abuse.

Scholarly research about domestic violence also ballooned in the 1990s. New journals, including the *Journal of Family Violence*, emerged, and many articles and books were published. The year 1990 saw the founding of the NNEDV, which sought to ensure that public policy was adequate to assist victims and their children. NNEDV also helps support the many domestic violence shelters and coalitions by offering community education and technical assistance. In 1993, the CDC began funding community-based prevention efforts, representing the beginning of a shift from response to prevention.

The 2000s saw the reauthorization of VAWA twice. The 2000 and 2005 reauthorizations continued the original grant programs and extended protections to sexual assault, stalking, immigrant victims, and victims of dating violence. Court training, assistance for child witnesses, and culture-specific programming were also included. At the same time, the decade started with a constitutional challenge to a portion of the original VAWA. In *United States v. Morrison* (2000), the Supreme Court declared the civil rights remedy for victims as unconstitutional, declaring that domestic violence was not an "economic crime" and therefore could not be regulated under the Commerce Clause.

As was noted earlier, the Supreme Court's decision in the case of Jessica Gonzales brought attention to the limitations in the criminal justice response to domestic violence in the United States. The decade also saw the passage of the Trafficking Victims Protection Act. While trafficking and domestic violence are different, there are some similarities in the power dynamics, and victims are at risk for trafficking. In addition, President Obama signed the Tribal Law and Justice Act in 2009 to acknowledge the unique needs of Native American victims of domestic violence and sexual assault. In 2013, VAWA was again reauthorized, and protections were extended to tribal

lands, although not to Alaskan Natives and Pacific Islanders. Although it never became law, the International Violence
Against Women Act (IVAWA) was introduced during the
111th congressional session. IVAWA

> would for the first time comprehensively incorporate solu-
> tions into all U.S. foreign assistance programs—solutions
> such as promoting women's economic opportunity, ad-
> dressing violence against girls in school, and working to
> change public attitudes. Among other things, IVAWA
> would make ending violence against women a diplomatic
> priority for the first time in U.S. history. It would require
> the U.S. government to respond to critical outbreaks of
> gender-based violence in armed conflict—such as the
> mass rapes now occurring in the Democratic Republic of
> Congo and Haiti—in a timely manner. And by investing
> in local women's organizations overseas that are success-
> fully working to reduce violence in their communities, the
> IVAWA would have a huge impact on reducing poverty—
> empowering millions of women in poor countries to lift
> themselves, their families, and their communities out of
> poverty. (National Task Force to End Sexual and Domestic
> Violence Against Women, 2014)

Another international effort involved the creation of UN
Women in July 2010, the result of a merger of several different groups. UN Women focuses on global gender inequalities,
providing funding and support for campaigns related to female
genital mutilation, domestic and dating violence, human trafficking, rape and sexual assault, and other issues. Further, 189
countries agreed in 2000 to address the millennium development goals, which include (1) ending poverty and hunger,
(2) providing universal education, (3) promoting gender equality, (4) ensuring child health, (5) providing maternal health,
(6) combating HIV/AIDS, (7) promoting environmental sus-
tainability, and (8) developing global partnerships.

Although there was more attention to especially vulnerable victims, some organizations still emphasized that not enough was being done to help poor women, women of color, Native women, and immigrant victims. In 2000, the organization INCITE! Women of Color against Violence was formed to address the many forms of violence women of color experience. Its leaders decided to disavow nonprofit status due to concerns that funders were too conservative. INCITE! believes that grassroots community organizing is the best way to help victims and to end abuse.

Prevention became a greater priority in the 2000s, with some domestic violence shelters establishing programs and other organizations emerging for this purpose. In 2002, the CDC established the Domestic Violence Prevention Enhancement and Leadership Through Alliances program to provide training and resources to agencies engaging in primary prevention. The emphasis was on the development of coordinated community responses (CCRs) that would include educators, social service providers, law enforcement, clergy, health-care professionals, and other stakeholders. CCRs are intended to address not just abuse but also related issues such as gender role norms, poverty and inequality, and homelessness.

Current Issues

Dating violence has begun to draw more attention, as an estimated 30 percent of teen relationships are abusive. As of July 2014, twenty-two states had some type of law related to dating violence (National Council of State Legislatures, 2014). Some of these criminalize dating violence, while other laws specify that schools must teach about abusive and healthy relationships. Several high-profile cases further put the spotlight on dating violence, including that of pop music star Rihanna, who went public with a black eye she received from her then-boyfriend, singer Chris Brown. She wrote and performed a song with rapper Eminem, "Love the Way You Lie," which was about the so-called stormy relationship she had with Brown. In addition, scholars, educators, and advocates have noted the importance of helping young people learn resiliency during breakups or dating rejections, as a number of school shooters during the 1990s and 2000s targeted girls who had rejected or broken up with them.

Another group that has begun to receive greater attention is male victims. Studies have shown that while more women are victims of domestic violence than are men, in dating relationships victimization is more equally split. Similarly, scholars and activists like Michael Kimmel and Jackson Katz continue to draw attention to the importance of involving men and boys in campaigns to end abuse. Katz's organization, Mentors in Violence Prevention, uses a bystander intervention approach that has been shown to be effective in changing attitudes about abuse and inspiring people to help disrupt it. Kimmel's work focuses on critiquing toxic masculinity and on the importance of gender equality. Although he has been highly regarded for his efforts, Kimmel has recently become controversial because he was accused in fall 2018 of sexually harassing a former student.

Given the ubiquity of technology in our modern lives, it is no surprise that abuse often involves the Internet or social media. Abusers monitor, stalk, threaten, and harass victims via Facebook and other sites. Forty-three states and Washington, D.C., now have laws prohibiting revenge porn. Abusers who have provocative photos and videos of their victims often share these, which can be devastating to victims. The Cyber Civil Rights Initiative cautions about the use of the term "revenge porn," however. It states, "The term 'revenge porn,' though frequently used, is somewhat misleading. Many perpetrators are not motivated by revenge or by any personal feelings toward the victim. A more accurate term is nonconsensual pornography (NCP), defined as the distribution of sexually graphic images of individuals without their consent." That organization provides services for victims, research, and political advocacy.

Yet, simultaneously, while the issue of domestic violence has gained more attention, it has also become more contentious as a result of the candidacy and then presidency of Donald Trump. During his candidacy, it was revealed that Trump has repeatedly made harassing and misogynistic comments about women, which he has generally defended as false or as "locker room talk." During his campaign, an *Access Hollywood* tape was released in which the president boasted about grabbing women's genitals. During the presidential debates, Trump made derogatory and sexist comments toward his opponent, Hillary Clinton, and toward female reporters.

One of Trump's first moves upon taking office was to reinstate the Global Gag Rule, which withholds federal funds from organizations that even discuss abortion as an option. The Gag Rule was previously in effect between 2001 and 2008, and during that time women's access to contraceptives decreased, the rate of unsafe abortions increased, and HIV prevention programs were significantly scaled back.

Trump is the first sitting president to address the antiabortion March for Life. The administration's removal of asylum status for victims of domestic violence may be deadly for women seeking to flee abusers. His family separation policy has ripped children from their mothers and forced pregnant women to sleep on floors. Trump himself has repeatedly mocked the #MeToo movement.

Twenty-two women have accused Trump of sexual harassment. Similarly, Donald Trump has been on record supporting Republican candidates who have been accused of sexual assault and domestic violence. In February 2018, President Trump was outspoken in his defense of two White House aides who had been accused of abuse by girlfriends or spouses. He backed Brett Kavanaugh for Supreme Court justice despite claims of sexual misconduct. Trump backed Rob Porter, the White House aide who was forced to resign after it became public knowledge that two of his ex-wives had accused him of abusing them. Although he was not elected, Trump threw his weight behind Roy Moore, the Republican candidate for U.S. Senate in Alabama, who had been accused of engaging in inappropriate contact with a fourteen-year-old girl. Trump tweeted that allegations of abuse can ruin lives, a sentiment many advocates and activists took issue with.

The government shut down in January, the longest ever, and the result of a fight between Trump and Democrats over funding for a border wall led to deep concern about federal funding for domestic violence shelters. VAWA was set to be reauthorized; the deadline extended twice during that time, and thus shelter administrators were scared that the lack of VAWA funds would seriously restrict their operational abilities. Some shelters did cut programs, at least temporarily (Kelly, 2019). While the government reopened and funding was again processed in March 2019, VAWA has yet to be reauthorized (as of June 2019). One of the barriers to reauthorization is lobbying by the National Rifle Association (NRA). The NRA opposes reauthorization because of new provisions that are designed to protect victims from abusers with firearms. One provision of the proposed bill would extend so-called red flag measures that prohibit individuals with a history of domestic violence, stalking, or sexual assault from owning or possessing guns. Several states have adopted such laws, which are often called extreme risk protection orders (ERPOs), which allow families and members of law enforcement to petition for a temporary seizure of someone's weapons if he or she poses a danger to self or others. Federal law also seems to allow ERPOs. 18 U.S. Code § 922 (g) prohibits individuals who are under court order "for harassing, stalking, or threatening an intimate partner" from possessing a firearm. The National Instant Criminal Background Check System, which was established in 1993 to collect more details about criminal incidents, provides information on state-level domestic violence convictions to the Federal Bureau of Investigation, although it is only on a state-by-state basis. The VAWA reauthorization would mandate that states provide relevant legal information to the federal government. In early 2019, New York became the fourteenth state, along with Washington, D.C., to pass ERPO measures, while twenty-nine other states already have similar restrictions for individuals convicted of domestic violence (Keller, 2019).

Data indicates that ERPOs are effective. A 2006 study found that states that adopted laws authorizing the confiscation of firearms from individuals subject to a domestic violence–related restraining order saw intimate partner homicides drop by 7 percent, while another study led by researchers at the Duke University's School of Medicine Center found that the EPRO measure enacted by Connecticut in 1998 ended up averting up to one hundred suicides, as well as likely dozens of violent homicides (Keller, 2019).

The NRA, however, has used what is its typical narrative to whip up concern about that provision of the reauthorization. It argues that proponents are "playing politics" and that ERPOs will lead to a slippery slope of broader gun confiscations and prohibitions. NRA spokeswoman Jennifer Baker told *National Journal*, "The NRA opposes domestic violence and all violent crime, and spends millions of dollars teaching countless Americans how not to be a victim and how to safely use firearms for self-defense. It is a shame that some in the gun-control community treat the severity of domestic violence so trivially that they are willing to use it as a tool to advance a political agenda" (Keller, 2019).

In addition, the VAWA reauthorization bill extends protections to transgender individuals, which is controversial among conservatives. In particular, it would codify Federal Bureau of Prison regarding sexual harassment, assault, and domestic violence for incarcerated transgender individuals.

Although it was started in 2006 by survivor and activist Tarana Burke, the #MeToo movement drew attention in 2017 to the issues of sexual harassment and assault, not just in abusive intimate relationships but in the workplace and in the daily lives of women. Burke began the movement on the social media platform Myspace, but it went viral after actress Alyssa Milano suggested on Twitter that women who have been sexually assaulted or harassed use the hashtag #MeToo. Milano's tweet came amid the allegations that filmmaker Harvey Weinstein had sexually assaulted and harassed many women during his decades in the industry. Burke's original idea was to use #MeToo as a way to connect survivors with needed resources and support, but it has now become a rallying cry to address sexual harassment and assault (Vagianos, 2017). One way to assess whether #MeToo has been successful is to analyze calls for help. From October to December 2017, calls to the Rape, Abuse & Incest National Network—a U.S. crisis hotline—rose by 23 percent compared with the same period in 2016. Some abuse survivors have cited #MeToo as a stressful influence, saying it resurfaced the pain of their abuse. Others have reported feeling less alone, saying it encouraged them to address past trauma by talking to loved ones, counselors, or people with similar experiences (Seales, 2018).

Some critics have asserted, however, that the movement has paid too little attention to domestic violence, which is as common as sexual harassment and assault. Others critique the focus on women, suggesting that #MeToo overlooks male victims. Still other critics have expressed concern for "soft sexism" among male allies of #MeToo and other feminist efforts to end domestic and sexual violence. Such criticism denounces the "knight in shining armor" approach, noting that women do not need "saving" or "rescuing." Albeit often nobly intentioned, men's so-called heroism undermines women's agency. As Matthew Johnson (2019) wrote, "Men should not fight for gender justice because they are men but because they are *human beings* who believe in a better world for other human beings. To appeal to the warrior archetype in support of the noble cause of liberating women from violence and sexism, and then otherwise condemn it as 'toxic masculinity' is not only inconsistent, it reinforces the same gender-based power dynamic that feminism seeks to transform."

Weinstein is being held accountable for his offenses, as are many other powerful men who were outed as harassers and abusers via #MeToo and other efforts. As of January 9, 2019, a reported 263 politicians, celebrities, CEOs, and others have been accused of sexual harassment since April 2017. A total of 101 are in arts and entertainment, the largest group. In New York, a judge ruled that an actress can sue Harvey Weinstein for violating state sex trafficking laws because the casting couch could be considered a "commercial sex act." The judge rejected Weinstein's lawyers' contention that nothing of value was exchanged when he saw a demo reel of one of Weinstein's accusers, Kadian Noble, being molested and then forced to watch him masturbate in a bathroom in Cannes, France, in 2014. Weinstein has also been indicted on criminal charges. He initially took a leave of absence from the Weinstein Corp and in October 2017 was fired from the company.

A wave of female politicians elected in 2018 are expected to help elevate gender-related issues in Congress. A record 110 women were elected to the House, most of whom are Democrats. This is a diverse group of women as well, including lesbians, Muslims, Native Americans, African Americans, and Hispanics. Further, a record six women are running for the 2020 presidential nomination. While women in political positions are not a cure-all, it could elevate gender-related issues to greater importance, including domestic violence.

Clearly, while many advances have been made in terms of understanding abuse, helping victims, holding abusers accountable, and changing social norms, much remains to be done. This reference book, then, can hopefully prove to be a timely and important resource to that end.

References

Animal Legal Defense Fund. (n.d.). The link between cruelty to animals and violence against humans. ALDF.

Retrieved May 30, 2019, from https://aldf.org/article/the-link-between-cruelty-to-animals-and-violence-toward-humans-2/

Arabi, S. (2018). The differences between abusers with narcissistic personality disorder vs. borderline personality disorder. *Psychcentral.* Retrieved September 11, 2019, from https://psychcentral.com/lib/the-differences-between-abusers-with-narcissistic-personality-disorder-vs-borderline-personality-disorder/

BBC. (2018). The women killed on one day around the world. BBC. Retrieved December 13, 2018, from https://www.bbc.com/news/world-46292919

Blount, W. R., Yegfidis, B. L., & Maheux, R. M. (1992). Police attitudes toward preferred arrest: Influences of rank and productivity. *American Journal of Police, 11,* 35–52.

Bonomi, A., Anderson, M., Rivara, F., & Thompson, R. (2009). Health care utilization and costs associated with physical and nonphysical-only intimate partner violence. *Health Services Research, 44*(3), 1052–1067.

Campbell, J. (2005). Commentary on Websdale. *Violence against Women, 11*(9), 1206–1213.

CBS News. (2014, October 31). 16 questions used to ID domestic violence victims likely to be killed. CBS News. Retrieved May 30, 2019, from https://www.cbsnews.com/news/16-questions-used-to-id-domestic-abuse-victims-likely-to-be-killed/

CDC. (2018a). Intimate partner violence: Risk and protective factors for perpetration. CDC. Retrieved November 25, 2018, from https://www.cdc.gov/violenceprevention/intimatepartnerviolence/riskprotectivefactors.html

CDC. (2018b). Intimate partner violence: Consequences. CDC. Retrieved December 13, 2018, from https://www.cdc.gov/violenceprevention/intimatepartnerviolence/consequences.html

Chelala, C. (2016, February 12). The public health impact of domestic violence. *CounterPunch*. Retrieved December 1, 2018, from http://www.counterpunch.org/2016/02/05/the-public-health-impact-of-domestic-violence/

Chemaly, S. (2012, December 6). 50 actual facts about domestic violence. *Huffington Post*. Retrieved October 4, 2017, from http://www.huffingtonpost.com/soraya-chemaly/50-actual-facts-about-dom_b_2193904.html

Coker, D. (2000). Shifting power for battered women: Law, material resources, and poor women of color. *UC Davis Law Review*, 33(1), 1009–1058.

Connell, R. W. (1987). *Gender & power*. Stanford, CA: Stanford University Press.

Cote, I., & LaPierre, S. (2014). Abortion and domestic violence: Women's decision-making process. *Affilia: Journal of Women and Social Work, 29*(3), 285–297.

Davis, L.V. & Carlson, B. E. (1981). Attitudes of service providers toward domestic violence. *Social Work Research and Abstracts, 17*, 34–39.

de Bocanegra, H. T., Rpstovtseva, D. P., Khera, S., & Godhwani, N. (2010). Birth control sabotage and forced sex: Experiences reported by women in domestic violence shelters. *Violence against Women, 16,* 601–612.

Dewan, A. (2018, June 26). India the most dangerous country to be a woman, US ranks 10th in survey. CNN. Retrieved December 13, 2018, from https://www.cnn.com/2018/06/25/health/india-dangerous-country-women-survey-intl/index.html

Dibble, U., & Straus, M. A. (1980). Some social structure determinants of inconsistency between attitudes and behavior: The case of family violence. *Journal of Marriage and the Family, 42,* 71–80.

Effects of Domestic Violence on Children. (2019, April 2). Office on Women's Health. Retrieved May 15, 2019, from https://www.womenshealth.gov/relationships-and-safety/ domestic-violence/effects-domestic-violence-children

Erickson, A. (2018, July 27). New Zealand will let victims of domestic violence take paid leave. *The Washington Post*. Retrieved December 13, 2018, from https://www .washingtonpost.com/news/worldviews/wp/2018/07/27/ new-zealand-will-now-let-victims-of-domestic-violence-take-paid-leave/?noredirect=on&utm_term=.6496ce94de6e

Ewing, C. P. & Aubrey, M. (1987). Battered women and public opinion: Some realities about the myths. *Journal of Family Violence, 2, 257*–264.

Faith Trust Institute. (2013, January 4). Guns + domestic violence = lethality. *Faith Trust Institute.* Retrieved May 30, 2019, from https://www.faithtrustinstitute.org/blog/158

Foshee, V., Bauman, K., Arriaga, X., Helms, R., Koch, G., & Linder, G. (1998). An evaluation of Safe Dates, an adolescent dating violence program. NCBI. Retrieved May 29, 2019, from https://www.ncbi.nlm.nih.gov/pmc/ articles/PMC1508378/pdf/amjph00013-0047.pdf

Gordon, L. (1988). *Heroes of their own lives: The politics and history of family violence, Boston 1880–1960.* New York, NY: Viking Penguin Group.

Hamby, S. (2014, October 1). Guess how many domestic violence offenders go to jail. *Psychology Today*. Retrieved December 13, 2018, from https://www.psychologytoday .com/us/blog/the-web-violence/201410/guess-how-many-domestic-violence-offenders-go-jail

Heavner, C. (2017, February 21). Switching the phrase "domestic violence" to "patriarchal violence." The Medium. Retrieved December 13, 2018, from https://medium.com/ applied-intersectionality/from-domestic-to-patriarchal-violence-92f973b5deb7

Hegewisch, A., & Hartmann, H. (2019, March 7). The gender wage gap: 2018 earnings differences by race and ethnicity. *Institute for Women's Policy Research.* Retrieved May 15, 2019, from https://iwpr.org/publications/gender-wage-gap-2018/

Heise, L. (1989, April 9). The global war against women. *The Washington Post.* Retrieved July 2, 2019, from https://www.washingtonpost.com/archive/opinions/1989/04/09/the-global-e01cd1d780ce/?utm_term=.1dca0773b580

Houston, C. (2014). How feminist theory became (criminal) law: Tracing the path to mandatory criminal intervention in domestic violence cases. *Michigan Journal of Gender and Law, 21*(2), 217–272.

HRC Staff. (2017, October 17). Common myths about LGBTQ domestic violence. Human Rights Campaign. Retrieved May 13, 2019, from https://www.usnews.com/news/best-countries/articles/2018-09-04/women-are-still-underrepresented-in-parliaments-around-the-world

Johnson, I., & Sigler, R. (2000). Public perceptions: The stability of the public's endorsements of the definition and criminalization of the abuse of women. *Journal of Criminal Justice, 28*(3), 165–179.

Johnson, I., Sigler, R., & Crowley, J. (1994). Domestic violence: A comparative study of perceptions and attitudes towards domestic abuse cases among social service and criminal justice professionals. *Journal of Criminal Justice, 22*(3), 237–248.

Johnson, M. (2019, March 29). The soft sexism of men's antiviolence efforts. The Good Men Project. Retrieved March 31, 2019, from https://goodmenproject.com/social-justice-2/the-soft-sexism-of-mens-anti-violence-efforts/

Jones, F. (2014, September 10). Why black women struggle more with domestic violence. *Time.* Retrieved May 14, 2019, from http://time.com/3313343/ray-rice-black-women-domestic-violence/

Kalmuss, D. (1979). The attribution of responsibility in a wife abuse context. *Victimology, 4,* 284–291.

Keller, J. (2019, March 29). The NRA's losing case against reauthorizing the Violence Against Women Act. *Pacific Standard.* Retrieved March 31, 2019, from https://psmag .com/news/the-nras-losing-case-against-reauthorizing-the-violence-against-women-act

Kelly, C. (2019, January 18). Shutdown panics domestic violence shelters despite temporary, eleventh hour reprieve. *USA Today.* Retrieved March 21, 2019, from https://www .usatoday.com/story/news/investigations/2019/01/18/ government-shutdown-domestic-violence-shelters-victims-funding/2612690002/

Klein, A., & Tobin, T. (1997). A longitudinal study of arrested batterers, 1995–2005: Career criminals. *Violence against Women, 14*(2), 136–157.

Kristof, N., & WuDunn, S. (2009). *Half the sky: Turning oppression into opportunity for women worldwide.* New York: Penguin.

Lisco, C., Leone, R., Gallagher, K., & Parrott, D. (2015). "Demonstrating masculinity" via intimate partner aggression: The moderating effect of heavy episodic drinking. *Sex Roles, 73*(1), 58–69.

Love Is Respect. (2017). Dating abuse statistics. Love Is Respect. Retrieved May 15, 2019, from https://www .loveisrespect.org/resources/dating-violence-statistics/

McLean, Gladys, & Bocinski, Sarah. 2017. The economic cost of intimate partner violence, sexual assault, and stalking. Institute for Women's Policy Research. Last modified August 14, 2017. https://iwpr.org/publications/ economic-cost-intimate-partner-violence-sexual-assault-stalking/

Morrison, A. (2006). Changing the domestic violence (dis)course: Moving from white victim to multicultural survivor. *University of California-Davis Law Review, 39,* 1061–1120.

Morse, D., Lafleur, R., Fogarty, C., Mittal, M., & Cerulli, C. (2012). "They told me to leave": How healthcare providers address intimate partner violence. *Journal of the American Board of Family Medicine, 25*(3), 323–332.

National Council of State Legislatures. (2014, July). Teen dating violence. NCSL. Retrieved March 21, 2019, from http://www.ncsl.org/research/health/teen-dating-violence .aspx

National Task Force to End Sexual and Domestic Violence Against Women. (2014, April 21). Action needed on international VAWA. *NCDSV.* Retrieved September 11, 2019, from http://www.ncdsv.org/images/NTFESDVAW_ Action-needed-on-IVAWA-Calling-for-bi-partisan-Senate-sponsors_4-21-2014.pdf

NCADV. (n.d.). Learn more: What is domestic violence? NCADV. Retrieved December 13, 2018, from https:// ncadv.org/learn-more

Parker, C. (2014). Women and children bear brunt of domestic violence, Stanford scholar says. *Stanford Report.* Retrieved May 1, 2019, from http://news.stanford.edu/ news/2014/september/domestic-violence-toll-092314 .html

Pearl, R. (2013, December 5). Domestic violence: The secret killer that costs $8.3 billion annually. *Forbes.* Retrieved September 11, 2019, from https://www.forbes.com/sites/ robertpearl/2013/12/05/domestic-violence-the-secret-killer-that-costs-8-3-billion-annually/#2686c0d14681

Pleck, E. (1987). *Domestic tyranny.* New York, NY: Oxford University Press.

Radu, S. (2018, September 4). Women still a rare part of world's parliaments. *US News & World Report.* Retrieved May 13, 2019, from https://www.usnews.com/news/

best-countries/articles/2018-09-04/women-are-still-underrepresented-in-parliaments-around-the-world

Rosay, A. (2010). Violence against American Indian and Alaska Native women and men. U.S. Department of Justice. Retrieved May 15, 2019, from https://www.ncjrs.gov/pdffiles1/nij/249736.pdf

Russia: One Woman an Hour Being Killed through Domestic Violence. (2005, December 14). Amnesty International. Retrieved July 2, 2019, from https://www.amnesty.org.uk/press-releases/russia-one-woman-hour-being-killed-through-domestic-violence-new-report-calls-action

Seales, R. (2018, May 12). What has #MeToo actually changed? BBC News. Retrieved March 21, 2019, from https://www.bbc.com/news/world-44045291

Sigler, R. T. (1989). *Domestic violence in context.* Lexington, MA: D. C. Heath.

Sinden, P. G., & Stephens, B. J. (1999). Police perceptions of domestic violence: The nexus of victim, perpetrator, event, self and law. *Policing, 22,* 313–326.

Stansell, C. (2010). *The feminist promise: 1792 to the present.* New York, NY: The Modern Library.

Stark, R., & McEvoy, J. (1970). Middle class violence. *Psychology Today, 4*(6), 107–112.

Toon, R., & Hart, B. (2005). *Layers of meaning: Domestic violence and law enforcement attitudes in Arizona.* Washington, DC: U.S. Department of Justice, Office on Violence Against Women.

UNICEF. (2008). Female genital mutilation. UNICEF. Retrieved October 15, 2019 from https://www.unicef.org/protection/female-genital-mutilation

USDOJ. (2018). Domestic violence. U.S. Department of Justice. Retrieved July 2, 2019, from https://www.justice.gov/ovw/domestic-violence

Vagianos, A. (2017, October 17). The "Me Too" campaign was created by a black woman ten years ago. *Huffington Post.* Retrieved March 21, 2019, from https://www.huffing tonpost.com/entry/the-me-too-campaign-was-created-by-a-black-woman-10-years-ago_us_59e61a7fe4b02a215b336fee

Ventura, L., & Davis, G. (2005). Court case recidivism and domestic violence. *Violence against Women, 11*(2), 255–277.

White, E. (1985). *Chain, chain, change: For black women in abusive relationships.* Berkeley, CA: Seal Press.

The World Bank. (2018, February 1). More than 1 billion women lack legal protection against domestic sexual violence, finds World Bank study. World Bank. Retrieved December 13, 2018, from https://www.worldbank.org/en/news/press-release/2018/02/01/more-than-1-billion-women-lack-legal-protection-against-domestic-sexual-violence-finds-world-bank-study

World Economic Forum. (2018). The global gender gap report, 2018. Retrieved May 15, 2019, from http://www3 .weforum.org/docs/WEF_GGGR_2018.pdf

World Health Organization. (2018, June 8). Elder abuse. World Health Organization. Retrieved May 13, 2019, from https://www.nrcdv.org/rhydvtoolkit/key-terms-resources/glossary.html

Zarya, V. (2017, November 7). 5 statistics that explain the link between domestic violence and mass shootings. *Fortune.* Retrieved December 13, 2018, from http://fortune.com/2017/11/07/domestic-violence-shootings-statistics/

2 Problems, Controversies, and Solutions

Introduction

While research has shed light on many facets of abuse, a significant number of questions remain. This chapter presents some of the most understudied or controversial issues in the field, using the best and most current data available to present the various perspectives on each. It includes segments on abusers, victims, responses to abuse, and prevention initiatives. In evaluating these controversial issues, the chapter also presents several proposed and actual solutions.

Do Athletes Commit More Sexual Assault and Domestic Violence?

According to one study by *ESPN*'s Outside the Lines, college athletes at Power 5 conference schools were three times more likely than their peers to perpetrate sexual assault and domestic violence (Lavigne, 2018). The increased risk of sexual coercion by athletes was linked to "traditional" beliefs about women and a higher belief in rape, which are used to justify rape. According to this study, rape and sexual coercion is a traditional belief, like a rite of passage into manhood. Other research has been done that has shown that male college athletes may be more likely than college students, in general, to commit sexual

Ray Rice with wife Janay Palmer after a hearing regarding his suspension from the NFL for domestic violence. (Andrew Burton/Getty Images)

violence or engage in sexual coercion. In a 2011 study on attitudes toward women that are key to higher rates of sexual assault by athletes, the U.S. Department of Education called for colleges and universities to institute efforts to educate athletes and address sexual violence (Sports and Sexual Assault, n.d.). Despite being overrepresented as assailants, athletes seem to be protected by everyone around them because of their potential and what they bring the university or professional team that they belong to. This is especially an issue when it comes to high-profile universities like Ohio State and Alabama, where football is everything and where schools make a lot of money from their athletes. College athletes are often protected by the college campus itself, and students may also turn a blind eye so that their favorite athletes and teams can continue playing. Athletes often have a sense of entitlement and may feel they can do as they please with little or no recourse.

There are many cases where athletes have been accused of sexual assault and rape, but the law hasn't done much to protect the victim. One case that has been documented according to Jessica Luther, author of a book called *Unsportsmanlike Conduct: College Football and the Politics of Rape*, occurred in 2016, when former Auburn tight end Landon Rice was accused of first-degree rape in an incident report with the Auburn Police Department filed on July 27 by an unidentified nineteen-year-old female. The incident allegedly happened in the late hours of April 12 in the South Donahue Residence Hall, a 209-room dorm located across the street from the athletic complex and housing most of the football team. Coach Gus Malzahn announced Rice had left the football program following the team's game on September 10 against Arkansas State for "personal reasons." Following a Title IX investigation, he was found "responsible" of sexual assault. Rice's attempt to appeal the ruling was denied.

Athletes are not just more likely to commit sexual assault; they are also likely to commit domestic violence and get a lighter sentence or even get their case dismissed. *USA Today* compiled a list of NFL players' arrests dating back to 2000, and it shows that domestic violence is one of the crimes players are most frequently arrested for. In particular, compared to men in the same age and income level, NFL players are much more likely to be arrested for domestic violence (NFL Player Arrests, n.d.). One of the most notable cases involves former NFL star O. J. Simpson, who was accused of murdering his former wife, Nicole Brown Simpson, and her friend. Simpson was acquitted of the murders, but evidence presented at his trial showed that he had abused Nicole and that she had called 911 several times.

Former Baltimore Ravens running back Ray Rice is an example of how the violent actions of a celebrity athlete often result only in minimal consequences. He was caught on camera in an elevator hitting his then fiancée (now wife). Rice was charged with third-degree aggravated assault, yet his attorneys described the punch that knocked his fiancée out as "little more than a misunderstanding." Atlantic City judge Michael Donio ordered a pretrial intervention that required Rice to pay $125 in fines and receive anger management counseling. After Rice completed this pretrial intervention program, Donio signed a dismissal order for the aggravated assault felony charges (Maske, 2014).

After a second surveillance video of the violent altercation at an Atlantic City casino was published by TMZ, Ray Rice was initially suspended for just two games but then was released by the Baltimore Ravens and suspended indefinitely by the NFL. Rice appealed his suspension and won, but he has yet to be signed by a team since the incident.

After the charges were dismissed, the National Domestic Violence Hotline said that it is common for first-time offenders to end up with no charges. The hotline wants to make sure that victims of domestic violence don't get discouraged because of the end result of this or other cases in which the offender was not charged.

NBA players are also overrepresented as abusers and assailants. Jeff Benedict chronicled many of these cases in his 2004 book *Out of Bounds: Inside the NBA's Culture of Rape, Violence and Crime.* Benedict reviewed the criminal histories of 177 NBA players in the 2001–2002 season and found more than 40 percent had a criminal record, with domestic and sexual violence being among the most common offenses.

World Wrestling Entertainment also seems to have a domestic violence problem. Many of its wrestlers have been accused or even convicted of abuse, including stars like Stone Cold Steve Austin. In 2007, Christopher Benoit killed his wife and seven-year-old son before committing suicide (Tessier, 2007).

When it comes to athletes, it seems the law is more lenient than with nonathletes who commit acts of sexual and domestic violence. In a study by Benedict (2003), found 32 percent of rapes reported to police in 1990 resulted in an arrest. More than half of these suspects were convicted. On the other hand, for athletes, the numbers are almost reversed. Out of the 217 felony rape complaints forwarded to police involving athletes between 1986 and 1995, only 172 resulted in an arrest. Out of those 172 arrests, only 53 resulted in convictions. In about forty-three cases, the accused athlete pleaded guilty to a reduced charge or entered a plea of no contest; only ten were convicted at trial. Another study focusing on the years 1991–2003 found that while there were 168 sexual assault allegations involving 164 elite athletes, only 6 cases resulted in convictions (Weir & Brady, 2003).

Many prosecutors are hesitant to bring cases against athletes to trial. The prosecutors who opted not to press charges revealed that in many cases they believed the accuser often had corroborating evidence to support her claim. The athlete's social environment provides him with both protection and support. Accused athletes have money, powerful lawyers, public relations specialists, high-profile coaches, and other popular personalities to come to their defense. Rarely do accused athletes deny sexual contact with their accusers; more often, they say it was consensual. Then the athletes can hold a press conference, making the accusers seem like they are just looking for fame or looking to gain some type of financial benefit from them. Many times the cases do not proceed because the athletes pay the victims to keep quiet and not pursue legal action. In 1992, twenty members of the Cincinnati Bengals football team were accused of gang-raping Victoria Crytzer. To protect the members of the team who were involved, the Bengals administration paid Crytzer $30,000 to not pursue legal action (Farry, 1993).

The determination that a report of sexual assault is false can be made only if the evidence establishes that no crime was committed or attempted. This determination can be made only after a thorough investigation. This should not be confused with an investigation that fails to prove a sexual assault occurred. In that case the investigation would be labeled unsubstantiated. The determination that a report is false must be supported by evidence that the assault did not happen. Even if the victim is telling the truth about the fact that an assault happened, if there is no physical evidence, it can be determined that it was a false accusation. False accusations are horrible but fairly rare; according to the FBI, between 2 and 8 percent of rape allegations are false, a rate lower than virtually any other crime.

It is important to note that it isn't all athletes who are overrepresented as abusers or sexual assailants. Rather, it is athletes in football, basketball, hockey, wrestling, and boxing who have the problem. This may be because aggression is rewarded in these sports; because these athletes tend to be idolized by fans and teams so they can get away with criminal behavior; because these sports often feature hypermasculine, misogynistic bonding, or because of other reasons. Literature has also focused on the role of steroids and the possibility that head injuries may partly explain the overrepresentation of these athletes.

In conclusion, it is hard to conclusively determine if athletes are more likely to commit a sexual assault, but when they are accused, they are less likely to face sanctions and tend to receive lighter sentences when convicted. Data does seem clear that, compared to men of similar ages and income level, professional athletes in certain sports are more likely to be arrested for domestic violence.

However, efforts have been made to address the problem of abuse and assault among athletes. Educational programs like Jackson Katz's Mentors in Violence Prevention (MVP) are aimed at athletes and attempt to challenge traditional gender role stereotypes and to encourage men to stand up to others who are mistreating or abusing women. Many argue that teams should not recruit players who have histories of abuse or assault. All the major sporting leagues have player conduct regulations and specific sanctions for violating them. This includes domestic and sexual violence, although critics argue they rarely go far enough. Fans can play a role as well, ensuring that teams know that they will not tolerate athletes who commit these crimes.

Are Men Abused as Frequently as Women?

Typically, men are considered to be the abusers and women the victims of domestic violence. Yet data is not entirely clear on whether men are victimized at similar rates. One issue related to this is when women abuse men, and another is when men abuse other men in same-sex relationships.

Most data shows that women are more frequently victimized by male intimate partners than the reverse. The National Coalition Against Domestic Violence (NCADV) (n.d.). states that one in four women and one in nine men experience several physical violence, sexual violence, or stalking by an intimate partner.

Yet some studies have found that men suffer from domestic violence by women at similar rates. According to a report by the Centers for Disease Control and Prevention (CDC) (2011), more men reported being slapped, pushed, or shoved by their female partner in the previous twelve months. Some 40 percent of the victims of severe physical violence—being beaten, burned, choked, kicked, or having their heads slammed into hard objects—were men (Birch, 2015). Another measurement of male victimization in domestic violence cases involves those who are abused by other males in same-sex relationships. Forty percent of gay men experience abuse by a partner (Vagianos, 2014).

One difficulty in discerning whether males are victimized by females at similar rates as females by males is that of underreporting. It is clear that domestic violence in general remains tremendously underreported, and research shows that male victims are even less likely to report than are female victims. Gene Feder and Potter Lucy, professors at the University of Bristol, United Kingdom (2017), conducted surveys and studies with victims of domestic violence in the United Kingdom and found that "only a third of men who had experienced domestic abuse thought they had been in an abusive relationship. This is much lower proportion than women" (p. 7). This is, in part, due to the dominant stereotype of femininity in the West, where the exercise of active violence is not considered an attribute of women. Men who are abused by female partners are considered to be "weak" and thus face tremendous stigma. As a result, many do not report the abuse nor seek help. Lisak (1993) argued, "The notion that men cannot be victims dovetails so well with the rest of the gender myth: 'Men can't be vulnerable, or helpless, or experience their pain.' The effect of these myths is to steer millions of victimized men away from the path of healing, to a continued denial of their pain, of their victimization, of their helpless vulnerability" (p. 6). There is evidence that even minor situations, such as the pronouns that are used to describe victims (she) and to refer to abusers (he), can have a negative effect on how likely male victims are to report abuse. The internalized notion that abusers are male and victims female only furthers the stigma around reporting domestic abuse by women (Lisak, 1993).

Research has shown that when females abuse males they tend to use different tactics which therefore result in different effects. According to Women as Abusers (n.d.), "Female abusers' common traits included being possessive, controlling and jealous; having unrealistic expectations of her partner; having high impulsivity, anger and rage; and not having enough outside support from female friends" (p. 12). Female abusers may use physical violence, but studies have shown that they inflict less damage in doing so than do male abusers.

There remains a dearth of resources for male victims of domestic violence. If resources are dedicated only to victims of a certain gender, it can have the negative effect of invalidating other victims. Even the titles of laws and the names of agencies can dissuade male victims from seeking help, such as the Violence Against Women Act (VAWA) which does provide for males as well. Studies also demonstrate that the impact of inadequate treatment or response to victims of abuse can have long-lasting effects. According to Douglas and Hines (2011), "Male help seekers in our sample had twice as many negative as positive experiences when searching for assistance with what we have documented as serious physical and psychological IPV victimization. Moreover, the quality of their experiences seems to have lasting implications for their mental health."

Which Groups Are Disproportionally Victimized and Why?

While anyone can be a victim of abuse, some groups are particularly vulnerable. In the United States, the group most at risk for experiencing both domestic violence and sexual assault is Native American, Alaskan, and Pacific Islander women.

Studies have shown that Native women experience all violent crime 2.5 times more often than other races and are twice as likely to endure rape or sexual assault. A recent study found that 94 percent of Native American women in Seattle had been raped or sexually assaulted at least once. While 29 percent of African American women experience domestic violence, as do 27 percent of white women, 21 percent of Hispanic women, and 10 percent of Asian women in the United States, an astonishing 39 percent of Native women are victims.

One of the complicating factors is the jurisdictional quagmire that exists on tribal lands. Supreme Court decisions and legislation have created a situation where tribal police and courts have been largely disempowered from responding to domestic and sexual violence. Reliance on state and federal authorities to do so has also been problematic, given the historic animosity between Native peoples and the white government, as well as logistical issues like the size of some reservations. Many reservations still lack resources for victims, and victims often fear reporting abuse because the populations on reservations tend to be so small and intimately connected that retaliation is a legitimate concern.

Until 2013, VAWA did not include Native women, thereby further limiting resources available to them. Although it now does, thanks to the heartfelt and tireless lobbying by many Native women and their allies, Alaska Natives and Pacific Islanders are still not protected by VAWA. The Tribal Law and Order Act of 2010 did expand funding for training and services in Indian country. The governmental shutdown in late 2018 and early 2019 obviously exacerbated the problem, however.

In addition, black women are overrepresented as victims. According to Maya Finoh and Jasmine Sankofah with the American Civil Liberties Union, about 22 percent of black women in the United States have been raped, 40 percent of black women have experienced domestic violence, and black women are killed at a higher rate than any other group of women. Black trans and nonbinary individuals are particularly likely to endure abuse, with some 53 percent experiencing sexual violence and 56 percent experiencing domestic violence. When such crimes occur, black women are less likely to be believed. "Adults view Black girls as less innocent and more adult-like than their white peers. Black girls are perceived to be more independent, more knowledgeable about sex, and in less need of protection" (Finoh & Sankofah, 2019).

Even when they are defending themselves, black women suffer tremendous consequences.

Cyntoia Brown was only sixteen years old when she shot and killed a man who picked her up for sex. Fearful of her life when the forty-three-year-old man took her back to his home and showed her his gun collection, Cyntoia tried to protect herself. The prosecution argued that Cyntoia's motive was robbery, not self-defense, and Cyntoia was tried as an adult. She was sentenced to life in prison with no chance for parole until she served fifty-one years, but in 2019 Tennessee's outgoing governor, Bill Haslam, commuted her sentence amid widespread activism on her behalf. She was released on parole in August 2019 after serving fifteen years behind bars (Finoh & Sankofah, 2019).

In 2017, Marissa Alexander was finally released from prison after being convicted of firing a warning shot into the ceiling of her ex-boyfriend's home. She spent nearly six years in prison or confined to her home after her 2012 conviction of aggravated assault. Alexander says her ex-boyfriend was abusive and that he threatened her just nine days after she had their baby. She had attempted to utilize a Stand Your Ground defense, but the court did not allow it. Alexander has gone on to become a vocal critic of the uneven application of Stand Your Ground laws and a domestic violence advocate (Hauser, 2017).

The reasons for the overrepresentation of women of color are complex. Historical racism, sexism, and colonialism, however, are clearly part of it. Historically, women of color have felt obligated to put racism ahead of sexism in movements for civil and human rights.

What Happens When Abuse Occurs within Progressive Groups or Organizations?

Survivors face a multitude of barriers when seeking assistance for domestic abuse. Further complexity is added when survivors are members of progressive organizations that disavow domestic and sexual violence and the punitive justice system. When the abuser is a member of community organizations that fight for social justice, responses to abuse allegations are often fraught with suspicion and shame. Leah Lakshmi Piepzna-Samarasinha, a queer Sri Lankan writer, revealed the responses from her community as follows: "Our men go through so much, it's no wonder—you can't be so hard on him." "What, you're going to call the cops? You're going to bring the prison-industrial complex down on a man of color?" "Have you tried healing him with love?" "It's so personal." "No one really knows what happens in a relationship but those two people." "You're a strong woman of color—you can take it" (Piepzna-Samarasinha, 2018). This being said, the question is raised, What course of action should be taken in lieu of the relying on the justice system?

The creation of a community-based accountability system is one mechanism for addressing domestic violence within progressive organizations/communities. INCITE!, a progressive domestic violence organization, argues that there are four main steps to a culture of community accountability: (1) create and affirm values and practices that resist abuse and oppression and encourage safety, support, and accountability; (2) develop sustainable strategies to address community members' abusive behavior, creating a process for them to account for their actions and transform their behavior; (3) commit to ongoing development of all members of the community, and the community itself, to transform the political conditions that reinforce oppression and violence; and (4) provide safety and support to community members who are violently targeted that respects their self-determination (INCITE!, 2018).

In 2014, INCITE! Women of Color against Violence held a meeting to address gender violence. During this sit-down, seven concrete principles were created to support community accountability of domestic violence.

(1) Understand the impact of unequal power

Unequal power structure causes a dynamic of abuse. One party holding the majority of power in a relationship can create an environment ripe for abuse (Incite-national.org, 2018, p. 13).

(2) Prioritize survivor safety

Safety of the survivor should take the highest priority, through support, safe spaces, and confidentiality (Incite-national.org, 2018, p. 13).

(3) Prioritize survivor self-determination

Creating priority of the survivor's needs and wants is an important factor in valuing the survivor. Some survivors may want to be a part of the process; others may not (Incite-national.org, 2018, p. 13).

(4) Collective responsibility and action

Domestic violence is a crime rarely reported. This leads to isolation of the survivor. By shifting the blame away from the survivor and onto the perpetrator, a power shift is created (Incite-national.org, 2018, p. 13).

(5) Collective accountability for oppressive, abusive, and violence organizational culture and conditions

INCITE! argues it is vital to create a culture of community accountability by members of a community personally holding one other accountable for their actions. This can be done by acknowledging collective community responses and creating a societal change (Incite-national.org, 2018, p. 13).

(6) Abuser accountability for oppressive, abusive, and violent attitudes and behaviors

Similar to point (5), abuser accountability *can happen by* acknowledging the abuse and creating consequences that are both short and long term (Incite-national.org, 2018, p. 14).

(7) Transformation toward liberation

"The overall goal for community accountability is to transform all individuals and collective groups towards gender equity and respect" (Incite-national.org, 2018, p. 14).

Creating awareness of the complexities of domestic violence in progressive organizations is only the first step. Once the issue is brought to light, the next question is, What is to be done about it? The following are four methods of change: exposing the perpetrator, education and awareness, self-defense, and systematic change.

Exposing the perpetrator, or the shame model, has become increasingly more prevalent with the development of social media platforms. Public or Internet vigilantism has often been suggested as a way of holding domestic abusers accountable when the criminal justice system fails to convict a perpetrator or as an alternative to the justice system altogether. However, the Internet can often be used as a form of anonymity. Karl Allen Wehmhoener stated, "People also partake in Internet vigilantism because they fear no repercussion" (Wehmhoener, 2010). Another form of transparency and accountability missing from the shame model is the spread of misinformation. The public beating of Jahir Khan, Gulzar Ahmed Khan, and Khurshid is an example of vigilante justice gone awry. Rumors that the men were "child abductors" quickly spread through the popular app WhatsApp. A mob formed around the three men, resulting in the death of Jahir Khan and the severe beating of Gulzar Ahmed Khan and Khurshid (Newsroom, 2018).

The education and awareness method has already grown dramatically within the past decade. By integrating anti-violence education curricula in schools, activists hope to increase awareness of domestic violence. The National Intimate Partner and Sexual Violence Survey in 2010 discovered that an estimated 11.2 percent of female rape victims first experienced rape below the age of ten years, and it estimated that 30.1 percent experienced rape between the ages of eleven and seventeen years (CDC, 2011). In response to these statistics, organizations like Break the Cycle have been educating children and young adults within the public school systems. Break the Cycle, formed in 1996, "inspires and supports young people to build healthy relationships and create a culture without abuse" (About Us, 2014).

In correlation with education, INCITE! recommends three practices for self-defense within the community:

1. Self-defense classes, including classes that teach "collective self-defense." That is, not just how you as an individual can fight back but how can you work with other people to fight back and hold perpetrators accountable.

2. Develop a community alarm "signal" that signifies immediate crisis.

3. Organize neighborhood watch groups to monitor not only strangers in the area but what is going on in peoples' homes (INCITE!, 2018).

The final method, systematic change, can arguably be included within the previous three methods because it can be defined as a change that pervades all or parts of a system. Oftentimes, change comes from a person or persons who hold a position of power. Take, for example, Reese Witherspoon. In 2011, Witherspoon launched the "Empowerment Bracelet" by Avon, with 100 percent net profits going to benefit Avon Foundation for Women programs dedicated to ending violence against women (Avon Foundation for Women, 2011). Increased societal awareness and celebrity advocacy can hold popular culture accountable for social issues. By creating a society against domestic violence, in theory, domestic abuse survivors may feel able to come forward.

Should Domestic Violence Be Automatic Grounds for Asylum or Refugee Status?

People from other countries seek refuge in the United States after fleeing persecution in their home countries. U.S. immigration laws allow people fleeing persecution to seek protection in the United States by filing for asylum. Victims of domestic violence are eligible for asylum based on whether their government is unwilling to protect them from the perpetrator. In these domestic violence cases, it is recommended to show the views in their home country concerning the victim's and the persecutor's social roles and status explain why their government is unable to protect the victim from domestic violence. It is also recommended to show why the victim is a target of persecution on the applicable ground. Depending on the country where the victim is from, they may be able to claim domestic violence–based persecution on the basis of their membership in a particular social group. Success in these asylum cases is very rare, however; for every approved applicant, ten are not approved, a rate that has increased under the Trump administration (Fact Sheet: U.S. Asylum Process, 2019).

The main case that recognized that domestic violence may be a basis for asylum was the matter of A-R-C-G. A-R-C-G had endured ruthless beatings, rape, burns on her body, and a broken nose from her husband. She also received death threats from her husband in her attempt to leave. The police of Guatemala refused to involve themselves in this "family dispute." The Guatemalan government failed to intervene in this situation or protect A-R-C-G (Jordan, 2018).

This case had the basic framework for this particular social group standard. Once a domestic abuse survivor seeks asylum, they must pass a credible fear interview to be allowed to pursue their claims. Once these claims are deemed credible, a series of hearings follow, which may take up to years to complete. People seeking asylum must meet the standards and show that they have suffered persecution. In seeking asylum due to domestic violence, women must provide the evidence of abuse, including police reports, expert testimony, hospital records, and corroborating statements. These victims also have to show the judge their membership in the social group and their persecution for being a part of it (Jordan, 2018).

Some areas of law, however, remain unsettled. Even though domestic violence could involve serious harm, it would not amount to persecution on the applicable ground unless it is perpetrated by someone that the victim's government will not or cannot control. In many of these countries, there is a huge neglect by authorities. Police turn a blind eye on cases, and courts do not issue restraining orders or follow through with the protection measures. Even though men are more likely to be victims of violent crime, 85 percent of the victims of domestic violence are women. Women are more likely than men to be victims of domestic violence due to male-dominated societies limiting women's social roles. Women are often forced to remain in a place where their abuse is allowed and sometimes even expected. For example, in some societies it is completely legal for a husband to rape, beat, and sexually assault his wife. Countries like Armenia, Congo, Egypt, Haiti, Iran, Latvia, Kenya, and Lebanon do not outlaw domestic violence. In these countries, domestic abuse is not treated like a crime; it has been ignored by governments and also is underreported by women. In 2014, Lebanon passed its first domestic violence law, but it has been stated that this law does not go far enough to protect the victims. The term "domestic violence" is very broad, leaving many women vulnerable to this abuse and unprotected by their government and police. Over one billion women lack legal protection against domestic sexual violence (The World Bank, 2018). Women are often not legally protected against specific types of harassment outside of their home in places such as school and work. Over the past couple of years, however, there has been progress in making this domestic abuse illegal. An example of this would be Saudi Arabia, a country known for its restraint on woman's rights, which passed a landmark bill in 2013 outlawing domestic abuse. Still, women's vulnerability to this domestic violence itself is not grounds for the basis membership in a particular social group. Group memberships in the perspective of domestic violence would be based on the inability of women to leave their relationship. They would need to have specific obstacles that keep them from leaving (acts or threats made by persecutor) and also ways in which the home country's laws or norms would make this problem worse.

However, victims of domestic violence and gang violence may not be eligible for asylum in the United States any more, since former attorney general Jeff Sessions reversed the grant of asylum in 2016 to a Salvadorian domestic violence survivor. This case is known as *Matter of A-B*. Ms. A-B was fleeing fifteen years of domestic abuse, including death and rape threats. Sessions vacated the decision made by the Justice Department's Board of Immigration Appeals that said she was eligible for asylum. "Generally, claims by aliens pertaining to domestic violence or gang violence perpetrated by non-governmental actors will not qualify for asylum," Sessions wrote. "The mere fact that a country may have problems effectively policing certain crimes—such as domestic violence or gang violence—or that certain populations are more likely to be victims of crime, cannot itself establish an asylum claim" (Sachetti, 2018). Many people were infuriated with this decision, saying Sessions was taking the country back to the era when the United States did not recognize women's rights as human rights and women fleeing gender-based persecution were denied refugee protection. Some, however, agreed with Sessions and believe that it has become too easy to seek asylum in the United States. They believe that it is the responsibility of the home country to protect its citizens from this domestic violence. Some say that many of these countries have created offices to deal with women's rights and domestic violence. However, these offices are not properly funded and/or are still dealing with cultural issues. Government attorneys argue that these home countries are trying to deal with domestic violence by creating these offices and shelter for the victims so the United States should not need to give them asylum. Many people who have applied or are in the process of applying for asylum in the United States have been affected by this decision.

The immigration courts are a part of the executive branch, which falls under the jurisdiction of the Department of Justice. The attorney general has the power to reverse asylum decision one at a time. The ability to grant asylum depends on who hears the case and where the case is heard. In Sessions's explanation of his reversal, he referred to domestic violence as "private violence" and "nongovernmental actors" to justify the decision to deny asylum to domestic violence victims as well as gang-based violence. Gang violence is also a huge reason people try to seek asylum in the United States. Nine years ago, a woman named Irene from Guatemala watched a gang murder her husband right in front of her after refusing to pay a fee to keep their business open. Once these men got out of prison, they threatened to kill Irene if she did not pay this fine. Irene and her seventeen-year-old daughter fled to the United States to seek asylum. On arriving at the border, Irene was detained, and her daughter was sent to a shelter. This was due to the Trump administration's "zero-tolerance border enforcement" policy. Irene now had to complete her credible fear interview to prove that she was in danger in her home country. The officer who conducted Irene's interview determined that she did not prove a "credible fear" of persecution if she did return to her home country. Due to Trump's new policy, several people are being rejected at the border and are not being granted asylum or refugee status (Brane, 2018).

One in three women worldwide have experienced either physical and/or sexual intimate partner violence or nonpartner sexual violence in their lifetime according to global estimates.

These domestic violence survivors flee their countries and come to the United States in hopes of living a life they did not fear. Several steps and interview processes are needed in order to fulfill this status. However, due to the Trump administration's policies, the United States may not be as welcoming as it once was.

On November 7, 2018, Jeff Sessions resigned his position as attorney general at President Trump's request. Matthew G. Whitaker, Jeff Sessions's chief of staff, was the acting attorney general, then William Barr took over in February 2019. It remains unclear the direction the new attorney general will take on this issue, but in October 2018, eighteen states as well as Washington, D.C., filed an amicus brief for a legal challenge to the policy (Powell, 2018).

Should Children Be Removed from Abusive Homes?

Every year, at least five million and as many as twenty million children in the United States witness domestic violence in their households (Emanuel, 2016). This results in a host of short- and long-term concerns, especially if the children do not receive therapy or some other type of intervention. In some cases, the children remain with their family until the victim can safely leave the situation or until the abuser changes his or her ways. In others, it is best to remove the children from the abusive home immediately. Obviously, every domestic violence situation is unique, and therefore it is always difficult to determine when it is the right time to remove a child or children from a home where domestic violence is occurring. Numerous factors need to be considered before determining that the removal of children is the best and safest option.

In most domestic violence cases, children are the silent victims of partner abuse: because they are young, they do not fully understand what is happening. In some cases, children are directly injured from the abuse, while in others children may just be frightened observers. Thirty to sixty percent of perpetrators of intimate partner violence also abuse children in the household (Emanuel, 2016). It is clear, however, that children who come from a family of violence are more likely to experience significant psychological problems short and long term. Children who have experienced domestic violence may suffer from emotional, physical, and mental abuse. Not all children will react the same way in response to a traumatic event such as domestic violence. The duration and type of domestic violence experienced affect how children will understand it. Gender may affect the way children cope with experiencing abuse, as will personality characteristics, including resiliency. Additional help from a loved one or supportive adult can heal a stressful event. Services such as guidance, attention, and support can help children who have been exposed to domestic violence, and services are increasing to be available to those who are in need of help from exposure to violence.

There is one core reason as to why it may be beneficial to remove a child from the home, and that is the dangerousness of the perpetrator. If the perpetrator is extremely harmful to the victims and children, then that may well be when protective child services take the initiative to step in. It is important to assess the risks carefully and report any type of physical evidence from the abuse on the children. Many state laws require police to open up child protective investigations in domestic violence cases in which a child below the age of twelve resides in the home. If abuse of the child is found, removal is often required unless the victim chooses to leave the abusive situation with the children. Documentation is crucial when making decisions on where to place children who come from abusive homes.

Unfortunately, in some situations, a victim of domestic violence will withhold certain information in fear of retaliation. Threats are made by the abuser that scare victims into thinking much worse will happen if they disclose information regarding their abuse. The survivor's main concern is usually the safety of her child or pet, so the thought of reaching out for help may be dismissed in order to protect them immediately.

According to one source, "CPS workers have asked if removal is appropriate in cases where adult victims lie, refuse to disclose details of abuse, or are seemingly uncooperative. While disclosures from adult victims are useful to CPS, the lack of them does not automatically demonstrate risk to children; in fact, in some cases an adult victim chooses not to disclose may be a strategy she uses to keep herself and her children safe for fear of the perpetrator's retaliation" (David Mandel & Associates, 2012).

Certainly, if a child is in imminent danger, they should be removed from that specific household. Child workers typically look to see if a child is not safe before taking the precautions of taking the child out of the home. "Imminent danger is defined as a specific family situation or behavior, emotion, motive, perception, or capacity within the family and home that is out of control and reasonably can be concluded to have severe effects on a vulnerable child" (Chill, 2009, p. 6). If there is danger that is active, then it is referred to as a present danger, whereas danger that is impending or inactive is referred to as impending danger. In many states, a certain threshold is required to be met before removing children.

The removal of a child from a home can result in negative effects. Reuniting a family later can be very challenging. Kids can end up in foster care for years and grow up without any family. Some advocates assert that Child Protective Services (CPS) are too quick to remove children from abusive homes. Statistics published by the U.S. Department of Health and Human Services in 2001 show that one in three children who were removed from their homes were found not to have been maltreated and thus it was an unnecessary removal. Also, the mentality of staff and agency leaders operating and justifying their actions and decisions has been described as "erring on the side of safety" (Chill, 2009, p. 3).

In some cases, CPS issues ultimatums to victims of domestic violence: either leave the abuser and flee with the children, or have them taken into protective custody. Domestic violence advocates caution against such an approach, as it exemplifies the same pattern of power and control that abusers are using against victims. Rather, domestic violence advocates wish to work with CPS to ensure that victims get to safety without unnecessary trauma to or removal of their children from their custody.

What Is the Connection between Pet Abuse and Domestic Violence?

Extensive research exists that shows that people who hurt animals don't stop with that and that what is called "the link"—the connection between animal cruelty and cruelty to humans—is very strong (Animal Legal Defense Fund, n.d.; Animal Welfare Institute, 2018). Advocates say law enforcement must pay attention to the link, as it can help protect both animals and humans. It is what many have called a "predictor crime" of domestic violence and child abuse. Likewise, health-care providers and domestic violence shelters should inquire about past animal abuse as a potential sign of lethality (Animal Welfare Institute, 2018).

A 1983 study found that animal abuse had occurred in 88 percent of homes in which physical child abuse was being investigated (Deviney, Dickert, & Lockwood, 1998. A study by the Massachusetts Society for the Prevention of Cruelty to Animals and Northeastern University in 1997 found that animal abusers are five times as likely to also harm other humans (Levin, Luke, & Ascione, 1999). A more recent study, in 2013, found that 43 percent of those who commit school massacres also committed acts of cruelty to animals—generally against cats and dogs (Madfills & Arluke, 2014). Another study in 2017 found that of the women who had companion animals during an abusive relationship, 89 percent reported that their abusers threatened, harmed, or killed the pets (American Welfare Institute, 2018).

Children who exhibit cruelty toward animals have often been neglected or abused. If children witness animal abuse, they are at significantly greater risk for becoming abusers. Pet abuse is considered one of the four most frequent and significant predictors of abusive behavior (American Humane Society, 2016).

Abusers use the threat of or actual violence against beloved animals as a tool of control. Some 49–71 percent of battered women report such threats or violence, according to the Animal Welfare Institute (2018). A national survey found 85 percent of victims seeking shelter for domestic violence reported pet abuse (American Humane Society, 2016). Women in domestic violence shelters are eleven times more likely to report pet abuse than comparable women who are not in shelters. Other research has shown that abusers who harm pets are more likely to use other controlling behaviors and to perpetrate serious harm. Questions about pet abuse are now included on most danger or lethality assessment tools.

For some time, there was no legal protection related to this. Now, all fifty states have felony animal cruelty statutes, and nearly two-thirds of states allow pets to be included on restraining orders. In some states, animal abusers must register in a fashion similar to that required for sex offenders. Several states require veterinarians to report signs of animal abuse, and some require the same of animal control officers. A few also require child and adult protection workers to receive training on the link and to report animal cruelty, abuse, and neglect (American Humane Society, 2016). As of 2016, the FBI began tracking crimes against animals in its National Incident Based Reporting System.

Yet, still, many shelters do not allow animals, which forces victims to make difficult choices about their own safety and that of their pets. As many as 48 percent of battered women report staying longer with an abuser out of concern for their pet. Some shelters make arrangements with local animal foster care, veterinary offices, or animal shelters (American Humane

Society, 2016). The American Humane Society provides information and training on the link and supports research and policy advocacy related to animal abuse and violence against humans.

Is Arming Victims of Domestic Violence an Appropriate Intervention to Stop Abuse?

Numerous instances of systematic failure to protect victims of domestic violence have prompted some critics to suggest more radical solutions to this problem. One such solution is to provide the victims with firearms so that they could protect themselves if their abuser threatens them. While such a measure can help victims to survive a confrontation with their abusers, it can also create serious safety risks.

The primary argument for providing at-risk household members with firearms is that such individuals will no longer be helpless if their abusers resort to extreme violence. Such benefit might become essential in situations when victims have no opportunity to flee or if the culprits themselves try to use guns and other tools. Indeed, Finley (2010) notes that when abusers resort to deadly violence, the police often might have no time to arrive and prevent the tragedy. Finley (2010, pp. 20–21) further describes examples of women assaulted and killed by their partners and a failure of governments to provide them with shelter or grant divorce or other protections. Such incidents show why law enforcement agencies cannot always address the problem. The fact that the victims often encountered disproportionate barriers to obtaining help might become another reason to question the efficiency of conventional policies for combating domestic violence. Critics could argue that such failures demonstrate the inability of the government to protect at-risk women and encourage abusive partners to keep mistreating victims.

In such conditions, providing victims with firearms might seem to be an attractive solution since it has a potential to reduce their dependence on governmental support. For example, one can reasonably assume that if a woman who fears her violent husband or partner cannot count on a quick response from authorities, she, at least, will have viable alternatives. For instance, she could use a firearm to protect herself, her children, and other family members in life-threatening situations. Indeed, male culprits often take advantage of their greater physical strengths to abuse women and children in their households. The presence of a gun could theoretically change the situation by depriving the aggressor of this advantage, thus giving the victim more realistic chances to protect herself and other family members. Zeoli and Bonomi (2015, p. 3) argue that such a worldview inspires laws that seek to "level the playing field." For that reason, some jurisdictions even encourage victims to obtain firearms. Notably, in Indiana, gun control legislation authorizes domestic violence survivors who enjoy a court order to freely carry firearms without a special permit for sixty days (Depompei, 2017). Such laws obviously intend to empower victims and deter potential abusers.

Such deterrence can be partially effective. For example, Sorenson and Wiebe (2004, pp. 1414–1415) investigate the role of firearms in the lives of battered women and observe that women occasionally use weapons to facilitate self-protection. Many women, according to the researchers, consider obtaining or using a gun to protect themselves from possible assault by an intimate partner. Such persons often think about the use of firearms not only for injuring or killing the attacker but also for intimidation. Interestingly, the respondents who faced domestic violence and used guns mainly sought to intimidate the intimate partner or threaten to kill him to secure the termination of hostile behavior. This circumstance is significant because it suggests that the presence of a gun might potentially help to prevent deadly violence in some cases. For example, if a woman threatens to use a gun to force her intimate partner to stop the aggressive behavior, she can avoid injuries or death, or gain an opportunity to call the police, or leave the house.

In such a scenario, both victims and culprits could survive and minimize negative impacts on children or medical costs caused by violent confrontation.

However, critics of such initiative argue that while scholarly evidence suggests the existence of benefits of arming victims of domestic violence, it does not offer consistent proof that such benefits outweigh risks. For instance, Zeoli and Bonomi (2015, p. 4) emphasize that scholarly evidence does not support the claim that guns aid victims in their attempts of self-defense. The research claims that guns, contrary to a widespread belief, can increase the risk of the deadly outcome if they end up in a household affected by domestic violence. Cases when abusers take guns that victims acquired for self-defense, and use them to commit their crimes, are also not uncommon. Since domestic violence involves intimate partners, it cannot be surprising that abusers often can learn about weapons their victims purchased. In essence, the proposed solution is more likely to increase the risk of violence than to eliminate it.

A review of statistical data and scholarly articles by the Harvard Injury Control Research Center (2018) results in similar conclusions. Specifically, women practically never use firearms for self-defense purposes. The researchers also found no statistical evidence that such a method of protection reduces the risk of injury in the first place. Opponents of providing women with guns emphasize that such recommendations rely on a belief that law-abiding citizens can use guns to protect themselves and are the main beneficiaries of gun ownership. However, multiple studies suggest that victims use guns in less than 1 percent of all crimes. Research by Hemenway and Solnick (2015, p. 25) further notes that the use of guns for self-defense is an extremely rare event. Even women who resort to firearms mainly use them in case of crimes against property, not sexual assaults or domestic abuse. Hence, critics might argue that the proposed recommendation relies on nothing but a myth.

Critics of the idea of providing domestic abuse victims with firearms further note that the risk of violence and death reduces only if one manages to remove weapons from at-risk households entirely. Unfortunately, many initiatives that seek to arm victims ignore this problem and fail to impose proportionate penalties on abusive partners. In most cases, such individuals continue enjoying the right to possess and buy new firearms even if they face restraining orders and despite existing laws that require their removal (Zeoli & Bonomi, 2015, p. 4). If men can freely acquire and use firearms, benefits of gun ownership for women become uncertain and can quickly render the initiative useless.

The benefits of gun-related initiatives might become particularly questionable in jurisdictions where owning or carrying a gun requires complex authorization procedures. For instance, Finley (2010, p. 21) mentions cases of women who died because competent agencies failed to provide them with necessary services in time due to bureaucratic difficulties. In essence, even if victims have the right to support, they do not always secure it. In such conditions, critics can reasonably ask how the government can guarantee that women who seek a permit for carrying or buying guns will not face similar delays. The implementation of such initiatives outside of the United States can be particularly challenging since most countries have strict gun control policies. While U.S. women usually have an unquestionable right to buy guns and keep them at home (without carrying), their foreign counterparts will have to go through complex procedures simply to obtain a gun. Even if the United States manages to transform this initiative into a success story, it will never be able to become a universal solution for all victims of domestic violence.

In conclusion, while domestic abuse victims might be able to use firearms to protect themselves and their families, the policy can increase the risk of violent and deadly outcomes or even help abusers to obtain weapons. Propositions to arm victims presuppose that firearms are an effective self-defense solution that reduces the likelihood of crime and its negative impacts. However, scholarly evidence challenges this assumption and reveals numerous risks of such a decision. Consequently, competent government agencies and communities might find it beneficial to test less radical solutions, including gun control measures and the removal of guns from households where domestic violence may occur, before arming victims. Such an approach could help minimize the risk of adverse effects.

Should Domestic Violence Offenders Be Allowed to Own Firearms?

Although there are many controversial issues about guns and gun control, one of the biggest surrounds the question of who should be able to have one. Some argue that domestic abusers should have to relinquish their weapons upon conviction and not be allowed to purchase or obtain additional guns. Others contend that this is an unfair restriction of the Second Amendment right to own weapons.

Critics contend that weapons in domestic violence situations dramatically escalate the chances of severe injuries or fatalities. Data shows that in a home with guns, domestic violence situations are often deadly. Abusers not only use the weapons but also control their victims by threatening to harm them, their family, or their pets or by otherwise brandishing the firearms. More than half of women who were once in a domestic violence situation had a partner who had threatened or harmed them with a gun (Shaw, 2016). Some studies have shown it is five times more likely that a victim will be killed when there is a gun in a domestic violence situation. Guns are the weapon of choice of abusers. Guns were used in 55 percent out of 1,352 intimate homicides in 2015. By 2011, nearly two-thirds of women killed with guns were killed by their intimate partner or ex-spouse (Shaw, 2016).

Federal law already says that those who have committed intimate partner violence cannot have or own a gun. In 1996, President Clinton signed into law the Lautenberg Amendment, making it illegal for individuals convicted of misdemeanor domestic violence assault to purchase or possess guns. Law enforcement officers (police) have the right to take any owned guns away from abusers in cases of domestic violence. State laws vary on the matter. In a domestic violence situation in Tennessee, for instance, police or law enforcement don't need to handcuff you to take your weapon away. Arrest is also not required in Alaska, Arizona, California, Hawaii, Illinois, Indiana, Maryland, Montana, New Hampshire, New Jersey, Ohio, and Utah. In other states, an arrest is required. Six states have court-ordered removal laws that specify gun use or threat as a condition of ordering guns removed. In three states, judges have the right to gun removal either temporarily or permanently depending on how the gun has been used as an instrument of abuse.

Another issue is that abusers may not just use their firearms on victims. Many mass shootings have occurred as a result of domestic violence. A study focusing on the period between January 2009 and July 2014 found that 57 percent of mass shootings involved the killing of a family member or a current or former intimate partner of the shooter.

These offenders have found their way around these laws. That is because there are loopholes in the law. For instance, the federal law does not apply to many abusers who victimize non-spouse partners. It also does not apply to abusers who victimize a family member other than a partner or child. Convicted stalkers are not included in the federal law related to firearm removal. Further, there is no specific provision in most states for abusers to surrender their firearms. Loopholes in the background check system also make it easy for abusers to acquire firearms. Persons purchasing guns from non-licensed dealers or online are not subject to background checks, for instance.

Oregon passed a new law banning people convicted of stalking or domestic violence, or under a restraining order, from buying or owning guns or ammunition. This closed a big loophole in the system that helped many assaulted women to be in more harmony. Oregon also passed a law expanding the waiting period to own a firearm from three days to ten days. This time, then, can potentially allow an abuser to cool off before utilizing a firearm against a victim, and it allows for a more detailed check by the National Instant Criminal Background Check System.

Others argue, however, that owning firearms is protected by the Second Amendment of the U.S. Constitution. Other offenders do not have to relinquish their firearms or face prohibitions on them.

What Role Does Mass Media Play in Domestic Violence?

Mass media is one of the biggest influences on people today. Many people use mass media for fun and as a distraction, while others use it for news. Mass media generally refers to news media, although increasingly people use social media, including sources like Facebook, Instagram, and Twitter, for these purposes as well. That does not mean, however, that mass media always covers certain issues fully or even accurately. Studies have repeatedly shown that mass media overrepresents violent crime, in general (Meade, 2015). One issue that doesn't seem to get too much attention is domestic violence. Despite public attention to the issue since the 1970s, the coverage it gets from the media is still lacking.

Several high-profile domestic violence cases have been covered by the media, however. Cases involving celebrities, athletes, and politicians tend to get the most coverage, but local sources typically cover other incidents, especially when someone is killed by an abuser. Some argue that media glorifies abuse, to the point that many times victims feel like the media coverage is like a second assault because of the insensitivity being used in using pictures and publishing names.

One of the most infamous domestic violence cases that received a great deal of media attention is the O. J. Simpson case. The case has to do with the ex-football player O. J. Simpson, who was tried on two counts of murder for the deaths of his ex-wife, Nicole Brown Simpson, and her friend, Ronald Goldman. This was a case that cut across class lines and demonstrated that domestic violence can happen to anyone, even to families that look like they have it all. The attention this case got from the media came from all angles and demonstrated racial disparities and issues related to class and wealth. According to Maxwell, Huxford, Borum, and Hornik (2000), O. J. Simpson was exploited with racial stereotypes because his wife—the victim—was an upper-class, white woman; it was more likely for this case to get media coverage than a domestic violence case involving a poor or African American victim or any other minority.

Since the 1970s, the media has used a variety of frames in covering domestic violence (Maxwell, Huxford, Borum, & Hornik, 2000). The press first "discovered" domestic abuse in the 1970s when it began to report incidents and ads that were posted around the country. According to Jacquet (2015), ads around the country would advertise bowling alleys and other places of fun and would say snarky phrases like "Have some fun, Beat your wife tonight. Bowling's a Ball at your BPA fun Center." Research has also shown that magazines often place the blame on the victim and that myths and stereotypes also blame the victim (Maxwell, Huxford, Borum, & Hornik, 2000). This ideology that women are the reason for anything that happens to them reflects the cultural myths and patriarchal assumptions about the role and behavior of women that are reinforced through mass media (Meyers, 1997).

The coverage of domestic violence doesn't stop at written media, like newspapers or blogs; it continues to reality-based television. This type of television often makes it seem as though domestic violence is a problem only for minorities and lower classes and that the blame always resides in the victim for not leaving the abuser. Popular culture, like movies and television, typically sends similar messages. For example, *Sleeping with the Enemy* (1991) is a movie that portrays the fault in the victim and the only way of her leaving the violent relationship is through faking her death.

The media also does what is referred to as "agenda setting," which is the "framing for content." Media coverage of abuse shifted from focusing on the victim to holding the batterer accountable for his or her actions. This too can be dangerous, as, many times, leaving or attempting to leave could be more lethal than staying and getting help in other ways. Maxwell, Huxford, Borum, and Hornik (2000) analyzed two Philadelphia publications that had the highest circulation—*The Inquirer* and *Philadelphia Daily News*—for coverage of domestic violence. The analysis covered the period pre– and post–O. J. Simpson trial with articles from January 1990 through August 1997. Of all the articles that dealt with domestic violence, half had domestic violence as their primary focus and the rest gave domestic violence a secondary mention. Coverage centered on the specific incident rather than the individual, and only a third of the stories mentioned criminal consequences for the abuser or recommended action for the victim.

The news is framed in ways that convey certain understandings of reality while excluding other understandings that may be important to the context of the story. News coverage of domestic violence often supports the status quo, which is designed to sustain male domination over women (Bullock & Cubert, 2002). Also, many times journalists see the police as a legitimate source, who can be neutral and balance the information from the people giving the opposing view. However, the police perspective many times is not neutral and often is focused on the offender instead of the victim or the case altogether. Another factor that is misleading from news coverage of domestic violence is the word "choice." A study by Benedict

(1992) found that the way the press covers crimes like domestic and sexual violence reinforces the use of certain vocabulary that promotes traditional images of women. Many times, in news coverage, domestic violence homicide is dealt with as just another murder, which completely ignores the context of battering and the background of domestic violence.

Media still reports the most salacious aspects of violence against women and provides the public with a view that is provocative but not representative, just as Benedict (1992) described. An example is the case of Gladys Ricart, which was broadcasted when her ex-partner killed her the day she was to wed someone else. Agustin Garcia shot Ricart multiple times on September 26, 1999, in Ridgefield, New Jersey. Media coverage of the case emphasized the titillating circumstances, and much of it questioned Ricart's decision to move so quickly into a new relationship after she and Garcia had broken up.

Carll (2003) states, however, that objective news coverage and dissemination of information may be one of the most powerful tools in reducing the problem of violence against women, and, more important, the way the information is crafted, if effective, can promote positive social change. For instance, Ricart's murder inspired Myhosi "Josie" Ashton to make a walk from Ridgefield, New Jersey, to Miami, Florida, in her own wedding dress to bring attention to the issues of domestic and dating violence. This has become an annual event in many cities, typically called the Brides' March, and for ten years, Ashton and others have coordinated a campus version in South Florida called the College Brides Walk.

Are Restraining Orders a Good Way to Protect Victims?

The motivation behind the restraining order is to shield victims from their abuser. Restraining orders, or orders of protection, specify limits on the abusers' actions, prohibiting them from making contact in person and typically via other methods.

There are many pros and cons to restraining orders in domestic violence cases.

One advantage of a restraining order is that it requires a battering individual to cut off contact with an injured individual. This is a valuable asset for victims who have effectively isolated themselves from the abuser. In the past, when a battered victim requested to have the batterer ousted from a common home, judges frequently denied the request, especially if the house was owned by the batterer or leased exclusively in the batterer's name. This left exploited people with little response other than escaping to a safe house. Since then, the standard in numerous states has changed to a desire that protective orders will incorporate stay-away arrangements. If the abuser follows the restriction made by the order around the victim, the victim may have peace of mind and safety.

The second advantage is that there are fewer costs (in both money and time) related to protective orders than with criminal cases. As a rule, criminal cases can be long and emotionally challenging for victims. Protectives orders are quicker and involve less emotional trauma. Once apprehended for violating a restraining order, penalties can be assessed more quickly than criminal proceedings (A Community for Peace, n.d.).

On the other hand, there are a number of disadvantages of restraining orders. These disadvantages suggest that forcing women to choose between getting a stay-away order and getting no protection order at all, as some courts now do, does a disservice to domestic violence victims.

In addition, while not impossible, enforcement of restraining orders in cases where the victim and abuser share children can be challenging. The courts typically grant contact between the abuser and the kids. Abusers frequently utilize their entrance to the child to execute abuse—for instance, while trading the kids for appearance periods. The abuser who is banned from seeing his victim will associate with the victim and probably have numerous chances to irritate and misuse her. Thus, victims with kids are at more serious risk than others without for encountering violence in the wake of accepting a security arrangement (Goldfarb, 2008).

Also, victims face the threat of separation assault, meaning the abuser may increase the frequency or severity of attacks in the wake of the victim attempting to leave. Women are most in danger in the wake of closure or while endeavoring to end the abuse. The order implies an end to contact between both parties, which might be the trigger for an increase of harm. The relationship might be finished, but the viciousness could continue. According to the Massachusetts protection study, individuals who had protective orders containing no-contact arrangements were, in reality, more inclined to experience additional harm than those whose protective orders allowed contact with the victim (Goldfarb, 2008).

Besides the danger of extra abuse, a protective order can force different kinds of harm on the victim. These include loss of access to the abuser's salary, loss of childcare help prompting the victim's powerlessness to keep an occupation, and loss of help from more distant family and community (Goldfarb, 2008).

More issues can emerge with the protective order if the victim needs to simply speak with her abuser. In the event that the abuser has been precluded from having contact with the person in question, any future correspondence between the two—regardless of whether the injured individual started it—can prompt a finding that he has contradicted the order, subjecting him to criminal punishments. In addition, when the victim has accelerated the infringement by starting contact with an abuser who is liable to a stay-away order, police, examiners, and judges might be unsympathetic to her and reluctant to make a move, regardless of whether genuine maltreatment has happened (Goldfarb, 2008).

In a surprising decision, the U.S. Supreme Court ruled in *Castle Rock v. Gonzales* (2005) that police in Colorado did not have a legal duty to enforce restraining orders. That case is described in Chapter 1. Jessica Gonzales (now Lenahan) and her attorneys brought that case before the Inter-American

Commission on Human Rights, which, in 2011, issued a strong critique of the Supreme Court's ruling and called on the United States to improve its procedures related to restraining orders. The transcript from that hearing is included in Chapter 5.

Do Mandatory Arrest Policies in Domestic Violence Cases Work?

The legal system responds to domestic violence in many different ways. One of these options is mandatory arrests for abusers.

State laws differ when it comes to domestic violence cases: in some states arrest is preferred, in others it is mandatory, or in some it is done at the officer's discretion. Many factors affect the arrest rates as well. One study found that police were 2 times more likely to arrest if there was an injured victim, 4 times more likely if the offender resided at the scene, and 1.5 times more likely if the crime took place in a large city (Hirschel & Buzawa, 2009). There has been a significant increase in the arrest rate for offenders over the years, and many studies have suggested that this is due to mandatory arrest policies. There is much debate about whether these mandatory arrests are effective or necessary in domestic violence cases.

Mandatory arrests policy is in place to help deter domestic violence from occurring and reoccurring. Such policies were ushered in around the United States in the 1980s and 1990s after the Minneapolis Domestic Violence Experiment, where researchers found that in cases where the offenders were arrested, the offenders were less likely to reoffend. Randomly chosen officers would report at domestic violence scenes and would be assigned a different method by which to respond to the incident. The different methods officers were assigned were (1) arresting the offender, (2) sending the perpetrator away from the scene for eight hours (if the incident occurred at home, the perpetrator was to leave home for eight hours), or (3) simply giving advice to the victim and suspect. Once the officers used their assigned method, there was a follow-up with the victims to analyze their situation post officer interaction. Findings showed that violence reoccurring in the six months after police involvement was the lowest when police conducted an arrest. It is also important to note that after six months, only 10 percent of suspects arrested repeated violence compared to the 19 percent who repeated violence after police advise and the 24 percent who repeated violence after the suspect was sent away for a period of time (Sherman & Berk, 1984). The best results came from the portion of cases that were subjected to arrests rather than advise or separation. Other cities such as Charlotte, Colorado Springs, and Metro-Dade conducted this experiment as well, and although they found that there is no policy that deters domestic violence long term, it is a better deterrent than no arrest at all.

One of the most compelling arguments against mandatory arrest would be the effect this has on the victim. Mandatory arrest policy may not be consistent with the wishes of victims. Although many victims may want their abusers to be arrested and separated from them, some do not. Victims may be in a particular situation within their relationship that deters them from calling the police or having the police arrest their partner. These situations could be that the victims are illegal immigrants or, in some cases, persons with visas or only legal residencies. In cases like this, victims fear that they will get arrested or may end up getting arrested themselves along with the abuser. Another reason a victim may not want to call can be due to their partner's immigration status, as domestic violence offenses allow for the deportation of undocumented individuals. If the abuser is the provider for the family, whether he or she be documented or not, the victim may not want to contact the police because their means of survival will practically be removed from their lives.

The effectiveness of mandatory arrests is questionable. Studies have found that when the abuser is arrested, there have been increased rates of repeat violence if the offender was unemployed, not married, had prior assaults, or was under the influence of drugs during the offense. The likelihood of an abuser having any of these is common, meaning that a good number of perpetrators are more likely to reoffend after being arrested. Incapacitating the abuser may result in making the situation worse (Iyengar, 2007).

Another criticism of this policy is that police officers cannot always effectively assess the situation when they are called onto a crime scene, which often leads to dual arrests. An unintended consequence of mandatory arrest policies is that more women are arrested in domestic violence cases in places where these laws were enacted. Not only is this faulty because the victim who called the police to get help is arrested along with the offender, but this also causes victims to not want to call the police again or call at all. Women of color are most likely to be arrested under mandatory arrest policies. When police are offered discretion, however, they may also use it in biased ways.

Another reason victims refrain from reporting their abuser is that many women do not want to subject their partners to a racist and prejudice justice system. Law enforcement, in general, lacks training to asses and address victims' conditions or environments effectively. A way to address this issue is to have a ready victim advocate to arrive at the scene as well as to address the victim while law enforcement addresses the offender, keeping both parties separate but equal. The organization INCITE! Women of Color against Violence has issued a statement opposing mandatory arrest, noting that it contributes to the prison industrial complex (Statement on Gender Violence and the Prison Industrial Complex, n.d.).

Many state governments that have adopted the mandatory arrest policy have taken further steps and implemented mandatory prosecutions or "no-drop" policies. These policies require that each suspect arrested for domestic violence be prosecuted in a court of law and further sentenced. This gives the survivors further relief because they are also relieved of the responsibility of pressing charges against their abuser. This makes it easier for the survivors because it is not the victims against their abuser but the state against the suspect. Some state governments have placed no-drop policies in which the survivors can even decide how much they are willing to participate in the case.

Is a Feminist Perspective the Best Approach to Domestic Violence Advocacy?

A feminist perspective on issues concerning violence against women and girls will typically cite the patriarchal society in which we live as a main source of the phenomenon. But before arriving to the notion of a hierarchical society based on gender, the feminist model must first examine gender as it exists in modern society. Taking into account gender roles both within and outside of the confines of a domestic partnership is essential to a feminist perspective on domestic violence. This model argues that because of the inferior status that women hold in society, along with the frequent manifestation of masculinity as dominance, women experience disproportionate rates of domestic abuse.

Gender roles are generally known as the socially assigned, and often strictly enforced, behavioral guidelines for men and women. These roles define the commonly held beliefs surrounding masculinity and femininity as they are known today and intend to dictate the positions that women and men occupy in society. Feminist theory argues that the gender roles placed upon women have limited them to lives of domesticity and social positions of inferiority for a large portion of human history. Conversely, the role of men in society has been understood as one of leadership, authority, and power. Their gender role has designated them the leaders of humanity. The feminist model cites this stringently enforced system of behavior for men and women as the source of the prevalent violence against women on a global scale. Gloria Steinem, a frequently referenced activist on the forefront of the feminist movement, stated that gender roles "are the deepest cause of violence in the world" (Interview: Gloria Steinem, n.d.). But far more than simply assigning power and freedom to one gender, feminists argue that gender roles have bred a form of "toxic masculinity" that has overcome modern society and has hindered our conception of what it means to be a man.

Connell and Messerschmidt (2005) discuss that to approach issues of gender and gender-based violence, we must form the conversation around masculinity instead of solely focusing on the term "gender issue" as exclusively referencing the special needs of women. Sociological studies show masculinity to exist in various forms across a global spectrum. Each culture has a different interpretation of, and ultimately the social role for, men and those considered masculine. For the purpose of discussing how feminism attributes gender-based violence to masculinity, Western hegemonic masculinity will be examined. "Hegemonic masculinity" refers to the dominant form of masculinity in any given culture. In various societies both in the West and in the East, masculinity is characterized by dominance and power, with an emphasis on leadership (Connell & Messerschmidt, 2005). Feminist theory will point to various examples of how this facet of masculinity has given birth to one in which these characteristics have translated into a violent form of manhood. These transformed characteristics have manifested themselves generationally through the relationships men have with women, whose gender role is largely defined by submission, and have left them susceptible to the violent manifestations of toxic masculinity. This conclusion leads to the phenomenon of what is known as "male-pattern violence." This term refers to the patterns of violent crimes and acts committed by men, one of the most notable being domestic violence. According to feminist literature on the topic, male-pattern violence is predominantly characterized by "motivations of aggression, revenge, competition for dominance, competition with other males (for example in drug- or gang-related violence)," or feelings of ownership or entitlement toward women, which is, what feminists argue, is typically the source of male-perpetrated violence against women (Ruby, 2004).

Just as important to this analysis is the examination of the gender roles placed on women in society. It is well documented that in contemporary culture, women have been ascribed a passive social role—one that has involved, for most of modern human history, the sole responsibility of tending to domestic issues and raising children. Along with informal cultural gender roles, actual laws deeming women as property of their fathers or husbands dominated Western society until roughly the turn of the twentieth century. Feminist theory argues that the application of rigid gender roles, as well as the legal oppression of women for centuries, has promoted the perpetuation of violence against women by deeming them the inferior sex. Flood and Pease (2009) argue that gender-based violence is inextricably intertwined with attitudes toward women and their role in society. They state that domestic violence is the product of a wider set of gender norms dictating that "men should be dominant in households and intimate relationships and have the right to enforce their dominance through physical chastisement, men have uncontrollable sexual urges, women are deceptive and malicious, and marriage is a guarantee of sexual consent" (Flood & Pease, 2009). Another important broader characteristic of the female gender role is the assumption of inherent sexual deviance. The classic trope of women as immoral seductresses who lure virtuous men to sins they would otherwise not commit has a long history. This archetype, which spans back to biblical times, is present in modern attitudes toward women and femininity and is also a fundamental aspect of the larger attitude toward women in society.

The feminist model is comprehensive in its explanation of domestic violence carried out against women by men, but many cite the inability to explain domestic abuse in lesbian relationships as a limitation of feminist theory. Critics of feminist theory believe that the prevalence of physical abuse

in lesbian relationships challenges the idea that domestic violence is a product of male socialization with violence (Miller
et al., 2001).

What Is the Role of Health-Care
Professionals in Domestic Violence Cases?

Many victims of domestic violence do not tell anyone about
the abuse. Trained professionals, however, can identify abuse
and can therefore help put victims in touch with needed resources. Physicians are often considered the "front line" when
it comes to domestic violence, as victims may disclose abuse to
them or, if the right questions are asked, abuse can be identified. Since 1992, the American Medical Association has called
on physicians to screen patients for abuse. Many other medical
bodies, including the American Academy of Family Physicians
and the American College of Obstetricians and Gynecologists,
have made similar recommendations.

Abuse takes its toll on physical and mental health, both in
the short and in the long term. Victims are more likely to suffer
from depression, post-traumatic stress disorder, anxiety disorders, eating disorders, substance abuse, chronic pain, and suicidal behavior. Adolescents who have been victims of dating
violence are more prone to have problems with drug and alcohol, engage in risky sexual behaviors, get pregnant, have low
self-esteem, suffer from depression and anxiety, and attempt
or commit suicide. As such, research has shown that victims
of domestic violence use health-care services more frequently
than do non-victims. According to one study, 14–35 percent of
women visiting an emergency department and 12–23 percent
of women visiting family practitioners had been physically
abused or threatened by their partners in the previous year
(Bradley et al., 2002).

Abuse is often overlooked by health-care providers, however.
Male physicians have expressed concern that female victims will
not disclose abuse to them if they ask about it. Some health-
care providers do not see screening for or addressing abuse as

part of their role, while others simply lack the knowledge or expertise to query patients about domestic violence. Domestic violence could also be overlooked by physicians who may themselves be perpetrators of abuse or who believe that religious laws allow men to control or sometimes beat their wives. Further, some physicians are afraid to open a "Pandora's box" by asking about abuse, or patients may find such questioning offensive (Usta & Talib, 2014).

Yet studies have found that women do not find questions about abuse to be offensive, and they are ready to talk about it when asked. The first step is using a tool for screening. Several scales have been tested on various populations and found to be valid and reliable. One of the most widely used is the HITS scale. It has four simple questions on a Likert scale: How often does your partner (1) physically hurt you, (2) insult you or talk down to you, (3) threaten you with harm, or (4) scream and curse at you (Sherin, Sinacore, Li, Zitter, & Shakil, 1998)? These questions can be asked verbally or in writing, and the screening can be conducted by the physician himself or herself or by a nurse or other staff during an intake process. They must, however, be asked in private. It is recommended that physicians or health-care providers establish a protocol for what happens after abuse has been identified. This typically includes a combination of health-care and social services. In addition, hospitals and other health-care settings can have pamphlets, posters, and other literature available to provide additional information about services. In some states, physicians are mandatory reporters of domestic violence, while in others they are not. Even if there is no reporting requirement, careful documentation and providing the victim information about resources can be very helpful. A danger or lethality assessment tool can also be used to identify those victims who are most at risk for serious harm. Such tools look at the history of threats of murder or suicide, attempts at both, increases in the frequency or severity of the abuse, attempts at strangulation, use of weapons, alcohol and substance abuse, and recent termination of the relationship or attempts to do so. If this questioning identifies a potentially lethal situation, the physician or another trained individual should assist the survivor with safety planning. This typically includes hiding money, clothes, keys, and important documents and identifying a safe place to flee.

Documenting the abuse properly is critical in case the victim needs that paperwork for legal cases, including restraining orders, prosecutions, and custody hearing. It is recommended that physicians avoid using words such as "claims" or "alleges," as these may make it appear that there is doubt about the verity of the claims. Physicians should include in the patient's file (1) what happened, when, and the nature of the injuries, using the patient's own words wherever possible; (2) any findings from a physical examination, including the nature, shape, and color of injuries—if possible, photographs should be included, but documenting the same on a body map could suffice if needed; (3) any lab work ordered, medications prescribed, or referrals made; and (4) comments on comorbidities, disability, or pregnancy, if relevant.

It is generally advised that physicians ask about weapons in the home, given the increased threat of serious injury or fatality. One legal challenge to this line of questioning came in Florida, where former governor Rick Scott signed a bill into law making it a misdemeanor for physicians to ask about gun ownership unless they had reason to believe "in good faith" that the information was medically relevant but not as part of routine screening. A team of pediatricians, backed by many other health-care providers and by the American Civil Liberties Union, challenged the law, and eventually a U.S. appeals court determined that it was a violation of the doctors' right to free speech in a case that came to be known as "Docs v. Glocks." Under the law, doctors faced fines and even permanent revocation of their medical licenses (Pierson, 2017).

For some time, insurance providers considered domestic violence to be a preexisting condition that could result in denial of coverage to survivors. As of 2010, forty-three states had adopted some form of legislation prohibiting such discrimination, and the health-care reform known as "Obamacare" specifically forbids it as well.

Some states have domestic violence training requirements for physicians. Since 2003, Florida has required this training, and evaluations have found that it has resulted in more physicians screening victims for abuse. Alaska, California, Colorado, Connecticut, Kentucky, Minnesota, New Hampshire, New Jersey, New York, Ohio, Oklahoma, Pennsylvania, South Carolina, Tennessee, Washington, and West Virginia also have state laws requiring domestic violence training for physicians. State laws also vary as to whether physicians are mandatory reporters of abuse in general or just in cases of serious injury. Doctors are mandatory reporters of child abuse and elder abuse (Family Violence Prevention Fund, 2010).

Is the Shelter Model of Domestic Violence Services the Best Way to Help Victims?

Emerging out of the 1970s' Women's Rights Movement and the Battered Women's Movement, the first domestic violence shelter in the United States was opened in 1973 in St. Paul, Minnesota. Originally based on a feminist understanding of abuse, today many assert that the shelter model has lost most of its feminist underpinnings and that perhaps a different model would be more effective.

One concern with the traditional shelter model is that, on any given day, many victims are turned away because domestic violence shelters are filled to capacity. Each year, the National Network to End Domestic Violence conducts a twenty-four-hour census of domestic violence programs in the United States and its territories. Ninety percent of certified domestic violence shelters responded to the 2017 Domestic Violence Counts survey, which found that while more than 72,000 victims were served in a day, there were 11,441 unmet requests, with the majority for shelter or housing (Domestic Violence Counts 2017 National Summary, 2017). While there is no clear data to show what happens to victims who are denied shelter, it is safe to assume that at least a portion of them stay with or return to abusers. Another portion likely ends up on the streets or in homeless shelters, not exactly safe locations when fleeing a dangerous assailant.

Some would argue that this means we need to fund more shelters. But critics note that another problem is that, as shelters have become increasingly bureaucratized, they have also become far more of a stopgap measure, less able to respond to the unique needs of victims and to help them develop ways and means of living alone safely. Funding for domestic violence services is scarce, and centers often compete for the same finite bundle of money. Each must therefore show that they are providing a specific set of services that funders have identified as "best practices." While most of these are indeed good (e.g., therapy, assistance in applying for state benefits), the need to document best practices inevitably results in services that cannot be provided because they were not included in the grant proposal or are supported by the funding agency. Further, the requirement for best practices means that funders rarely support unique or innovative programs. A radical, feminist perspective that challenges societal patriarchy, gender inequality more broadly, and traditional gender role norms is not necessarily what conservative funders want to support.

Certain services are rarely provided by domestic violence shelters, for instance, legal assistance. Victims who need legal assistance (and most do) are generally sent elsewhere. Therefore, rather than a one-stop shop that can help a victim navigate the many systems with which she or he must interact, domestic violence shelters often simply make referrals, leaving the already-traumatized person to fend for themselves, all this while grant monies are sometimes being spent on nonessential items, like fancy office furniture, because the funding source allowed it but did not authorize legal help.

Another issue is that the increasing bureaucratization of domestic violence shelters has led to a more professionalized work service. While in some ways that may be beneficial, as shelter staff may be more educated about the issue, it has also resulted in a more cold and clinical approach to a problem that requires a supportive and flexible response. Staff at many nonprofit agencies are overwhelmed, often juggling fund-raising, completing paperwork required for funders, and still trying to assist victims. Less like a grassroots, people-centered movement, oftentimes these nonprofits look more like the corporate world, with its hierarchies and cutthroat strategies. Victims often complain that shelters feel like prisons and that they must beg for any personalized assistance. Advocates working at domestic violence agencies are often prohibited from engaging in political advocacy, yet that is a key component of social change. When they get it, many say they are treated as though they are a burden. One victim who sought help at a South Florida domestic violence shelter said this about her experience: "If I had been any weaker than I am I would have probably committed suicide after talking to the person on the hotline" (Finley, 2011).

An alternate model could be more individualized, for instance, housing victims in hotels if needed during crises but then finding and helping pay for safe housing of the victim's choice. During this time, advocates can work with victims to help them with all other required resources, from medical to legal, educational to economic. Some organizations that help victims have even disavowed 501(c)3 nonprofit status so that they no longer have to spend time appealing to and pleasing funders. Rather, all monies they generate go directly to services for victims. Two of these organizations—No More Tears and INCITE!—are included in the profiles in Chapter 4.

What Role Can Self-Defense Classes Play in Efforts to Prevent Sexual or Domestic Violence?

Many people believe that women can protect themselves from abuse or sexual assault. Likewise, media and popular culture tend to promote self-defense as a solution. Films like *Enough*, starring Jennifer Lopez, show victims learning self-defense tools and using them to successfully fight off a batterer. In reality, however, most domestic violence and sexual violence organizations disavow self-defense training.

Self-defense alone does not change the underlying causes of abuse or assault. As such, to market them as "prevention" tools is entirely disingenuous. Further, it continues to place responsibility for change on the victim rather than on the offender (Hollander, 2014). Many self-defense courses are merely profit driven and pay little attention to the specific needs of victims or of women, in general (McCaughey & Cermele, 2015). In addition, many assert that self-defense programs are dangerous, as it is difficult for someone to use those strategies against an acquaintance or loved one, and thus victims may feel they are more equipped to stave off unwanted advances than in reality they are.

On the other hand, advances in understanding abuse and assault have resulted in changes in how some self-defense courses operate. Some courses now use a trauma-informed perspective that teaches not only physical defense skills but also psychological skills and assertiveness training. Early research of these classes has found that victims report feeling less fearful, having more self-confidence, feeling better about their bodies, and having a general sense of empowerment and self-worth. Rather than prevention, these classes can be considered part of a risk-reduction strategy that includes many other elements (Stahl, 2016). One agency that provides such an approach is Peace Over Violence in Los Angeles.

Others recommend that self-defense courses should take an explicitly feminist perspective that emphasizes broader gender inequalities (Gidycz, 2014). Some argue that discouraging women from preparing to defend themselves plays into gender role stereotypes about women as the weaker sex (Hollander, 2014).

How Accurate Is Battered Woman Syndrome?

Many factors influence how a particular victim will respond in an abusive situation. In the early 1970s, psychologist

Lenore Walker coined the term "battered woman syndrome" (BWS) to describe the more common experiences and behaviors of women who have been abused by intimate partners (Walker, 1979).

BWS refers to women's experiences that result from being battered, which is typically referred to as "learned helplessness," as well as the actions of the abuser, referred to as the "cycle of violence." BWS also describes the mental health effects of abuse, including post-traumatic stress disorder. Many believe it to be a legal defense, but in reality, there is no special "battered women's defense" or "battered woman syndrome defense."

Walker intended BWS to help explain why many women stay with abusers. She wrote that many abusive relationships were characterized by the following three-phase cycle and that this cycle resulted in learned helplessness. The cycle included (1) a tension-building phase; (2) an acute battering incident; and (3) a contrition phase, where the batterer showers affection on the woman with promises never to repeat the abuse. Later research suggests that, over time, the contrition phase may end up being less about apologizing and more a simple lull in the hostilities. The victim is scared to leave regardless. In her work, Walker also attempted to correct a number of myths about abuse, including that it was uncommon, that middle- and upper-class women were not victims, that abusers were masochists, that victims could easily leave abusers, and that women deserved to be beaten. Before BWS, many believed that women brought on the abuse and that victims were vulnerable because of low self-esteem.

The concept of learned helplessness was adapted from the work of Martin Seligman in the 1960s. Seligman studied dogs that learned that either side of a cage in which they were stuck contained an electric shock no longer tried to avoid the shock, as they had learned there was nothing they could do. Repeated beatings, like the shocks, Walker argued, resulted in victims feeling as though any attempt to end the abuse would be futile. Many, therefore, became passive and accepting that the abuse would be their norm.

Critics contend that BWS undermines victims' autonomy, as it makes it seem as though victims are helpless and can thereby stigmatize victims (Dutton, Osthoff, & Dichter, 2009). Further, there is no standard and valid definition of BWS that can be used in expert testimony in legal cases. Others note that BWS fails to incorporate scientific data that shows an array of other responses to battering (Chan, 1994).

Although there is no special legal defense, experts in abuse cases can testify that a woman may have used self-defense as a last straw, fighting back before the abuser kills her. To successfully use this type of defense, an expert must show that the battered woman is a normal, reasonable person who is responding the only way possible in a difficult situation. The emphasis is on the fact that anyone could behave similarly in such circumstances. There is an apparent contradiction here, in that if one suffers from learned helplessness and sees no point in fighting the abuser, how could one bring oneself to use self-defense? Proponents of BWS maintain that this simply means the abuse has escalated and the victim is now in survival mode, thinking she will likely die if she takes no action.

How Effective Are Batterer Intervention Programs?

Given the frequency of domestic violence in the United States, it is necessary not only to establish facilities that provide protection but also to analyze the effectiveness of treatments in regard to the perpetrators. Education is a key factor to prevent abuse, since in many cases early signs of aggression and violence are present during childhood. Most abusers are exposed early on to abuse in the household and learn this behavior that they may carry into adolescent and adult relationships. Early intervention would reduce domestic violence and might even prevent homicides.

Another strategy that had been used to address domestic violence is batterer intervention programs (BIPs). The first step of the intervention is the intake assessment, a process that can span one to eight weekly sessions (Healey, Smith, & O'Sullivan, 1998) The purpose is to explain the terms and conditions of treatment to the client and to examine the batterer's abusive behavior. The next step involves contacting the victims to ensure their safety. Batterers often deny or minimize their actions, so contact with their victims also provides insight into the behaviors that need correction (Healey, Smith, & O'Sullivan, 1998).

The most commonly used model of intervention is the Duluth Curriculum, which utilizes a coordinated community response to domestic violence (Healey, Smith, & O'Sullivan, 1998). Topics such as nonviolence, respect, partnership, negotiation, and fairness are discussed during sessions along with visual illustration such as videos. Another method that is common is the EMERGE model, which targets not only physical but also emotional and psychological abuse and includes exercises to develop respect and empathy for the victim (Healey, Smith, & O'Sullivan, 1998). It is a forty-eight-week program that is divided into two stages. Orientation and group work are the key stages for intervention with group leaders using confrontation during sessions to correct behavior.

Prevention and intervention for perpetrators of domestic violence is a field that has not been thoroughly evaluated. While forty-five states have developed formal standards for BIPs (Morrison, Hawker, & Miller, 2016), much debate exists on the fundamental elements of such programs and their success rates. Evaluations must to be done in order to measure the effectiveness, as the results of many studies to date are inconclusive because of methodological problems (Arias, Arce, & Vilarino, 2013).

Some characteristics of successful BIPs have been identified, though. It is generally agreed that group size should be relatively small in order to be able to effectively manage programs, but there's debate about what exactly is the perfect number of clients to have in such groups. The duration of the program is also relative not only to the effectiveness of the program but also to the batterers in reform. More sessions do tend to promote behavior change, but the problem is establishing the essential time that is needed—a factor that is subject to each client in the most effective type of program due to the complexity of multiple backgrounds. "Most agreed that it's important for batterer intervention programs to have a curriculum to work with; however, participants felt strongly that imposing a strict curriculum on clients was largely ineffective" (Morrison et al., 2016). That is, while there needs to be some program specifics, the intervention also needs to be flexible enough to address each batterer's unique needs. Qualification requirements for program leaders are also a key factor that needs to be taken into consideration.

Studies have shown that a woman is less likely to be reassaulted by a man who was arrested, sanctioned, and sent to a batterers program than by a man who was simply arrested and sanctioned. "Working with an estimated population of 100,000 batterers, this would equal 5,000 fewer batterers" (Arias, Arce, & Vilarino, 2013). Far from conclusive, it does seem to suggest that such programs have impacted and prevent the reoccurrence of abuse.

A suggestion to improve the effectiveness of the program is co-facilitation. "Having two people co-leading groups was believed, allowed facilitators to better manage the group and attend to clients" (Morrison et al., 2016). The idea is to demonstrate multiple points of view and gain more insights in order to reform individuals. The aspect on gender is always a crucial issue in domestic violence, which is why some BIPs have facilitators of both genders (Morrison et al., 2016). This exposure allows well-trained members of co-ed teams to interact with one another and is viewed as an effective strategy to model desired behaviors (Morrison et al., 2016).

Before the behavior of the perpetrators can change, their mentality needs to be addressed. A common trait among batterers is victim blaming. Many put all of the blame and responsibilities of their actions on the women they targeted and abused. The goal of BIPs is to ensure that the participants understand that they were responsible for the actions against their victims (Morrison et al., 2016). Using co-ed facilitators gives them an opportunity to change this mentality and allows batterers to see and experience positive, respectful interactions with women (Morrison et al., 2016). While all these techniques might hold the potential for reforming perpetrators, the question still at hand is, What is the success rate and effectiveness of this program?

Research to date has not found BIPs to be effective, as recidivism rates are high as are dropout rates (Aaron & Beaulaurier, 2017). One study of 620 men mandated to BIPs under threat of incarceration found that 50 percent did not complete the program or never attended at all (Aaron & Beaulaurier, 2017). For those who did participate in the program, a study of offender recidivism after BIP completion found that 41 percent reassaulted within a thirty-month follow-up period, nearly 60 percent reassaulted within the first six months after treatment, and approximately 20 percent of the men repeatedly reassaulted their partners. While these results don't support the finding that the program is effective, many factors that might contribute to these issues need to be taken into account. Reasons such as different curriculums between states, lack of inclusion of individualized cultural background components, the influence of gender roles, and the degree of violence the perpetrator was responsible for are factors that can shape the effectiveness of BIPs.

It is important that we understand that more effort needs to be put into effective strategies to change offender behavior, as victim safety often hinges on effective BIPs (Aaron & Beaulaurier, 2017). Improving the effectiveness of BIPs could mean the difference between life and death to a victim of domestic violence. Some argue for different approaches to batterer intervention depending on the type of violence (Aaron & Beaulaurier, 2017). Explaining how different roles of power and control change depending on the context, therefore, requires different treatments. Aaron and Beaulaurier (2017) explain how the "typology of domestic violence requires further explorations to determine how and whether it is useful to practitioners." Other solutions that are being suggested are implementing and analyzing more behavior modifying techniques. A more personalized approach might yield higher success rates. Further, critics note that most offenders in BIPs are court-mandated to attend. They do not do so willingly, which likely impacts the success of the effort. BIPs outside the United Sates typically do not mandate perpetrators into treatment. Instead, they focus on creating change in the broader society rather than changing the behavior of the individual perpetrator (Aaron & Beaulaurier, 2017).

In sum, there have been many advances in the field since the 1970s, and scholars, practitioners, and activists know much more about the scope and dynamics of abusive relationships. More is needed, however, to better understand the behavior of abusers, to identify the most effective strategies for changing batterers' behavior and for keeping victims safe, and especially for changing social norms that underlie abuse. Primary prevention programs that address gender role norms and patriarchy and that teach young people about healthy relationships and about nonviolent conflict resolution seem to be the most promising practices. Some of these programs are discussed in other chapters.

References

Aaron, S., & Beaulaurier, R. (2017). The need for new emphasis on batterer intervention programs. *Trauma, Violence, & Abuse, 18*(4), 425–432.

About Us. (2014). *Break the Cycle.* Retrieved September 12, 2019, from https://www.breakthecycle.org/about-us

American Humane Society. (2016, August 25).
Understanding the link between animal abuse and family
violence. *American Humane Society.* Retrieved July 1,
2019, from https://www.americanhumane.org/fact-sheet/
understanding-the-link-between-animal-abuse-and-family-
violence/

Animal Legal Defense Fund. (n.d.). The link between
cruelty to animals and violence against humans. *ALDF.*
Retrieved June 2, 2019, from https://aldf.org/article/
the-link-between-cruelty-to-animals-and-violence-toward-
humans-2/

Animal Welfare Institute. (2018). Facts and myths about
domestic violence and animal abuse. *AWI.* Retrieved
June 2, 2019, from https://awionline.org/content/
facts-and-myths-about-domestic-violence-and-animal-abuse

Arias, E., Arce, R., & Vilarino, M. (2013). Batterer
intervention programmes: A meta-analytic review of
effectiveness. *Psychosocial Intervention*, 22(2), 153–160.

Avon Foundation for Women. (2011). Reese Witherspoon
launches the Avon Women's Empowerment Bracelet to
honor the 100th anniversary of International Women's
Day. *People.* Retrieved September 12, 2019, from https://
people.com/style/reese-witherspoon-launches-the-avon-
womens-empowerment-bracelet/

Benedict, H. (1992). *Virgin or vamp: How the press covers sex
crimes.* New York: Oxford University Press.

Benedict, J. (2003, August 5) Athletes and accusations. *New
York Times.* Retrieved September 12, 2019, from https://
www.nytimes.com/2003/08/05/opinion/athletes-and-
accusations.html

Birch, J. (2015, October 26). The number of male domestic
abuse victims is shockingly high—so why don't we hear
about them? Yahoo! Retrieved May 31, 2019, from
https://www.yahoo.com/lifestyle/the-number-of-male-
domestic-1284479771263030.html

Bradley, F., Smith, M., Long, J., & O'Dowd, T. (2002). Reported frequency of domestic violence: Cross-sectional survey of women attending general practice. *British Medical Journal, 324*(7332). Retrieved September 12, 2019, from https://www.ncbi.nlm.nih.gov/pmc/articles/PMC65059/

Brané, M. (2018). Woman fleeing domestic violence deserve asylum. *The Washington Post.* Retrieved October 20, 2018, from https://www.washingtonpost.com/news/global-opinions/wp/2018/06/13/women-fleeing-domestic-violence-deserve-asylum/?noredirect=on&utm_term=.489279ed989f

Bullock, C. F., & Cubert, J. (2002). Coverage of domestic violence fatalities by newspapers in Washington State. *Journal of Interpersonal Violence, 17*(5), 475–499.

Carll, E. K. (2003). News portrayal of violence and women: Implications for public policy. *American Behavioral Scientist, 46*(12)s, 1601–1610.

CDC. (2011). The National Intimate Partner and Sexual Violence Survey: 2010 Summary Report. CDC. Retrieved October 27, 2018, from https://www.cdc.gov/violenceprevention/pdf/nisvs_report2010-a.pdf

Chan, W. (1994). A feminist critique of self-defense and provocation in battered women's cases in England and Wales. *Women and Criminal Justice, 4*(1), 39–65.

Chill, P. (2009). Burden of proof begone: The pernicious effect of removal in child protective services. *Family Court Review, 41,* 1–42. Retrieved October 29, 2019, from http://action4cp.org/documents/2009/pdf/April_Why_We_Remove_Kids.pdf

A Community for Peace. (n.d.). Domestic violence restraining orders: The pros and cons. ACPA. Retrieved October 28, 2018, from https://acommunityforpeace.org/uncategorized/domestic-violence-restraining-orders-the-pros-and-cons

Connell, R., & Messerschmidt, J. (2005). Hegemonic masculinity: Rethinking the concept. *Gender & Society, 19*(6), 829–859.

David Mandel & Associates. (2012). When do we remove children? FCADV. Retrieved September 12, 2019, from http://fcadv.org/sites/default/files/4When%20Do%20 We%20Remove%20Children.pdf

Depompei, E. (2017, February 23). Indiana House passes gun bill easing requirements for some. *News and Tribune.* Retrieved November 1, 2018, from https://www .newsandtribune.com/news/indiana-house-passes-gun- bill-easing-requirements-for-some/article_469f9d30-f956- 11e6-86b0-4372082c8332.html

DeViney, E., Dickert, J., & Lockwood, R. (1998). The care of pets within child abusing families. In R. Lockwood and F. R. Ascione (Eds.), *Cruelty to animals and interpersonal violence.* West Lafayette, IN: Purdue University Press. (Reprinted from *International Journal for the Study of Animal Problems*, 4 [1983]: 321–329.)

Domestic Violence Counts 2017 National Summary. (2017). NNEDV. Retrieved June 3, 2019, from https://nnedv.org/ mdocs-posts/2017-national-summary/

Douglas, E. M., & Hines, D. A. (2011). The help-seeking experiences of men who sustain intimate partner violence: An overlooked population and implications for practice. *Family Violence, 26,* 473–485.

Dutton, M., Osthoff, S., & Dichter, M. (2009). Update of the "battered woman syndrome" critique. VAWNet. Retrieved June 2, 2019, from https://vawnet.org/material/ update-battered-woman-syndrome-critique

Emanuel, G. (2016, September 3). How domestic violence in one home affects every child in a class. NPR. Retrieved July 1, 2019, from https://www.npr.org/sections/ed/2016/09/ 03/491204888/how-domestic-violence-in-one-home- affects-every-child-in-a-class

Fact Sheet: U.S. Asylum Process. (2019, January 19). National Immigration Forum. Retrieved September 12, 2019, from https://immigrationforum.org/article/fact-sheet-u-s-asylum-process/

Family Violence Prevention Fund. (2010). Compendium of state statutes and policies on domestic violence and healthcare. Family Violence Prevention Fund. Retrieved June 2, 2019, from https://www.acf.hhs.gov/sites/default/files/fysb/state_compendium.pdf

Farry, T. (1993, November 12). Seattle woman takes her case on *20/20*—new details revealed in case against Bengals. *Seattle Times.* Retrieved September 12, 2019, from http://community.seattletimes.nwsource.com/archive/?date=19931112&slug=1731372

Feder, G., & Potter, L. (2018, September 19). Why gender can't be ignored when dealing with domestic violence. *The Conversation.* Retrieved November 1, 2018, from https://theconversation.com/why-gender-cant-be-ignored-when-dealing-with-domestic-violence-74137

Finley, L. L. (2010). Examining domestic violence as a state crime: Nonkilling implications. Center for Global Nonkilling. Retrieved October 28, 2018, from http://citeseerx.ist.psu.edu/viewdoc/download?doi=10.1.1.168.4641&rep=rep1&type=pdf

Finley, L. L. (2011, May 6). Being human. *New Clear Vision.* Retrieved July 2, 2019, from http://www.newclearvision.com/2011/05/06/being-human%E2%80%A6/

Finoh, M., & Sankofah, J. (2019, January 28). The legal system has failed black girls, women, and non-binary survivors of violence. ACLU. Retrieved May 31, 2019, from https://www.aclu.org/blog/racial-justice/race-and-criminal-justice/legal-system-has-failed-black-girls-women-and-non

Flood, M., & Pease, B. (2009). Factors influencing attitudes to violence against women. *Trauma, Violence & Abuse, 10*(2), 125–42.

Florida Coalition against Domestic Violence. (2012). When do we remove children from abusive homes? FCADV. Retrieved November 1, 2018, from http://www.fcadv.org/sites/default/files/4When%20Do%20We%20Remove%20Children.pdf.

Gidycz, C. (2014). Feminist self-defense and resistance training for college students: A critical review and recommendations for the future. *Trauma, Violence and Abuse, 15*(4), 322–333.

Goldfarb, S. F. (2008). Reconceiving civil protection orders for domestic violence: Can law help end the abuse without ending the relationship? NCDSV. Retrieved November 1, 2018, from http://www.ncdsv.org/images/ReconceivingCivilPOs_Goldfarb_2008.pdf

Harvard Injury Control Research Center. (2018). Gun threats and self-defense gun use. Retrieved October 29, 2018, from https://www.hsph.harvard.edu/hicrc/firearms-research/gun-threats-and-self-defense-gun-use-2/

Hauser, C. (2017, February 7). Florida woman whose "Stand Your Ground" defense was rejected is released. *New York Times.* Retrieved May 31, 2019, from https://www.nytimes.com/2017/02/07/us/marissa-alexander-released-stand-your-ground.html

Healey, K., Smith, C., & O'Sullivan, C. (1998). *Batterer intervention: Program approaches and criminal justice strategies.* Washington, D.C: National Institute of Justice.

Hemenway, D., & Solnick, S. J. (2015). The epidemiology of self-defense gun use: Evidence from the National Crime Victimization Surveys 2007–2011. *Preventive Medicine, 79,* 22–27.

Hirschel, D., & Buzawa, E. (2009). An examination of the factors that impact the likelihood of arrest in intimate partner violence cases. Paper presented at the Annual Meeting of the Justice Research Statistical Association, St. Louis, October. Retrieved July 2, 2019, from http://www.jrsa.org/events/conference/presentations-09/David_Hirschel.pdf

Hollander, J. (2014). Does self-defense training prevent sexual violence against women? *Violence against Women, 20*(3), 252–269.

INCITE!. (2018). Community accountability. Incite! Retrieved October 21, 2018, from https://incite-national.org/community-accountability/

Incite-national.org. (2018). Community Accountability within the People of Color Progressive Movement. Incite! Retrieved October 21, 2018, from https://incite-national.org/community-accountability-within-people-of-color-progressive-movements/

Interview: Gloria Steinem. (n.d.). PBS. Retrieved September 12, 2019, from https://www.pbs.org/kued/nosafeplace/interv/steinem.html

Iyengar, R. (2007, August 7). The protection battered spouses don't need. *New York Times.* Retrieved July 2, 2019, from https://www.nytimes.com/2007/08/07/opinion/07iyengar.html

Jacquet, C. (October 15, 2015). Domestic violence in the 1970s. Circulating now: From the historical collections of the National Library of Medicine. Retrieved October 21, 2018, from https://circulatingnow.nlm.nih.gov/2015/10/15/domestic-violence-in-the-1970s/

Jordan, M. (2018). Her husband's killers told her she was next. These days, that's not enough for asylum. Nytimes.com. Retrieved October 20, 2019, from https://www.nytimes.com/2018/08/07/us/asylum-aclu-migrants-border.html

Lavigne, P. (2018, November 2). OTL: College athletes three times more likely to be named in Title IX sexual misconduct claims. ESPN. Retrieved September 11, 2019, from https://www.espn.com/espn/otl/story/_/id/25149259/college-athletes-three-s-more-likely-named-title-ix-sexual-misconduct-complaints

Levin, J., Luke, C., & Ascione, F. (1999). The relationship of animal abuse to violence and other forms of antisocial behavior. *Journal of Interpersonal Violence, 14*(9), 963–975.

Lisak, D. (1993). Men as victims: Challenging cultural myths. *Journal of Traumatic Stress, 6*(4), 577–580.

Madfills, E., & Arluke, A. (2014). Animal abuse as a warning sign of school massacres. *Homicide Studies, 18*(1), 7–22.

Maske, M. (2014, November 28). Ray Rice wins appeal of NFL's indefinite suspension, is eligible to play immediately. *The Washington Post*. Retrieved November 8, 2018, from https://www.washingtonpost.com/news/sports/wp/2014/11/28/ray-rice-wins-appeal-of-nfls-indefinite-suspension-is-eligible-to-play-immediately/?noredirect=on&utm_term=.8bbb393b0317

Maxwell, K. A., Huxford, J., Borum, C., & Hornik, R. (2000). Covering domestic violence: How the O. J. Simpson case shaped reporting of domestic violence in the news media. *J&MC Quarterly, 77*(2), 258–272.

McCaughey, M., & Cermele, J. (2015). Changing the hidden curriculum of campus rape prevention and education: Women's self-defense as a key protective factor for a public health model of prevention. *Trauma, Violence and Abuse, 18*(3), 1–16.

Meade, A. (2015, November 24). Media often distort domestic violence. *The Guardian*. Retrieved October 20, 2018, from https://www.theguardian.com/society/2015/nov/25/media-often-sensationalise-domestic-violence-reporting-study-finds

Meyers, M. (1997). *News coverage of violence against women: Engendering blame.* Thousand Oaks, CA: Sage.

Morrison, P., Hawker, L., & Miller, P. (2016). The operational challenges for batterer intervention programs: Results from a 2-year study. *Journal of Interpersonal Violence, 34*(13), 2674–2696.

Newsroom. (2018). One man lynched to death in Tripura on child-lifting rumors spread through WhatsApp, two others severely injured. HuffPost India. Retrieved October 26, 2018, from https://www.huffingtonpost.in/2018/06/29/one-man-lynched-to-death-in-tripura-on-child-lifting-rumours-spread-through-whatsapp-two-others-severely-injured_a_23470812/

NFL Player Arrests. (n.d.). *USA Today.* Retrieved May 31, 2019, from https://www.usatoday.com/sports/nfl/arrests/

Physicians for Human Rights. (2018). Domestic violence is a form of persecution. PHR. Retrieved October 20, 2018, from https://phr.org/news/domestic-violence-is-a-form-of-persecution/

Piepzna-Samarasinha, L. (2018). Where the revolution started: An introduction [online]. Criticalresistance.org. Retrieved October 20, 2018, from http://criticalresistance.org/wp-content/uploads/2014/05/Revolution-starts-at-home-zine.pdf

Pierson, B. (2017, February 16). U.S. appeals court strikes down Florida law in "Docs v. Glocks" case. Reuters. Retrieved June 2, 2019, from https://www.reuters.com/article/us-usa-florida-guns-idUSKBN15V2YX

Powell, C. (2018, October 16). States are challenging new policy that denies asylum to victims of domestic violence. Council on Foreign Relations. Retrieved May 31, 2019, from https://www.cfr.org/blog/states-are-challenging-new-policy-denies-asylum-survivors-domestic-violence

Ruby, J. (2004). Male-pattern violence. *Off Our Backs,* *34*(9/10), 21–25.

Sachetti, M. (2018, June 11). Sessions: Victims of domestic abuse and gang violence generally won't qualify for asylum. *Washington Post.* Retrieved September 12, 2019, from https://www.washingtonpost.com/local/immigration/ sessions-signals-that-victims-of-domestic-abuse-and-gang-violence-generally-will-not-qualify-for-asylum/2018/06/ 11/45e54602-6d9e-11e8-bd50-b80389a4e569_story.html

Shaw, K. (2016, August 22). 12 facts that show how guns make domestic violence even deadlier. *The Trace.* Retrieved May 31, 2019, from https://www.thetrace.org/2016/08/ domestic-violence-gun-facts/

Sherin, K., Sinacore, J., Li, X., Zitter, R., & Shakil, A. (1998). HITS: A short domestic violence screening tool for use in a family practice setting. *Family Medicine, 7* (July/August), 508–512.

Sherman, L., & Berk, R. (1984). The Minneapolis Domestic Violence Experiment. *Police Foundation Reports.* Retrieved July 2, 2019, from https://www.policefoundation.org/ wp-content/uploads/2015/07/Sherman-et-al.-1984-The-Minneapolis-Domestic-Violence-Experiment.pdf

Sorenson, S. B., & Wiebe, D. J. (2004). Weapons in the lives of battered women. *American Journal of Public Health,* *94*(8), 1412–1417.

Sports and Sexual Assault. (n.d.). CQ Press. Retrieved November 8, 2018, from https://library.cqpress.com/ cqresearcher/document.php?id=cqresrre2017042800

Stahl, K. (2016, March 1). What role can self-defense classes play in our efforts to prevent sexual violence? VAWNet. Retrieved June 3, 2019, from https://vawnet.org/news/ what-role-can-self-defense-classes-play-our-efforts-prevent-sexual-violence

Statement on Gender Violence and the Prison Industrial Complex. (n.d.). INCITE! Retrieved July 2, 2019, from https://incite-national.org/incite-critical-resistance-statement/

Statistics. (n.d.). National Coalition Against Domestic Violence. Retrieved November 1, 2018, from https://ncadv.org/statistics

Tessier, M. (2007, October 1). Wrestling murder highlights violence-suicide link. Women's Enews. Retrieved May 31, 2019, from https://womensenews.org/2007/10/wrestling-murder-highlights-violence-suicide-link/

Usta, J., & Talib, R. (2014). Addressing domestic violence in primary care: What the physicians needs to know. *Libyan Journal of Medicine, 9.* Retrieved June 2, 2019, from https://www.ncbi.nlm.nih.gov/pmc/articles/PMC3957738/

Vagianos, A. (2014, October 23). 30 shocking domestic violence statistics that remind us it's an epidemic. Huffington Post. Retrieved May 31, 2019, from https://www.huffpost.com/entry/domestic-violence-statistics_n_5959776

Walker, L. (1979). *The battered woman.* New York: Stringer.

Wehmhoener, K. (2010). Social norm or social harm: An exploratory study of Internet vigilantism. Graduate Theses and Dissertations, Indiana State University. Retrieved November 1, 2018, from https://lib.dr.iastate.edu/etd/11572

Weir, T., & Brady, E. (2003, December 22). In sexual assault cases, athletes usually walk. *USA Today.* Retrieved September 12, 2019, from http://www.ncdsv.org/images/InSexualAssaultCAsesAthletesUsuallyWalk.pdf

Women as the Abusers. (n.d.). Domestic Shelters. Retrieved November 2, 2018, from https://www.domesticshelters.org/domestic-violence-articles-information/women-as-the-abusers

The World Bank. (2018). More than 1 billion women lack legal protection against domestic sexual violence, finds World Bank study. World Bank. Retrieved October 20, 2018, from https://www.worldbank.org/en/news/ press-release/2018/02/01/more-than-1-billion-women-lack-legal-protection-against-domestic-sexual-violence-finds-world-bank-study

Zeoli, A. M., & Bonomi, A. (2015). Pretty in pink? Firearm hazards for domestic violence victims. *Women's Health Issues, 25*(1), 3–5.

3 Perspectives

Introduction

Survivors have been leaders in the efforts to address domestic and dating violence and sexual assault. Through telling their stories, they have corrected myths and misconceptions and have lobbied for important legislation and policy changes. Many survivors have become advocates in the movement and now provide critical services to victims. Several survivors share their perspectives in this chapter. Yet not all who have helped advance the movement are themselves survivors. Also included in this chapter are perspectives from a variety of people about what prompted them to get involved and what they have contributed.

Why I Am an Advocate against Domestic Violence in the Bahamas: We Must Continue to Strive
Camille Smith

Having served as a volunteer counselor at the Bahamas Crisis Center for approximately fifteen years and as a social worker and counselor at the Department of Social Services and the University of the Bahamas in the Bahamas for thirty years, I have learnt from the stories of many women and children who have suffered domestic and sexual violence; stories that

---

Lisa Brunner, twice a victim of domestic violence, and her daughters Samantha and Faith. Samantha (left) was raped on White Earth Reservation. (Linda Davidson/The Washington Post via Getty Images)

persons have poured out as they sought assistance, counseling, and resources to find a salve for their trauma; stories from adults who were manipulated in domestic violence as children who are now trying to navigate life as adults, still carrying remembered trauma; stories of women, mostly, who were beaten and had their spirits broken at the hands of partners from whom they expected better. These people, with their stories and their will to survive, are motivation for me as I serve as an advocate against domestic violence in the Bahamas and in the surrounding region of the Caribbean. I seek to help address a huge wrong being perpetuated in society, that people should be expected to accommodate abuse from their partners as par for the course in normal society.

As for what could be considered normal regarding domestic violence in the Caribbean, literature reveals that there is a significant presence of domestic violence in the Caribbean, sometimes referenced in Caribbean research as family violence, for which there is a long history and an array of contributing factors. A study conducted by the United Nations Development Program (UNDP, 2012) with 11,155 respondents from various Caribbean countries regarding the extent to which they faced domestic violence (deliberately hit with fists or a weapon, kicked, or faced violence from a family member) revealed that individuals from Guyana (17.3 percent), Barbados (9.6 percent), Jamaica (5.9 percent), and Trinidad and Tobago (8.3 percent) reported that they had experienced domestic violence in their homes.

Throughout the Caribbean, violence against women has been categorized as a public health problem against women and extended to include children. The incidence of gender-based violence documented in the Caribbean and Latin America is troubling; findings indicate that one in four women are physically abused in their residence, two times higher than the global average (World Bank, 2007). These statistics show cause for concern regarding the incidence of domestic violence in the Caribbean.

According to the U.S. Census (2010–2014), it was estimated that 135,928 Jamaicans, 20,312 Trinidadians and Tobagonians,

13,093 Bahamians, 2,714 Barbadians, and 1,320 Grenadians were estimated to be residing in the Broward, Miami/Dade, Monroe, and Palm Beach counties of South Florida. The prevalence of domestic violence in the Caribbean countries could be an impact on the incidence of domestic violence in Florida as a sizable diaspora from the region has migrated to South Florida. My research project for the dissertation for PhD in social work at Barry University, Miami, Florida, focuses on the experiences of Caribbean survivors of domestic violence who have sought help in South Florida because it is an area where many Caribbean nationals have relocated.

The purpose of this study is to examine the layers of meaning and lived experiences of Anglophone (English-speaking) Caribbean women survivors of domestic violence living in South Florida who are currently seeking or have sought and accepted help from human service agencies providing services to women having experienced domestic violence. The information gleaned from this study will inform practitioners working with diverse populations, particularly those from the Caribbean, about factors that impact decisions related to help-seeking behaviors. Of particular interest is the extent to which there is a difference in help-seeking behaviors among women from the Caribbean who have experienced domestic violence after living in South Florida. The role that cultural factors may play in the decision to seek help is also a central question in this study.

The questions to receive focus in this research are the following: What has it been like for Anglophone Caribbean women living in South Florida who have experienced domestic violence to access domestic violence services in South Florida? To what extent were there any barriers to accessing services, and what were those barriers? What stood out for the participant as particularly memorable about the experience of seeking and receiving services? To what extent did the historical and cultural background of the participant play a role in the decision to seek help? This writer believes that the importance of giving a voice to underrepresented populations cannot be overstated.

This qualitative study will attempt to capture the lived experience of persons who have faced this issue and to acknowledge the meaning they make of those experiences.

Anecdotal evidence reveals that women from the Caribbean sometimes escape to the United States to flee domestic violence in the Caribbean. Initial contact with several domestic violence services and shelters in South Florida also reveals that Caribbean women actively seek help through those services. I am interested in learning the stories of those women who seek assistance for domestic violence in South Florida: What are they experiencing? Do they feel safe when they seek help in South Florida? Do they delay seeking help because they have certain fears as immigrants in South Florida? Would they recommend others to seek such assistance?

There is much that can be learned from sitting with Caribbean women in South Florida. I am interested in giving voice to their experiences and sharing a collective version of their stories, with the hope that their stories can positively impact services for the diaspora in South Florida and in the Bahamas and Caribbean in the future. I am conducting this research to provide a means of release for the stories, the cries, and the voices of the Caribbean women who face such abuse and yet seek help in South Florida with the hopes of being empowered to healing and strength; that is a very important work.

Camille Smith is a native of the Bahamas and mother of two. She has completed all coursework except her dissertation and will be earning a PhD in social work from Barry University.

Moving On from Dating Violence
Amanda Pagano

When I was fourteen years old, I started dating a boy the same age the summer before we both entered our first year of high school. We were friends first. He was a good friend to me, and we used to talk for hours on AOL Instant Messenger (AIM) about life, music, and things we liked. We had a connection I hadn't felt with anyone else before. He was my first serious boyfriend, so everything in our relationship was new for me. As a child of divorced parents I didn't have a successful relationship to base anything on. I went into this blind to the differences of what was right and wrong in a relationship. Before I knew it, the person he was as a friend changed into a controlling and jealous boyfriend. The change was gradual. It started with him telling me not to talk to someone he hated that would be in a class with me. I never met this person before, so I accidentally befriended this hated person, and when I was seen talking to him, my boyfriend forcefully dragged me away while berating me in front of everyone. That was my first lesson that defying him would end in some form of pain for me. I listened mainly because I felt it was out of love, and he was jealous because of this love for me. This jealous love soon wanted me to talk to no guys at all, not my friends or his. One of my best guy friends was pushed to the ground by him for talking to me. He even punched one of his own friends in the face for asking me a question. I soon avoided talking to any guys in fear that he would hurt them or me. The more control I gave him, the more control he took. He wanted me to be with him at all times, talking to nobody else but him. Soon I had no time for any of my friends. I didn't realize he was isolating me until it was too late. He learned the public bus schedule to my home so he could come over when I was all by myself. Even if I said no, he would come and make a scene if I didn't let him in. Behind closed doors he was able to pressure me into doing things I was not ready to do. But I thought I would lose him, or worse feel his wrath, if I didn't give in to his requests. My first year of high school was a blur. All my time was spent with him. Before class, between class, and after school, he was always there. If I tried to walk a different way from him between classes, he would pinch my skin so hard that I'd have to walk with him to stop the pain. Anytime he wasn't physically with me, I had to be on the phone with him or on AIM. He needed to know where I was and what I was doing 24/7. I tried breaking up with him multiple times over the school year, but he would threaten to kill himself, me, or my friends and family. One time I made the mistake of trying to break up with him in person while he was in my home. He grabbed a knife from the kitchen and held it in front of his throat telling me he would kill himself if I didn't stay with him. When I didn't react, he quickly put the knife up to my throat until I agreed to still be his girlfriend. While I gave him control over my life out of fear, I still had times where I resisted. Unfortunately, anytime I did stand up for myself, my actions were met with painful consequences. When I did fight back or argue against him, it would result in head-butting, getting choked, or even getting pushed down the stairs in my own home. Our ultimate breakup was near the end of our freshman year of high school. We had a huge, public fight at school next to my bus to go home. He had forbidden me to go to a concert for one of my favorite bands, a band whose music kept me afloat during this stressful and emotional time of my life. I spoke up and said I wasn't going to listen to him. He told me I'd suffer the consequences if I went as he pinned me against the chain link fence in front of my bus for everyone inside to see. I remember crying my eyes out that he wouldn't leave me alone, and I didn't understand why everyone stood by as he hurt me. That was the hardest thing to accept. Nobody was going to help me. I had to help myself. I had to end this. While I doubted this decision along the way, I managed to find the courage to stand my ground. My mother and I had just moved to a new address he didn't know, which made it a lot easier for me to finally end it. I changed my phone number so he couldn't harass me with nonstop texts and phone calls. At school I made new friends he didn't know and made sure I was never alone, avoiding him as much as possible. He still sent e-mails with declarations of love followed by death threats. But soon he moved on and started to leave me alone. However, the next three years of high school were not easy. Every day at school I would have to see him, and it kept the pain a fresh memory. But I was thankful to no longer be under his control. That's my story, and I know I'm very lucky I was able to break free. I hope my story is able to help people understand a little more about domestic violence, especially for teens.

Amanda Pagano is a survivor of teen dating violence and is involved with Forget Me Not Advocacy Group in South Florida.

Rolling with the Punches
Amy Daumit

Each time I tell my story, it begins the same way. "Over the course of several years I have been on a bit of a journey, if you would like to call it that. This journey took me far away from the person I am. So far away, in fact, that I didn't recognize the person in the mirror. She looked the same on the outside, but if I really looked into her eyes, I didn't know the person staring back. She was empty. She had little interest in anything. She found no joy in the happiest of occasions. She was a shell."

And, every time I read it, my stomach turns in on itself, shooting a course of nauseating pain that screams of anxiety. I fight through it, reminding myself that my life is now different, that I'm in a better place, and that he (my abuser) is no longer a part of me.

Although I had lost the notion of who I was, what was more difficult for me was that I couldn't comprehend how I had let it come to this. I was a strong, independent, ambitious woman. I had a plan for my life, and this was not it.

They say it takes half the time you were in a relationship to get over it. For me, that would be eight years. I was over him within months, but being over how the relationship affected me is an entirely different matter. The damage that I incurred over those sixteen years has created a few obstacles that I've had to overcome. But before delving into that, let me start at the beginning.

It all began as a blissful, high school romance. But, within months, there were signs I refused to see. It seemed that everything he did included trying to control me. With every good thing that came of our relationship, his behavior and anger escalated. It started with guilting me for wanting to spend time with family and friends, to putting me down and calling me names, to manipulating circumstances to hurt me and raise himself up. Soon, everything he didn't like about his life was my fault, and I paid for my "wrongdoing" with emotional and physical attacks.

I didn't look right, cook right, clean right, make enough money, work enough, exercise enough, eat right, or lose enough weight. His temper would flare over the simplest of things, resulting in broken keepsakes, slaps, arm bars, wrist locks, chokes, being slammed against walls, being kicked and punched, being pinned down, emotional abuse, and my broken spirit.

Through all of it, I lied to friends and family, covered for his actions and absences, and protected him with all I had. I learned that nothing you can to do will change someone who does not wish to change.

It took me sixteen years to decide I could take no more and several months to walk out. It was something as simple as being accused of cheating that was the catalyst that propelled me out the door. I had done nothing but be faithful, in every way, while he treated me like the dirt beneath his feet, and I could take no more. I didn't realize the damage that had been done and what I had waiting for me. I had to work through health issues and psychological issues. I had to learn to interact with others again and start picking up the pieces of my life.

As I write today, I can say with confidence that I am no longer looking at that same reflection, but I am still learning to live with me. Learning to live with yourself is no small task. It has been more than ten years since I faced my fears and walked out the door. A decade since I said I was done and made the heart-wrenching, terrifying decision to leave my marriage. And, even though so much time has passed, I find myself at war with my own insecurities, dealing with anger and bitterness and often fighting to be happy in my own skin. Old habits, and emotions, die hard. And yet, I am also aware of how far I have come.

This journey has been like none other, bringing me to places I never comprehended, lows I don't wish on my worst enemy, and love I never knew existed. But isn't that what life is? A journey? Every day is a new start, a new adventure, and another day where I chose my happiness. No one said the journey would be easy, but there is a profound beauty in the lessons I have learned along the way.

Everyone deserves to be treated with respect. It takes some of us longer than others to realize that. But, no matter how long you have stayed and endured, there is a beautiful life that can be had. Believe in yourself and find it.

Amy Daumit is the founder of Forget Me Not Advocacy Group, an organization devoted to providing education and awareness about dating violence.

Abuse from a Male Survivor's Perspective
Dustin LeBrun and Erin Moloney

My childhood cannot be boxed into any standard definition of normalcy. When people learn that I have post-traumatic stress disorder, they typically tend to ask me what branch of the military I toured in or thank me for my service, but my wounds originate from much further back. Beyond the pale of personal choice and life-making decisions, nestled deep within the boundaries of what should be considered sacrosanct and sacred, my trauma springs from the earliest years of my memory. During a time when the protection and love of a parent or two could have fended off the worst attacks that could harm a child, I was left alone to wade deep into the waters of adult decision-making and defend myself against threats.

My mother was a stripper, and my father was in and out of my life. During the times we all lived together, my life was a blur of coke-fueled, drunken all-nighters, fist fights, and orgies, where my younger brother Jeff and I would often be left to our own devices for long periods of time. Before I was ten years I was nearly shot when a drunk guy, who was carrying Jeff on his shoulders, fell and knocked Jeff's head on the ground. My father charged him as the man pulled a gun and shot twice, luckily missing everyone within range. My father beat the hell out of him.

When our father was gone, and mom was at work, sometimes a couple of boys from the neighborhood would babysit us. Their names were Bill and TJ. They were brothers, sixteen and fourteen, and spent two long summers watching over Jeff and me. Bill was older and took on the role of ringleader.

It's always overwhelming to bring this back up. I remember having my face stuffed into my mother and father's bed with a pillow over my head. I remember Bill's smell, his breath on the back of my neck. When I fought him, he would threaten to rape and kill Jeff or my mother if I didn't relax.

So I did. And he had his way with me.

I know it happened several times over those two summers. I remember hiding when they would come over; I remember running into the woods. My mother saw how I would react when they would arrive, but she never asked if I was okay. She never investigated why her son was terrified all the time.

Horribly, this wasn't the only trauma that I experienced during my childhood. Once my father had more permanently left the picture, my mother went through a string of boyfriends with easily questionable morality. One, named Steve, was an ex-police officer with an immense power issue. He was a customer at the strip club my mother worked at; she brought him home, and he stayed there. It didn't take long for him to get comfortable enough to use his fists on us both. A distinct memory I have is of him commanding me to kiss his cowboy boots while he drunkenly held a 50-caliber Desert Eagle at my head. I was eight. I was still incontinent at night by this point, and Steve took to dragging me off my top bunk by my ankle each morning to see if I had wet the bed. When he found I had, he used the cowboy boots I kissed to kick me until I cried and pleaded for him to stop.

It was just a daily beating. I shut off. That's why I have memories only in flashes; a part of my brain had broken. One summer Jeff and I got lice, and Steve told my mother that gasoline was the cure for this particular affliction. He buzz cut our hair, got us both in the shower, and dumped gas on our heads. We both screamed while my mother just stood there in the doorway, silent. Blank.

It was shortly after that, the summer I turned nine, when I had a real mental break for the first time. Jeff and I were horsing around, and I slammed my ear into a doorknob. I came unglued and beat Jeff bloody: tore his shirt to shreds, punched, slapped, scraped; I just lost it. All in front of Steve, who finally got up and punished me in the only way he knew—with his fists and his boots.

Part of you gets cut off inside. You have to cope or die. An experience this traumatizing internalizes a belief of personal uselessness and worthlessness. I truly thought (and part of me still believes) that I was weak for letting this happen to me, and I have to remind myself that I was a seven-year-old boy. I had been left to my own devices, but I wasn't old enough to decide what was best for me. I didn't understand how the world worked, and in the end I learned in the worst way a child could.

In 1998 I had a second breakdown. My brain couldn't contain the level of trauma I had been avoiding anymore. Trying to hold it all in had an explosive effect; by avoiding and not addressing what I had been through for so long, I had effectively shaken the soda can and thrown it on the rocks. Even attempting suicide was just a last-ditch effort at running away, making the pain and confusion end.

By the time I hit my thirties, I couldn't avoid it anymore. I finally stopped running and started to look inward. I began meditating and slowly, steadily dealt with the onslaught of emotions that came up when I quieted my mind. It took direct investigation of my emotions and experiences on a regular basis, a continual peeling back of layers to expose what I had been harboring. This process, as painful as it has been to relive, has allowed me to truly understand my current actions and feelings, and I have been learning to forgive myself and feel compassion for the boy who was abused, instead of hatred for the man I had become.

Dustin LeBrun is a medical marijuana cultivator living in New Boston, New Hampshire, with his wife of fourteen years, Erin Moloney. They are currently working on a memoir of his life and the effects of childhood PTSD.

Why I Volunteer with Victims of Domestic Violence
Anya Finley

From the ripe young age of four I was exposed to what it means to treat everyone as an equal. While I didn't fully understand what domestic violence was until a much later age, I saw people who had clearly suffered and needed someone to help. Many times women would call No More Tears in search of an escape or for help rebuilding a broken life. Many times these women had children around my age.

When I think of these children, one specific girl comes to mind. Her name was Jane*, and she and her mother had escaped her abusive father. She had beautiful dark hair, cut into a bob, and like me enjoyed strawberries. That was enough for us to become friends. I never saw her or her mother as victims. I saw them as my friend and my friend's mother. On Easter my mother (who is a board member for No More Tears) and Somy Ali, the organization's founder, took me and Jane to the Miami Zoo. While it was hot beyond belief, and sweat ran down our faces in streams, Jane and I enjoyed ourselves in a way I remember more than ten years later. A picture from that day still hangs in my mother's office. It shows Jane and me in our swimsuits, smiling so much our eyes were squinted.

This wasn't the only day of its kind. Through the years I went to many Thanksgiving and Christmas dinners with those receiving help from No More Tears. I became friends with the other children and spent hours playing with them. Throughout this time I never once felt like I was "volunteering." I just felt like I was meeting new friends. I believe that this has contributed to a thought I still hold. All of these people were victims, but they were also smart, kind, and caring—some of them artsy, some analytical. While they had one uniting factor and commonality—they had endured abuse—they were very different people. This taught me that one's circumstances do not define one as a person.

Over time some of the memories have faded, but my knowledge about domestic violence has grown. My involvement with No More Tears created an interest in advocacy efforts, and I do what I can to help. It has shown me red flags to watch for in my friends and my relationships. And, most important, it has taught me an overall theme of tolerance toward others.

*Name changed to respect privacy.

Anya Finley finished her sophomore year at Florida Virtual School, where she serves on the student government. She is also an actor with South Florida theaters and a long-time volunteer with No More Tears.

Abuse Is Everywhere, But We Can Stop It
Somy Ali

My name is Somy Ali. I was born in Karachi, Pakistan, but have lived and worked in the United States and in India. I grew up in a home where domestic violence was rampant. I am a multiple-time victim of sexual abuse. But more of all, I am a victor who has overcome these circumstances to dedicate my life to helping others.

As a child, I remember Karachi as a modern city with the hustle and bustle of a mix of fancy cars, rickshaws, trucks, motorcycles, taxis, and bicycles. There were people everywhere on the streets walking or squatting down on a sidewalk engrossed in conversation. There were men selling fruits and vegetables on carts and children holding onto their fathers' waists as they rode on the back of motorcycles. There were women riding in the back of taxis covered in burkas mostly accompanied by a man sitting in the passenger seat. There were beggars everywhere, beggars of all ages at every traffic light. I remember this one guy who was mentally handicapped; my father always gave him money each time we stopped at the light that led us home. Then there were little girls and little boys who begged at every light, many of them Afghan refugees. I remember that my father always gave money to the kids, but he would tell them to go find work somewhere as opposed to begging. It is inconceivable to me now to instruct a five-year-old girl to go find work rather than to beg. But this was the way of life in Pakistan, and unfortunately little has changed.

Blue Square was the name of my house in Karachi, located on Sherea-e-Faisal Road in a wealthy section of Pakistan. I don't know why it was named that except that it was partially blue but not at all shaped like a square. In fact, I don't know why the house needed a name at all. Nonetheless, it was by far the most beautiful and palatial home I have ever seen in my life. It had twenty-six rooms and was a three-storied home. The main entrance of the house was through a nine-foot-tall white grille gate with two guards carrying AK-47s to protect themselves and us from robbers and kidnappers. I remember my father always saying that there was a fear of children being kidnapped for ransom.

As a child, I was terrified of my mother. My father was my favorite in comparison. I would always wait for him to pull into the driveway; he would get out of the car and greet me with a huge smile. He never said that he loved me, but I assumed he did because I was his daughter. Anytime I was hurt or my mother was mad at me, I looked for my father. But the interactions with my father were always quick. I would run to him and he would smile then immediately and say, "Now go and play, *beta*, Daddy has lots of work to do." *Beta* means "my child" in Urdu. It has a similar meaning to that of uncle so and so, and anyone younger or children, in general, are often referred to as *beta*. The servants would simply be called by their names.

Despite this affluence, all was not well in my life. It was a day off for my father's staff, and I was on the first floor of our house. There was no one around in any of the offices, not a single soul. I was so bored. I took a peek out at the gate, and the guards were pacing back and forth holding on to their rifles. I went into the editing room on the first floor and pulled out the reel of one of my father's commercials waiting to be edited from the editing machine, curious to see how far it would stretch out. I went in to my father's office and glanced at all of his magazines, all about advertising and films. I noticed a fax that had come in; I pulled it out and tried to see how far the role of fax paper would stretch. When all of this did not cure my boredom, I ran in to Uncle Mushtaq's office and opened up his drawers. I found a bunch of red markers and decided to draw a house for him on his white canvas office wall. While I was in the midst of drawing on the wall, Abdul, our Bangladeshi cook, who must have been forty-five or forty-six at the time, walked into the room. He sat on the chair across from Mushtaq's desk and asked me what I was doing. I don't remember what I said.

All I remember from that moment was Abdul asking me if I wanted to see baby chicks. I stopped drawing and said, "What do baby chicks look like, and what do they feel like?" He said that if I would stand up on the chair and lift up my frock he would show me. I said okay. Then Abdul touched my panties and started crumbling them together. I asked him what he was doing, and he said that the baby chicks felt like my panties, very soft. Then we heard one of the guards walking in, and Abdul got up and said that if I wanted to actually see baby chicks, I would need to go to his servant quarters. He told me to meet him there in a few minutes because he had to find them and get them ready for me. I decided to go toward the back of the house to get to Abdul's quarters. When I got there, he told me to sit on his bed and lift up my frock again. I asked him why we couldn't see the baby chicks. He said first he wanted me to see what they would feel like. I told him "no" and that I have to go back upstairs and ran out of his quarters. I decided that I would not go back there until he told me for sure that the baby chicks were there.

The next day Abdul told me to meet him again in his quarters and that, in addition to the baby chicks, he had another surprise for me. I was really excited and went to see what it was he had for me. When I walked in, he told me to sit down, and then he removed his pants and then his underwear. He asked me if I had ever seen a penis before and I said "no." I told him that it stank in there and asked where my surprise was. He said that if I would touch his penis and come closer he would give me the surprise. I told him "no," because it smelled really bad. He yelled at me and told me to come closer to him or else he would tell my parents that I had been a bad girl. I was terrified, and so I moved closer to him. He said to put my hand on his penis. I took my hand and touched it, and then he told me to kiss it. I said "no" and ran out of his quarters. I ran to the bathroom and washed my hands really hard for a long time.

The next time I saw Abdul, he had two baby chicks in his hands, and he promised to let me have them if I met him again in his quarters. I said "okay" and that I would meet him there right away. I walked in, and Abdul said that I needed to take my panties off if I wanted to play with the baby chicks. I asked him why, and he just said that it was the condition. I said okay and took my panties off. Abdul then threw the baby chicks on the floor and took his pants off. He began to lift up my frock, and I started crying. I told him that I needed to go and didn't like him touching me. He said that if I didn't let him touch me, he would tell my parents that I and been really bad and that I was drawing on Uncle Mushtaq's wall. I said I didn't care and ran out of there without my panties. I ran up to my mother's room and told her everything. My mother was livid. She immediately picked up the intercom and told my father.

My father called me down to his office and told me to sit in his chair. Then Abdul walked in, and my father said that I needed to stay put in the chair no matter what happened. My father approached Abdul and began pounding on him. Then two of my father's staff began hitting and kicking him. I was shaking and crying because I did not know what was going on. My father kept yelling at Abdul, telling him to say he was sorry to me and to accept me as his daughter. Then, after beating him unconscious, my father's staff threw him outside our tall white gate. My father came to me with his fists covered in Abdul's blood. He knelt down on the floor and looked straight at me. He said, "I never want anyone to know what happened to you. I want no one to know that Abdul touched you or what he did to you. Do you understand me?" I simply nodded, still trembling and crying, and then ran upstairs to my mother. She said exactly the same thing about the incident with Abdul: don't ever tell anyone.

It was typical to hide from everyone the sexual abuse of a child. It was meant to protect the child, especially if you had a girl who was sexually abused. Sexual abuse drastically decreased the chances of one's daughter ever getting married, as no one wanted to marry a girl who had been touched by another man. My brother and I were also beaten and ordered never to tell anyone that we were abused. I learned not too long ago that when my brother informed my mother that he had been sexually abused by one of our cooks, Hashim, who was thirty-five, she beat him and told him never to bring it up again. It makes me physically sick to know that because of my mother's fear, my brother, who was only three or four years old at the time, suffered numerous incidents of sexual abuse at the hands of Hashim.

Several years later in a different house, a similar incident occurred. Our mother was not home, and we had no clue where our father was; in fact, I recall that we had not seen him in several days. My brother and I were playing with the guards at the main gate and the servants from the townhouse on the right. The servants told me to come up to their quarters, as they wanted to show me something. I remember every inch of the spiral staircase that I climbed to see what they wanted to show me. I told my brother to wait and that I would be right back. When I got up there, the servants pulled out a magazine and showed me naked pictures of men and women in sexual poses. I was only nine years old and had never seen anything like that before, but I knew that it was bad and dirty. I asked them why they were showing me dirty pictures, and one of them said, "Because we want you to do what they are doing in the pictures." I remember getting really scared, the same fear I had in the servant quarters with Abdul. I told them I had to go downstairs because my brother was alone and I tried to leave.

One of the servants grabbed my shoulders, and the other lifted up my frock and pulled down my panties. I don't know what prompted my five-year-old brother to shout my name at that moment, but he did, telling me to come downstairs. It was perfect timing to pull up my underwear and run down the stairs to him. I held his hand really tight and told him, "Come on, we are going home. We're not playing here anymore." My little brother seemed scared and confused. I still remember the expression on his face clearly. When we got to our front door, we found that we had locked ourselves out of the house and had no way to get in. We sat on the doorstep for probably five hours before our mother finally got home. We were more terrified of what she was going to do to us for locking ourselves out than the servants coming to get us and hurt us. My brother eventually fell asleep in my lap while we waited, squatting on the ground Indian style.

When our mother pulled up and saw us on the doorstep, we were convinced it was going to be our last day on earth. She unlocked the door, and when we told her what happened, she just beat us both and told us we were stupid. After that we never stepped outside of the townhouse. I was afraid of the servants next door, and my brother feared our mother's beatings. Soon we learned that we were again moving to a different home. This pattern continued throughout our years in Pakistan until the day a woman showed up with a baby, and I learned that my father was also its father. His tense and abusive relationship with my mother had run its course, and I contacted my uncle in the United States to see if we could move there. At first it was just me who moved, and I lived with my half sister Tina and her boyfriend.

I did not fit in well at school, and other kids made fun of me because of my accent. I was getting terrible grades and hanging out with the kids who skipped school a lot and spent most of their time stoned. Our circle of friends increased with the entry of a new boy, Mark, who at age seventeen was much older than the rest of us. Mark became a regular in our group, and one day when I was standing alone outside the school waiting to be picked up, he told me that he thought I was really pretty. It was the first time a boy—anyone for that matter—had told me I was pretty. I did not know how to act and became extremely nervous and shy. The next day I told my group of friends about what Mark had said. Literally all of my friends told me to be careful of him. They said that he had an arrest record for drugs and that I should never be alone with him. My first thought was that the girls in my group were jealous because Mark had chosen me.

One evening Tina and her boyfriend went out to the movies, and I was home alone. I received a call from Mark, who said he was downstairs and needed to talk to me about something really important. I told him that I couldn't come down and that if my sister and her boyfriend showed up, they would kill me for leaving the apartment. Mark was persistent, saying that it would just take five minutes. Therefore, I went downstairs to see him. He said that we should not talk in front of the building, as we would get caught. Instead, we should walk toward the woods that were across from the apartment building. I agreed, and soon we were deep in the woods. We both sat down under a tree, and I could literally hear my heart beating out of fear and nervousness. I told Mark to hurry and tell me what he had to say. He said that he never liked a girl the way that he liked me and that he really cared for me. He asked me if I had ever been kissed, and I said "no." He then reached over to kiss me. It felt weird, but I liked it. We were soon lying down, kissing under a tree, and he began to lift up my shirt. I immediately got up and said that I had to go, as my sister would be home soon. He said, "You don't like me, do you?" And I said, "It's not that I don't like you. I am just really scared and I need to get back upstairs before my sister comes back." Mark begged me to stay for a few more minutes and held my hand to sit back down. He began kissing me again and once again reached under my shirt. This time I stood up, irritated and angry. Then I saw a look on Mark's face that I had never seen before.

With a look of deep anger, he yanked me down by my arm and threw me to the ground. He got on top of me, and I kept saying, "No, please, I have to go, please let me go." He told me to shut up, or I would regret it. I tried to wiggle my way out from under him, but he was a lot stronger. He held my hands back with one hand and pulled down my pajamas with the other one. I began to scream, and he punched me in my left leg, the one I had been operated on and was sensitive still. I had never felt such severe pain in all my life, not even when I woke up from surgery after they removed the tumor in my legs years prior. I was crying hysterically, and he told me to lay still and then punched me in my left hip, where I had bone grafting. I was in unbelievable pain and was trembling in fear. He forced himself into me and in less than a minute left me on the ground, crying, bleeding, and covered in his semen. I lay there alone on the ground in the woods for a long time, unable to move due to the pain and the shock.

Eventually I walked back to the apartment and called one of my friends. I told her what happened, and she called another friend via three way. My friends said, "Somy, you have been raped! Call 911 right how and tell them what happened!" One of my friends came over to the apartment and called the police for me. Soon the cops came and were taking my statement. My sister showed up and was shocked to see the police there. One of the officers told Tina, "Your sister has been raped. We found semen in her and blood. We are taking her to the hospital right now." Tina did not know how to react and began crying.

A month had passed, Mark had been arrested, and we had to go to a court hearing. Tina, with the intention of protecting me, said, "Look, I did not expect you to stay a virgin forever. If you want to put this behind you, we can drop the charges and move on like this never happened." I looked at her and said, "No! We are going to court no matter what!"

We walked into the courthouse in Miami, and I went to use the bathroom. Mark's sister, who was standing by the sink, approached me and begged me to drop the charges and let it go, as it would ruin Mark's life. I just stared at her, terrified of what was happening. I wished so badly at that moment that my father was there to hold me. I walked out of the bathroom without saying a word to her. Mark's attorney asked me if I consented in any way to Mark. I did not even know what the word "consent" meant but assumed its meaning. I said "no." I was a thirteen-year-old girl from Pakistan and was completely lost in the midst of a new culture and naive enough to believe that this boy actually liked me.

I don't remember what happened after that, but Tina kept telling me to put it behind me and never ever say a word about this to anyone in the family, especially my parents. Once again, I was being told to stay quiet about sexual assault. I never received counseling or professional assistance to deal with the emotional trauma. I was not going to school again and would barely come out of my room. I would remain in bed listening to Bon Jovi's album again and again, staring at his posters all over my walls. I don't understand why his music was comforting to me, but it always made me feel better.

Eventually, I followed my dreams, somehow with my father's support, and moved to India when I was seventeen. I was smitten with Bollywood star Salman Khan and vowed to meet him and make him my husband. The world works in mysterious ways, and almost as soon as we arrived in India, I met a photographer who took professional shots of me and distributed them. They somehow landed in front of Salman Khan and thus began my career as an actress and model and my engagement to the man of my dreams. I do not wish to speak ill of Salman, but I eventually ended my career and left India to return to the United States. My mother was here as well, and I spent time with her and cared for her, as she suffers from severe depression. I was lost at first but eventually enrolled at Nova Southeastern University to study psychology. It was at this time that I realized that perhaps I could do some good for all those women I saw being abused and assaulted.

I decided to form a nonprofit organization that would assist victims of domestic violence. It was my mother's idea to call it No More Tears (NMT). I wasn't really sure how to start, but I learned as much as possible and, fortunately, had bought two rental properties with my savings from India, so I did not need to make money for the work. I invested most of the remainder of my savings in NMT. I even sold the jewelry Salman had given me to fund the work. I knew that I wanted NMT to be welcoming and to be a place where victims are not treated like numbers or bounced between different agencies as they seek freedom and safety. I surrounded myself with others who could help with different components of the work, from attorneys to doctors, movers to English instructors, and more. NMT continually expands this network.

To date, NMT has helped 815 adults and nearly 29,000 children. Although it is impossible to measure the full scope of our impact, we know that we are successful because compared to national figures showing that the average victim leaves her abuser seven times before getting completely free, we know of only three who have returned to abusers. I take great pride in the fact that NMT is not corporate or bureaucratic, like a lot of other help agencies. I personally work with every victim, not only helping to arrange the assistance they need but also holding their hands when they cry, hugging them when they are sad, and celebrating when they achieve. I have worked really hard to develop a network of caring professionals who help me provide whatever help these victims need. I take no salary for this work because it is a labor of love.

I hope that my story can help more people realize that abuse and assault happen in all cultures and among people from all socioeconomic statuses. Rather than hide abuse by refusing to talk about it, we need to talk more frankly about these problems so that we can develop community-based prevention efforts and better respond to the needs of victims. I believe that NMT is one small part of that effort. I am proud that I, and my organization, have won several awards for our commitment to helping victims. I implore people to get involved in their communities to help in whatever way they can.

Somy Ali is a former Bollywood actress and model and the founder of No More Tears, a South Florida–based nonprofit organization that assists victims of domestic violence and human trafficking.

A Counselor's Perspective
Alison Morris

My passion and motivation to become an advocate for domestic violence education and prevention came as a result of my role as a counselor to the students of Barry University (2002–2010). In response to the growing number of individuals sharing their stories of domestic violence in the therapy room, my colleague Jennifer Mathis-Fisher and I established an annual Domestic Violence Awareness and Prevention Month campaign on the Barry campus. I had the honor of cochairing the Programming Committee within the Division of Student Affairs and engaged various agencies such as Women In Distress (where I had the privilege of meeting Laura) in furthering educational and preventative activities. Our primary objective was to heighten the awareness of domestic violence in the Barry community and provide critical information for victims of abuse and help students process their experiences. Upon moving into private practice, I was eager to continue this work and joined the committee to plan the College Brides Walk on an annual basis. It has been a powerful experience volunteering alongside my committee members and has served to enhance my work with my clients in creating the life and relationships that they will find ultimately fulfilling.

Alison Morris is a licensed counselor who has worked in university and private settings. She is also one of the founding organizers of the College Brides Walk, a dating violence awareness event.

How Abuse Can Turn You into Something You're Not and How to Reclaim Yourself
Rebecca Smith

Domestic violence is, oftentimes, a vicious and destructive cycle. Whether it takes the form of a child learning via the behavior of an abusive parent on how their eventual family "should" be treated, or a partner in a romantic relationship becoming convinced that the treatment they receive is somehow warranted and deserved on their part, the abuse finds a way to perpetuate itself in the lives of those it affects. All too frequently the abusers themselves take no responsibility for their behavior—they excuse it as perfectly normal; perhaps they view it as some sort of inherent right to impose their fists, words, and will on their loved ones, or the blame for their actions is placed on the person being abused. "Why do you make me act this way? Why do you make me do these things to you?" The mind of an abuser is an ill one, as are any relationships it attempts to construct. This very same illness also infects those it is focused upon, the abused party.

As for my own experience, I've been on both sides of this horrendous phenomenon. This particular relationship took place during a very dark time in my life—overwhelming active addiction ruled every aspect of my existence and turned me into a person I had never intended or wanted to become. I was diagnosed with mental illness at a somewhat young age, in my teens; and my partner at the time also struggled with mental illness. When I say I've been on both sides of an abusive relationship, I mean that I not only suffered emotional, verbal, mental, and sometimes physical abuse at the hands of this partner but was returning it in spades via manipulative behavior, lying, my own personal brand of emotional and verbal abuse, and sometimes, yes, even physical.

When I was angry over some perceived slight, or being denied money to feed my addiction, my first course of action was usually to throw an actual temper tantrum, including, but not limited to, screaming and crying, and throwing things at my partner (sometimes with the intent to actually strike him with the object and other times just to try to "make a point" by just barely missing him with my aim). I knowingly and intentionally took advantage of his feelings for me in order to obtain my own ends—money for drugs, usually, but sometimes just to win arguments or prove points. At the time it was impossible for me to examine my own behavior. Looking back I've realized that it was also incredibly difficult for me to see that I was being abused as well. He was very controlling, accused me of cheating when other men would approach me without invitation or provocation, was manipulative in his own ways, and also at times used the promise of drugs and/or continued money for drugs as a way to convince me to stay in the relationship.

As I eventually dragged myself out of the depths of my addiction, I began to recognize and examine my patterns of behavior. As it turns out, this was *not* the only relationship in which I had ever engaged in emotionally, verbally, and mentally abusive tactics. I also realized that the relationship I had been in during that time was not the first of that sort for me—of that intensity and frequency, yes, but by far not the first abusive relationship I'd ever been involved in. I've since wondered if my behavior is what dictated the behavior of my partner. Were his responses involuntary, knee-jerk reactions to the abuse I inflicted upon him? I don't think I blame myself, I've come to believe that it's a mixture of two factors—his responses to my behavior compounded with abusive tendencies of his own. I don't know if this is common or even heard of. I just think that it's what has happened in my life. And maybe even that is wishful thinking on my part, a subconscious way of removing the totality of the blame from myself. Since parting ways with both active addiction and that relationship, I've noticed that I tend to be hyperaware of red flags, for better or for worse. It might in truth be something totally innocuous, such as a potential partner asking what I'm up to that evening that will set off alarms in my brain—he is trying to control my behavior; he is trying to monitor my activities. It is always a struggle to discern what his true motives are, although nine times out of ten it is a simple inquiry meant to show interest in my life. I also do my best to be just as hyperaware in those tendencies within myself.

For reasons I've never been able to ascertain, there have been people who have just brought that behavior to the surface in me. Of course, to be sure, that has also been due to external factors. I am in no way placing blame on these individuals. Life stressors, poor mental health at the time, and so many factors assuredly play a part in that. But, at any rate, I've been careful and quick to cut off communication and any possibility of a relationship with these people, for fear that I will be dragged—by my own brain or something else—back into that sort of behavior. I don't want to hurt anybody, least of all myself.

Funny enough, my partner in the aforementioned relationship is now one of my two very best friends in this world. As friends, we could not be closer to one another. We spend a ton of time together, go on outings, talk to each other all day every day, and have not had an argument of any sort in over two years—coincidentally, also the amount of time we have not been together in a romantic sense, as a couple. I also often wonder what it is about that differentiation that has such an effect on our interactions with each other. It is almost as if a flip switched—one day we were terrible for each other and next we were just very best friends. In a lot of ways it's like so much of the abuse, from either end, never happened. I harbor no ill will toward him for it, nor he toward me. In fact, we are able to call each other on those behaviors if we see one another engaging in them in the course of other relationships in our lives—not just romantic relationships, also friendships and familial relationships. In all of these ways, I know that our relationship is a *gross* outlier, entirely out of the normal realm when it comes to abusive relationships and their aftermath.

I don't know how common it is for someone to feel as though they have lived through both sides of an abusive relationship, that is, being both the abuser and the abused. I'm not up to date on statistics or case studies about that particular phenomenon. All I can really speak of is my own personal experience. It took a lot of inward reflection, self-examination, and painful, difficult revelations on my part to finally come to terms with the fact that I was both a survivor of abuse and an abuser myself. They are both categories I always swore I would never fall into, anytime the topic ever presented itself, be it in the guise of someone I knew experiencing abuse or being an abuser, or in media such as news articles, television/movies, and books. Certainly, neither are things I ever *set out* to identify as. The descent into their individual brands of lunacy was gradual, not readily noticeable, even insidious I would say—a slow, creeping evil that has a vice-like grip on you before you've even noticed its actual presence to begin with. I know that I am lucky to never have been seriously physically harmed, as so many abusive relationships end with grievous injuries or even death. And, again, I know that the fact that I now have an amazing friendship with a person who at one time was an abusive person in my life is something more or less unheard of; most people, understandably so, cut all contact and ties with their abusers and actively strive to never have any interaction with them again. I don't have a good explanation for that, just like I have no good explanation for my abusive behavior in the first place. It's just how my life ended up working out.

I am thirty-five years old, live and work in central Florida, and am by most measures a completely normal woman for my age group. I volunteer with organizations that help felons keep from becoming recidivism statistics and also donate my time to rescues for unwanted/abused horses—two of my passions in life.

Rebecca Smith lives in central Florida, where she was born and has resided most of her life. She has a dog and a cat, a BA from the University of South Florida, and a food service job.

References

UNDP. (2012). Caribbean human development report, 2012: Human development and the shift to better citizen security. UNDP. Retrieved September 10, 2019, from https://www .undp.org/content/dam/undp/library/corporate/HDR/ Latin%20America%20and%20Caribbean%20HDR/C_ bean_HDR_Jan25_2012_3MB.pdf

World Bank. (2007). Crime, violence and development: Trends, costs and policy options in the Caribbean. World Bank. Retrieved September 10, 2019, from http://site resources.worldbank.org/INTLAC/Resources/Caribbean C&VExecutiveSummary.pdf

4   Profiles

Many individuals and organizations have offered and continue to offer important perspectives, research, advocacy, and services to victims. The profiles in this section begin with some of the most influential individuals, ranging from scholars to activists to celebrities. The second portion of the chapter focuses on many of the most critical organizations that work nationwide on domestic and dating violence. Both portions are organized alphabetically.

People

Jimmie Briggs

Jimmie Briggs is an award-winning African American journalist, a teacher, and a human rights leader. Briggs wrote stories about troubled kids, gang culture, and the impact of urban violence on innocent children as a result of a lot of taunting and racial abuse he endured when he was young. Due to this he came to the realization that he wanted to help those who tend to not have a voice and also people who are not always respected or protected.

Briggs founded the Man Up campaign in 2009 after he wrote *Innocents Lost*, a book about child soldiers forced to fight and rape in the wars of central Africa. Briggs felt that men were not standing up on this issue or standing up alongside women. He believed he should do something that will encourage men

Erin Pizzey, founder of Chiswick Women's Aid in England, in 1979. (Manwaring/Evening Standard/Getty Images)

to take action. Man Up is a global campaign to stop violence against girls and women and to also put a halt to child-related violence. Briggs established Man Up as being led by youth. He believes that engaging the youth with this issue dares them to alter history. Briggs argues that stopping violence against women must be through the grassroots efforts of both young men and women. In other words, it is important to start with the men and women while they are young, to educate them about what domestic violence is, how to avoid it, and what to do about it. His Man Up campaign has been recognized by President Obama's Ambassador-at-Large of Global Women Issues. In addition, the Man Up campaign developed new partnerships with Dash Gallery and Creative Control TV, a New York–based online TV network. As well, he gained a partnership with the J Dilla Foundation, which is a nonprofit charitable organization to help fund the making of music in the inner city and give scholarships to students who are in schools with progressive music curricula. Furthermore, he gained recognition from the United Nations Development Fund for Women, which provides financial and technical aid to create programs and more ways to promote women's rights. All of these organizations may not be related to women in the way that Briggs's campaign is, but they help promote awareness with their platform and help children as well.

The campaign has been effective. It has exposed young individuals to many more organizations dealing with this issue along with opening their minds and making them aware of domestic violence in general. The campaign holds summits, which bring more people together to address the issue. Partnering with other organizations for support is another way it has been effective because it gives it more platforms to spread the awareness. The campaign does not have many controversies except the name in itself. The term "man up" embraces the sexist stereotype that men have to be tough, strong, brave, macho, leaders, and way more independent than any female.

Briggs has traveled extensively to continents and countries outside the United States, including many places in Africa, the Middle East, and Asia. The mission is for the campaign to be widespread globally and to remind people that domestic violence is indeed an issue and it is something people must stand up for, especially men. The next steps for Briggs and the Man Up campaign are to continue to raise awareness and to create more services and programs for the victims all the while getting guys to step up and use their "powerful" voice, in a patriarchal sense, that these women lack.

Sarah Deer

Statistics show that one out of every three Native American women will experience sexual violence at least once in their lifetime. Native women face similar rates of domestic violence. Research also indicates that these assaults are typically being committed by non-Native American men. This phenomenon often goes unreported or is not acknowledged, due to the fact Native American reservations must follow federal law, which specifies that they are not to prosecute anyone who is not of Native descent.

Sarah Deer has been a vocal and active agent of change for Native women. Deer's book *The Beginning and End of Rape* (2017) is an edited collection that focuses on domestic and sexual violence. Deer's work has received many accolades and influenced colleagues, both Native and non-Native. Her work also helped include Native women in the 2013 reauthorization of the Violence Against Women Act (VAWA) and in ushering in the Tribal Law and Order Act, which provided additional resources for Native victims and for training law enforcement.

Sarah Deer's work has influenced Native law and activism as well as the broader domestic violence movement. Her work bridges the gap between Indian law and feminist thinking, showing how intersectional approaches are vital to addressing the rape and abuse of Native women. Deer emphasizes the importance of Native voices in the movement, and her work honors the wisdom and lived experiences of Native women.

Salma Hayek

Salma Hayek Jiménez is as an Emmy Award–winning Mexican director, actress, and producer. Born in Coatzacoalcos, Veracruz, Mexico, in 1966 to immigrant parents, her mother is from Spain and her father from Lebanon (Hayek, 2018). The family immigrated to the United States when Hayek was twelve years, residing in Louisiana. As Catholics, Hayek attended a girls-only convent school. In her teens, she moved to Houston, Texas, to live with her aunt (Hayek, 2018). Hayek went on to study at the University of Mexico City but soon withdrew from the university in order to follow her passion for acting (Hayek, 2018).

At the start of her career, Hayek pursued roles in Mexican soap operas, becoming a telenovela star (Hayek, 2018). Hayek moved to Los Angeles (Hayek, 2018). In her 1991 breakout role, she costarred in *Desperado* (1995) with Antonio Banderas (Hayek, 2018). Hayek began her own production company, Ventanarosa, to produce and star in the 2002 film *Frida*, which followed the life of Frida Kahlo de Rivers, legendary Mexican painter and wife of Diego Rivera (Hayek, 2018). The film launched Hayek to Hollywood stardom, earning her an Emmy and Oscar nomination. Following *Frida*, she starred in *The Maldonado Miracle*, *Once upon a Time in Mexico*, and *After the Sunset* and served as the executive producer of the popular television series *Ugly Betty* (Hayek, 2018). In addition to her Hollywood career, Hayek is a fighter for domestic violence and sexual assault awareness (Hayek, 2018).

Hayek cites her father as a role model who established in her a problem-solver mentality (Warner, 2016): "This creates, I think, a very easy environment to preserve the empathy that you are born with as a child and to always put yourself in the shoes of others and then care for the others" (Warner, 2016). One of the stories that Hayek tells to express how she became an activist describes the first time she saw domestic violence. "The first time I saw domestic violence firsthand was when I was in Mexico, taking a walk with my family, and we came upon a man beating up this woman. My father intervened and fought the man and won. I remember thinking, 'Oh my God, my father is a hero'" (Salma Hayek Delivers Anti-Domestic Violence Speech, 2013). But the part of the story that impacted her most was that after her father stopped the violence, "the woman turned around and started beating up my father. I couldn't comprehend what was happening. After that, I became very intrigued with what makes a woman stay in an abusive relationship. How does her spirit break?" (Salma Hayek Delivers Anti-Domestic Violence Speech, 2013).

In 2005, Hayek testified before the U.S. Senate Violence Against Women Act Committee (Salma Hayek Delivers Anti-Domestic Violence Speech, 2013). She testified in order to encourage the extension of the Violence Against Women Act, which produced a $3.9 billion allocation to U.S. agencies that work with domestic violence. In 2006, she donated $17,722.36 to shelters for women who are victims of domestic violence in Mexico (Salma Hayek Delivers Anti-Domestic Violence Speech, 2013). Hayek is involved with many organizations such as the Kering Foundation, which fights domestic violence against women, and Chime for Change, in which the legendary brand Gucci leads the campaign for women's rights (Warner, 2016). Avon is another organization that Salma works with (Salma Hayek Pinault and Avon CEO Sheri McCoy, 2016). She created a charm necklace for Women's Day 2016 with Avon; One hundred percent of the sales of that necklace would be put into the Avon Speak Out against Domestic Violence program (Salma Hayek Pinault and Avon CEO Sheri McCoy, 2016). The charm has an infinity symbol to represent the infinitude of potential that women have when free from violence.

With Chime for Change, Hayek works with women and children's education and health on a global scale (Cartner-Morley,

2015). Some of those projects include creating schools for refugees from Syria in Turkey and Lebanon (Cartner-Morley, 2015). Hayek is a self-described feminist: "I am a feminist because I love women and I am ready to fight for women. I am a feminist because I am proud to be a woman, and I am passionate about making the world a better place for women. I am a feminist because a lot of amazing women have made me the woman I am today. I am inspired by women every day, as friends and such as colleagues" (Cartner-Morley, 2015). Hayek has also worked with the Brides Walk campaign in which people dress up in wedding dresses to fight against domestic violence. It is inspired by the shooting of Gladys Ricart, who was murdered by an envious, abusive ex-boyfriend (Anderson, Botton, Gest, & Ogunnaike, 2002). About 34 percent of the Latino community suffers domestic violence, and Hayek, as a Mexican-born woman, wants to stand up for her community (Anderson, Botton, Gest, & Ogunnaike, 2002). Hayek has also called on Congress to increase the funds provided for organizations that deal with domestic violence (Anderson, Botton, Gest, & Ogunnaike, 2002).

Although Hayek has not been a victim of domestic violence, she has been a victim of sexual harassment and has been involved with the #MeToo movement. When news broke out about the sexual assault allegations against noted film producer Harvey Weinstein, many celebrities spoke out about their experience with him (Hayes, 2018). When *The New York Times* asked Salma Hayek about it, she initially remained quiet because she felt that her story was not as important as others (Hayes, 2018). "I felt my pain was so small." She thought, "There's no point for me to talk because it happens to everyone," but then she realized that when all of the voices of the #MeToo movement come together, they can become powerful enough to produce change" (Hayes, 2018). In her #MeToo story, she reports how although there was no sexual assault involved with Weinstein in her case, she was sexually harassed for five years during the *Frida* era (Hayes, 2018). Hayek received the Award for Individual Achievement at the 2015 Kahlil Gibran Spirit of Humanity Awards for her contributions to the education, health, and justice for women around the world (Producer, Actress, and Activist Salma Hayek Pinault to Receive Award for Individual Achievement, 2015).

Francine Hughes

Michigan housewife Francine Hughes is best known for setting her husband, James "Mickey" Hughes, on fire in their home on March 9, 1977. Francine had endured thirteen years of emotional and physical abuse that started shortly after the couple's November 1963 wedding. She was just fifteen when she met Mickey, who was eighteen. Francine dropped out of high school a year later, married Mickey, and the two lived in his parents' home in Dansville, Michigan. It was only a few weeks after the wedding that Mickey beat Francine because he felt that her outfit was too revealing. She sought help from family, friends, police, and social workers numerous, but the abuse continued and Francine felt increasingly fearful for her life. She did manage to leave Mickey once, in 1994, and sought refuge with her parents, but her mother encouraged Francine to reconcile with her husband. Her father abused her mother as well, which likely impacted her lack of support for her daughter, as did the fact that Francine was pregnant with the couple's first child. Mickey was employed only sporadically, which made the abuse more constant and relentless. The couple eventually had three other children. When Francine applied for welfare for her and the kids, she was told she had to divorce Mickey to receive benefits. She did, but he still refused to leave the home. After she set fire to Mickey's bed while he was passed out drunk, Francine was arrested and charged with first-degree murder for his death. Earlier that day, Mickey had locked Francine and the kids out of the house and refused to allow her to feed them. Mickey was resentful that Francine had begun taking classes at Lansing Business College, so he ripped up her books and demanded that she burn the others. She said, "I remember he was pulling my hair and he was hitting me with his fist and he had hit me on the mouth and my lip was bleeding." At the time, there were few resources for victims, and police often did not take domestic violence seriously. When police arrived then, Francine testified that they did very little and that Mickey continued to beat her after they left. After pouring gasoline on his bed and lighting a match, Francine drove to the police station and confessed. She was acquitted on the grounds of temporary insanity.

An important element of the case was the testimony that battered women are often too fearful to leave and that they may repress their anger at abusers. Dr. Berkman, a clinical psychologist, testified that Francine was terrified that Mickey would kill her if she tried again to leave him. Berkman maintained that Francine "was overwhelmed by the massive onslaughts of her primitive emotions. Emotions she had suppressed. . . . She experienced a breakdown of her psychological processes so that she was no longer able to utilize judgment . . . no longer able to control her impulses . . . unable to prevent herself from acting in the way she did." A psychologist, Dr. Anne Seiden, corroborated Dr. Berkman's testimony, while another, Dr. Blount, wrote that Francine's behavior did not meet the legal definition of temporary insanity in the state of Michigan. The jury deliberated for just five hours before announcing the verdict. After being released on November 4, 1977, Francine returned home to Jackson, Michigan, and enrolled in nursing school. She eventually remarried.

At the time of the trial, self-defense was rarely successful in murder cases, and Francine's attorneys did not believe it would have been successful. Many critics felt that Francine got away with murder and that she should have retreated instead of killing Mickey. Some women's rights groups were also troubled by the verdict, not necessarily because they wanted Francine to be convicted but because they believed that the temporary insanity argument made it seem as though victims of domestic violence are mentally ill.

The case continued to receive attention after Francine's acquittal, and in 1980, author Faith McNulty (1980) used the trial records and interviews to tell the story in the best-selling book *The Burning Bed*. Four years later the book was used as the basis for a movie of the same name that starred Farrah Fawcett as Francine Hughes. It was one of the highest-rated television movies of the time. The trial, book, and movie all helped draw attention to the issue of domestic violence and the need for better laws and more support for victims.

Jackson Katz

Jackson Katz has been a leader in efforts to address domestic violence, not only with his studies, speeches, and books but also with the movements he supports. He is the founder of a bystander intervention initiative called Mentors in Violence Prevention (MVP). Although the #MeToo movement was initiated by Tarana Burke, Katz has lent his support vocally and in writing.

Jackson Katz is a man of many accomplishments. He is an educator, author, and cultural theorist. He was born on May 7, 1960, in Swampscott, Massachusetts. Katz had a rough childhood, as his dad died at the age of two. His mom remarried, and Katz was raised by his stepfather, which was no easy ordeal. Katz said he grew up fearing "not of being brutally beaten, but fear of being pushed up against the wall and yelled at. It was more a fear of violence happening than it actually happening" (Burleigh, 2014).

Although at an early age he played football and was successful, Katz ended up taking a greater interest in society and its problems. Also, Katz currently writes for the *Huffington Post*, and according to an article published by Nina Burleigh (2014), he is "media savvy." According to Nina Burleigh (2014), "He's also the first man to graduate from the University of Massachusetts Amherst with a degree in women's studies, back in 1982." A social problem that gets downplayed in the United States is that of sexual assault, which has been one of Katz's primary focuses throughout his career. He has published several books dealing with these social issues, including *The Macho Paradox* in 2006, followed by *Leading Men: Presidential Campaigns and the Politics of Manhood* in 2012 and his last book *Man Enough?: Donald Trump, Hillary Clinton, and the Politics of Presidential Masculinity*, published in 2016.

Katz is well known for MVP, a program many colleges and schools use today. The MVP program was cofounded by Katz in 1993 in Northeastern University's Center for the Study of Sport in Society. Katz's work has been quite successful, and MVP has been used with military, fraternity, and sport groups as well. One evaluation of MVP, funded by the Department of Education, involved 468 students in 2007 and 2008. Participants reported significantly lower sexist attitudes after completing the program and improved sense of self-efficacy (Cissner, 2009).

Most of Katz's work revolves around violence against women and enlisting men to help end it. He consistently draws attention to the gendered nature of most criminal offense. For instance, in a TED talk, Katz discussed why violence against women is a problem for men. In his writings and in the documentary *Tough Guise*, Katz emphasizes that traditional gender roles that require males to be aggressive and nonemotional contribute to violence against women. Furthermore, these gender role norms are not healthy for men either, as many men suffer from not being able to express their emotions. In regard to school shootings, for instance, Katz (2006) said, "There was not one mention of men, masculinity, or violence in their coverage, yet all of these school shootings have been perpetrated by young men. The first thing we should be talking about is the gender of the perpetrators, not gun control, school security, and the school's responsibility."

Nicole Kidman

Nicole Kidman, born in Honolulu, Hawaii, and raised in Sydney, Australia, is an internationally recognized, award-winning actress who has won many awards for her many successful movies and/or TV shows. She is also a victim of sexual assault. Despite the lack of information on the actual incident(s), renowned film director Harvey Weinstein is alleged to have sexually assaulted Kidman and other actresses, including Gwyneth Paltrow, Angelina Jolie, Meryl Streep, Jennifer Lawrence, Kate Winslet, and Minnie Driver. In light of this scandal, which was brought to attention as part of the #MeToo movement, Kidman said, "As I've stated before publicly, I support and applaud all women and these women who speak out against any abuse and misuse of power—be it domestic violence or sexual harassment in the workforce. We need to eradicate this behavior" (Wagmeister, 2017).

Kidman has also been appointed as the goodwill ambassador of UN Women. UN Women works at a global level with countries to advocate for ending gender-based violence, increasing "awareness of the causes and consequences of violence and build capacity of partners to prevent and respond to violence," along with "changing norms and behaviors or men and boys and advocate for gender equality and women's rights" (About UN Women, n.d.). As the goodwill ambassador for UN Women, to which she was appointed in 2006, Kidman is now "raising awareness on the infringement of women's human rights," specifically focusing on violence against women (UN Women). Kidman is also the spokesperson for the global advocacy effort Say No-UNiTE to End Violence against Women initiative. Kidman has traveled to many countries alongside UN Women to meet with and support women who have suffered due to this issue by giving them a voice through the media and raising funds for violence against women (UN Women). With her position as goodwill ambassador, Kidman stated that she has "seen that there is no limit to what women can achieve when given the opportunity. . . . To me, these women embody resilience, strength, dignity—and hope" (UN Women).

Since 2007, there has been a draft legislation that never passed Congress called the International Violence Against Women Act. If enacted, it would require the U.S. government to become involved "in anti-violence campaigns . . . through both diplomacy and funding" (IVAWA Summary, n.d.). In 2009, Kidman spoke before the House Foreign Affairs sub-committee on International Organizations, Human Rights and Oversight, which considered this legislation. In her state-ment to Congress, she mentioned that succeeding in ending violence against women, "requires political will at the highest levels . . . after all, a life free of violence is a human right" (Ellis, 2002, p. 24). Kidman further explains that Hollywood is a significant factor in dismissing gender-based violence: "I can't be responsible for the whole of Hollywood, but I can certainly be responsible for my own career," she adds (Ellis, 2002, p. 24). Although the legislation was not passed, Kid-man using her voice and celebrity role had hundreds of people lined up to hear what she had to say about violence against women.

As an actress, Kidman has played many roles in which she portrayed women suffering from gender-based violence. One of her most recent roles was as Celeste Wright in *Big Little Lies*, a woman who seemed like she had a perfect life but, in reality, was in an extremely abusive relationship that she referred to as simply being "volatile." Her husband, Perry, would tell her how to dress, would tell her when she should be home, questioned her love for her children, and beat her on a near-daily basis. Kidman's role depicted a very clear picture for viewers, showing how easily someone can fall into an abusive relationship and how many do not even realize it until it is too late.

Nicole Kidman has been a great contributor to ending gender-based violence, which she refers to as her passion. At a fund-raising dinner that marked the twentieth anniversary of the UN Trust Fund to End Violence against Women, Kid-man asked the guests to "undo your wallets" because there are women out there who "need us who have the ability, who have the money to help them" (Associated Press, 2016). The din-ner itself raised over $105,000 along with a $50,000 donation from Kidman. The organization also has funded grants which have "risen from $1 million in 1997 to supporting $57 million in grants in 2016" (Associated Press, 2016). At another fund-raising event in Hong Kong for the United Nations Development Fund for Women (UNIFEM), Kidman raised more than $175,000 to promote gender equality and funding for UNIFEM projects in China. The funds raised for this event in China will "support shelter and legal protection for survivors" (Associated Press, 2016).

More recently, Nicole Kidman gave a speech on domestic violence after receiving her Emmy for her role in *Big Little Lies*. She referred to domestic violence as a "complicated, insidious disease that exists far more than we allow ourselves to know" (Li, 2017). Kidman continues to be an advocate and grand spokeswoman for violence against women.

Michael Kimmel

An American sociologist, Michael Kimmel is best known for his work on gender studies and masculinity. Kimmel earned a bachelor's degree from Vassar College in 1972, a master's degree from Brown University, and a PhD from the University of California at Berkeley in 1981. He is a SUNY distinguished professor of sociology and gender studies at Stony Brook University.

In 2013, with support from MacArthur Foundation, Kimmel founded the Center for the Study of Men and Masculinities at Stony Brook. He is the author of many books, chapters, and articles and is often featured in various news media, including the *Huffington Post*. Kimmel is a highly sought-after speaker, having lectured at more than 300 high schools, colleges, and universities, and has delivered the International Women's Day lecture at the European Parliament, the European Commission, and the Council of Europe. In addition, Kimmel has worked with the ministers for gender equality in Norway, Denmark, and Sweden, helping to create programs for men and boys. According to his website, the *Guardian* named Kimmel "the world's most prominent male feminist." Kimmel has faced challenges professionally and personally, however, due to allegations of sexual harassment.

Kimmel identifies as a feminist and argues that gender equality benefits not only women but also men. In a 2015 talk for TEDWomen, Kimmel articulated why. He pointed to studies showing that men are healthier, businesses are more productive, and societies are less violent when there is more gender equality. Kimmel has long argued that more men need to be involved in gender equality efforts and, in particular, in ending violence against women.

Kimmel's eleven books include several titles related to gender equality and ending violence against women. His 1996 book *Manhood in America: A Cultural History* was nominated for a Pulitzer Prize for Nonfiction and the National Book Award. In 2000 *The Gendered Society* was published, followed by two books in 2005: *The History of Men: Essays on American and British Masculinities* and *The Gender of Desire: Essays on Masculinity and Sexuality*. In 2008, *Guyland: The Perilous World Where Boys Become Men* was published, followed by *Misframing Men: Essays on the Politics of Contemporary Masculinities* in 2010, *The Guy's Guide to Feminism* in 2011, and *Angry White Men: American Masculinity at the End of an Era* in 2013. In addition, Kimmel has edited a number of books on gender, sexuality, masculinity, and privilege. His journal articles are also focused on these issues, as are many of his pieces for the Huffington Post and other news sources.

Kimmel's 2002 paper "Gender Symmetry" in *Domestic Violence: A Substantive Methodological Research Review* is perhaps his most significant piece specifically related to domestic violence. Kimmel countered other researchers who maintain that men and women experience abuse at similar rates. He argued that these numbers were used for political purposes by persons opposing funding for women's shelters and asserted that the studies showing gender symmetry were fundamentally flawed. Researchers asked only cohabiting couples about abuse in their homes, thus leaving out those who have separated. Few same-sex couples were included, and the framing of the questions may have underestimated both physical and nonphysical forms of abuse. Kimmel also took issue with the fact that a punch by a man was tallied as equally violent to a slap by a usually smaller woman and argued that women are socialized not to use violence and thus may be more likely to feel guilt and remorse and subsequently to report when they do it. In contrast, men are socialized, according to Kimmel, to be in control and thus may not report using violence to researchers because it would appear that they had lost control. Similarly, women are taught to justify and accept men's violence, so many do not report all of it. Like many, Kimmel maintains that women's violence is often actually self-defense and that women suffer far greater physical damage than do men.

His book *Guyland: The Perilous World Where Boys Become Men* (2008) offers a detailed example of the cultural world of young men in today's America. Kimmel asserts that young men today are passing through a different stage than other generations, which he calls "Guyland." Guyland involves largely male-to-male peer interactions, a sense of entitlement, and little care for the criticism or concern of female peers, parents, or other authority figures. From boyhood, Kimmel argues, men engage in violence with one another as a test of masculinity. Hazing, especially by fraternities, is one example, as is sexual violence against women. These young men feel entitled to sex and often use derogatory language and aggressive behavior to get it.

In August 2018, allegations of sexual harassment were leveled against Kimmel by a former graduate student at Stony Brook. Initially the student reported the harassment anonymously, but shortly thereafter, she released their (the individual's preferred pronoun) name. Bethany M. Coston, now an assistant professor of women's, gender, and sexuality studies at Virginia Commonwealth University, alleged that Kimmel routinely used explicit sexual talk, made homophobic comments, was transphobic, and generally lacked respect for anyone who didn't identify as a heterosexual cisgender male. When Coston came forward, Kimmel was poised to accept a sociology award from the American Sociological Association but asked the organization to defer the award for six months. Kimmel was criticized by many for referring to the allegations as "rumors" (Flaherty, 2018).

Paul Kivel

Paul Kivel is a social justice educator, writer, and activist who has been involved in fighting for the oppressed for more than forty-five years. He speaks about many social justice issues, from racism and diversity, the challenges of youth, teen dating and family violence, raising boys to manhood, and the impact of class and power on daily life. Kivel's work on violence mainly comprises traveling the globe and speaking on the subject to millions of listeners and attendees while also opening projects and organizations, such as the Oakland Men's Project. That effort was started in 1979 and helps young men combat violence in their lives.

Domestic violence has also been a huge component in Kivel's work. He created exercises and tips for people to identify domestic violence if they see it, experience it, or are a domestic violence perpetrator. Kivel also wrote many books, on the subject of not only domestic violence but also ending violence of all sorts. Summing up his feeling toward such injustices, Kivel explains: "We need to provide services for those most in need, for those trying to survive, for those barely making it. We need to work for social change so that we create a society in which our institutions and organizations are equitable and just and all people are safe, adequately fed, adequately housed, well educated, able to work at safe, decent jobs, and able to participate in the decisions that affect their lives" (Kivel, 2002). Like an economic pyramid, he explains, the social justice of those less fortunate is the same, with the straight white males being at the top and trickling down to the poor white males, minorities, women, and, at the very bottom, women of color. The same goes with domestic violence, with power predominantly residing with the males at the top and then trickling down to women, women of color, and the almost forgotten group of men who do experience domestic violence as well.

In the 1970s when the women's movement was in full force, Kivel was a significant contributor. "His experience made it clear to him that men, perpetrators of a disproportionate number of murders, assaults, and rapes, had an important role to play in stopping abuse" (Villines, 2015). The impact that it left on him made him pursue the lifelong career of teaching men to avoid violence and teaching anti-violence seminars to different demographic groups, especially men who have had a history of abusing women.

Gender role conditioning plays a huge role in the development of children; according to Kivel, this is where it all starts. People develop a list of traits that they associate with sons and daughters, and that phrase "act like a man" is typical for boys. "Dominance, being in control, winning at all costs, athleticism, sex, aggression, and being tough top the list. These traits become a central part of men's identities and render them likely to commit violent acts, particularly when their masculinity is threatened" (Villines, 2015). Kivel points out the fact that our society does not teach males healthy ways to react to stress except with aggression and violence. The factors that do help with combating stress we associate only with feminism and females include showing emotion, expressing compassion, and opening up. In his seminars, Kivel tells men that aggression does not have to be a main part of masculinity. There is room to be gentle and compassionate as well.

Another problem with domestic violence that Kivel points out is that men are not actively involved in ending it when they are the key. "Kivel believes that men have a moral obligation to work to end violence. They also have a personal interest in the subject because many men's lives are ripped apart by violence. While outreach to women is necessary, stopping abuse at its source is the true recipe for sustainable change" (Villines, 2015, p. 4). Domestic violence does not harm just women, as he points out; men also get abused. By hindering their relationships with others, it removes their ability to be nurturers, which, in turn, hurts the future offspring in the process. It is also not fair to a woman's future partner when their loved one has come from an abusive relationship and now may have trust issues and problems with intimacy.

Nicholas Kristof and Sheryl WuDunn

Married couple Nicholas Kristof and Sheryl WuDunn are authors and activists for gender equality globally. Both are acclaimed in their own right but together are best known for their award-winning journalism and, most recently, for their book and documentary, *Half the Sky: Turning Oppression into Opportunity for Women Worldwide* (2009). Kristof is an award-winning columnist for the *New York Times*, where he writes generally about human rights issues. He has been a regular columnist at the *Times* since 2001 and has twice won the Pulitzer Prize. Kristof is a graduate of Harvard College and earned a law degree as a Rhodes Scholar at Oxford.

Kristof has written numerous times about domestic violence. In a March 2014 Op-Ed for the *Times*, Kristof told the story of a woman who was jailed for the murder of her abusive boyfriend when she grabbed a knife and stabbed him during a particularly brutal attack. With help from the Women's Resource Center to End Domestic Violence, her charge was reduced to manslaughter and she received probation. Kristof uses the story to highlight the need for earlier intervention in domestic violence cases and notes that American women are twice as likely to suffer from domestic violence as from breast cancer.

WuDunn earned a bachelor's degree from Cornell University, an MBA from Harvard Business School, and an MPA from Princeton University's Woodrow Wilson School. WuDunn also holds honorary doctorates from the University of Pennsylvania and Middlebury College. She worked at the *Wall Street Journal* and then *The New York Times* as its Beijing bureau correspondent. In addition, WuDunn has taught at Yale University's Jackson Institute for Global Affairs. A regular commentator on global affairs, especially related to China, as well as on gender issues, WuDunn is often featured on National Public Radio, *The Colbert Report*, and *Charlie Rose*, among other news sources. WuDunn has extensive experience in business and banking and has won several journalism awards.

With WuDunn, who also worked for the *Times*, Kristof won the 1990 Pulitzer Prize for their coverage of the Tiananmen Square protests. They were the first married couple to win a Pulitzer.

Kristof and WuDunn's work *Half the Sky* focuses on gender-based violence, situating it in the global oppression of women. Starting even before birth with sex-selective abortion, Kristof and WuDunn maintain that oppression of women is the twenty-first century's greatest injustice. In the book they also discuss inadequate medical attention to and nutrition for girls, rates of rape and sexual assault, acid attacks, domestic violence, and sex trafficking, noting that poverty and lack of adequate education of girls are key factors. More than just statistics, the book shares the stories of women and girls who have been trafficked, who have suffered horrendous violence by family members, and who have been forced into prostitution. Yet Kristof and WuDunn also make clear that women and girls are not "the problem"; they are the solution. That is, women and girls globally have great power to help remedy these issues. As such, they lobby for the economic, educational, and political empowerment of women. The book received much praise and was expanded into a movement with a concomitant website. Kristof and WuDunn have solicited celebrities to help in the efforts to combat violence against women and gender oppression, so the website features several short videos by celebrities who have been involved. It also features additional information and resources for communities. *Half the Sky* was made into a PBS television series that aired in October 2012. It also includes several celebrities and was shot in ten countries: Cambodia,

India, Kenya, Sierra Leone, Somaliland, Afghanistan, Pakistan, Vietnam, Liberia, and the United States.

Erin Pizzey

In 1971, Erin Patricia Margaret Pizzey founded the first nationally and internationally recognized women's shelter in Chiswick, England, which was later renamed the Refuge. She also fell victim to domestic abuse earlier in her life as she had an abusive mother; given this background, it was easy for her to empathize with the inhabitants of the women's shelter. The women's shelter opened up at a very difficult time in the world, a time when domestic violence was taboo. It was not discussed or even considered a real issue because it was simply "domestic" or, in other words, not anybody else's business. That is what made the shelter opening so significant; it sent a message to society that causing harm to your partner shouldn't be tolerated. Soon came the death threats and public protests against Pizzey and her organization. It wasn't until her family dog was shot that she decided to relocate, along with her children. Pizzey was one of the pioneers of the women's movement in the United Kingdom. Pizzey received backlash for multiple opinions, one of them being that teaching feminism was also teaching Marxism. She responded in an interview:

> Yes, but most of them don't even know anything about the beginning of this movement. And the thing I have to point out, very simply, the beginnings of the women's movement happened way back when a lot of women were fighting for the rights of people, of Americans, to end the apartheid that was going on at that time. When they had finished marching for the civil rights movement—There's a whole storied history that you can read it. They came back and decided that the leftist women wanted their own movement. So instead of it being Capitalism, which everyone was against in the left wing movements, they simply changed the goal posts and said it was Patriarchy.

Everything was because of men, because of the power that men have over women. And then the second part of their argument was that all women are victims of men's violence because it's The Patriarchy. And that is such a lot of rubbish. Because, we know, and everybody in the business knows, that both men and women in interpersonal relationships can be violent. And that's in every single study all across the Western world. All this time—40 years— we've been living a big lie led by these Feminist women who essentially have created a huge billion-dollar industry all across the world and they have shut the doors on men. No men can work in refuges; no men can sit on Boards; boys under the age of twelve often can't go into the refuges. A mother has to make a difficult choice of what she should do. (Esmey, 2012)

Another controversial position Pizzey holds is the act that men are as much victims of domestic abuse as women, which she articulated in her book *A Terrorist within the Family*. Pizzey discouraged attitudes that blame men for all abuse. Pizzey says that women are more prone to direct anger inward; the violence is covert or not openly displayed. Men direct their anger outward and hurt others, but either way, it is violence. "They weren't allowing women to have a choice: I knew that a woman who ends up with a violent armed robber has at some level chosen to be with him—but the feminist movement only allowed women to be victims" (Rabinovitch, 2001). Almost right after opening the women's shelter, Pizzey wanted to open a shelter for men, and to her surprise she was given a house by the council. She went to the millionaires who helped fund her women's refuge, and they refused to help fund the men's shelter.

Pizzey further explains that if someone comes from a family that is dysfunctional, violent, and sexually abusive, then that is what they are familiar with and what they carry with them for the rest of their life; they simply don't know any better and are not taught accordingly. Magnetic resonance imaging (MRI) scans were first used in 1977 (years after Pizzey had already endured the abuse). With the MRI scans, parents can finally see the actual damage that abuse can cause to the brain, specifically the part of the brain that controls all of the emotions.

In a 2012 interview, Erin Pizzey explained how she was abused by both her parents; when the interviewer apologized for having experienced that, she declined his pity and said, "No, you have to remember that's why I know what I know and that's why I can do what I do" (Esmey, 2012).

As of today, Refuge is the largest provider of services in the United Kingdom for victims of domestic violence, modern slavery, human trafficking, forced prostitution, rape, forced marriage, and "honor"-based abuse (punishment that is given as a result of bringing dishonor). It provides buildings, facilities, open spaces as well as services, advocacy, counseling, information, and sponsors. Refuge supports over 4,500 children, women and men, elderly people, and people with disabilities. Pizzey made it her duty to mention in an interview: "In my refuge, half the staff are always men because they're so important for children who haven't known good, kind men . . . and some of the mothers" (Esmey, 2012).

Pizzey's work influenced the early leaders of the shelter movement in the United States.

Tony Porter

Born in New York, Tony Porter has grown and developed into a world-renowned activist. He has become a leading voice when it comes to male socialization, its role in domestic violence, and combating violence against women. Tony Porter has established his position in the world of social justice. Porter is also an author and educator whose work influences many organizations working on violence prevention and dealing with the issues of masculinity. Porter also serves as an advisor to multiple professional sports organizations, including the National Basketball Association and the National Football League. However, his range of influence spans far beyond the United States, as he has presented at the United Nations Commission of the Status of Women, along with lecturing in many foreign countries, including Brazil and Africa.

Tony Porter is the cofounder of A Call to Men, a nonprofit organization that aims to educate men about healthy manhood (Fessler, 2018). Porter was driven to create a new journey toward the prevention of violence due to having past experiences that related to sexual assault toward women. A Call to Men aims to end violence against women. The organization itself has partnered with multiple communities and other organizations where they seek to prevent domestic violence through education on their manhood and about masculinity.

Labeling himself a feminist, Porter connects many issues of domestic and sexual violence to masculinity. He aims to create a world where every woman is respected and loved by all men. Shifting the mind-set that women are inferior to men is a common topic of Porter's lectures, which he presents virtually anywhere there is a male population. He also claims that continuing to believe in the stereotypical idea of manhood is a constant threat to the future of men in America. He goes on to state that the idea that men should suppress their emotions is very harmful to their future relationships. Men who suppress their emotions have been found to be one-third more likely to suffer from unhealthy coping mechanisms and even a premature death.

Tony Porter presented a TED Talk concerning men and breaking out of what he called the *Man Box*. He starts off by describing that while he was growing up, he was taught to show no emotion except anger and that men were superior to women and held a higher value. Introducing the Man Box, he describes it as being the socialization of men, stating that there are pros and cons to this belief about manhood. The Man Box contains many values that men are taught at a young age concerning how they are supposed to be and how they should view women, consequently leading to the devaluation and objectification of women, which also leads to domestic and sexual violence (Porter, 2010a, b).

Connecting this idea to several of his experiences, Porter realizes the influence of the Man Box and why he must free himself from it. One instance he compares his reaction to is that of his children crying. While they were only months apart, he would handle both of them differently. If his daughter were to come to him crying, he found himself comforting her and having a more passive atmosphere. On the other hand, if his son were to come to him crying, he would be more aggressive and loud, telling his son to "be like a man" about the situation. In another instance, he found his uncle refused to cry in front of the women at his son's funeral, but as soon as they left, he could not hold it in anymore, even praising Porter for not crying and apologizing for it. Through both of these occurrences, Porter decided to liberate himself from the Man Box, and through this, he states that men can also help liberate women.

Through A Call to Men, Tony Porter has given many informative speeches and lectures at universities and schools throughout the United States, including the United States Military Academy and the United States Naval Academy. He has also worked with *Law & Order: Special Victims Unit* as a script consultant. Having written *Breaking Out of the Man Box* and playing a role in *NFL Dads: Dedicated to Daughters*, Porter has a widespread of influence with both the average man and those that are looked up to by many.

Porter's vision is to bring an end to men inflicting domestic and sexual violence toward women. He blames traditional ideologies being pushed onto men during their youth as being the root of this behavior. It is common for fathers to tell their son to "not be like a girl," thus diminishing the strength and value of women and creating room for the thought of men being greater than women. The idea of men being superior and women being inferior causes many instances of abuse. Tied into this is the mind-set of women being objectified and primarily used for sexual actions, thus leading to an increase of sexual violence. In order to end this, Porter plans to educate young men, the future generation, about handling their masculinity properly and respecting women and for them to continue teaching these lessons to those to come. He believes that a large amount of gender discrimination is because of men. Therefore, educating about the cause of the problem, men and their traditional beliefs, would help bring an end to the issue, violence with women being the victims.

On average, one in three women fall victim to being sexually assaulted, a third of all female homicides have a partner committing the crime, and out of all of this, only 27 percent of women report sexual violence they've experienced, meaning there is possibility for plenty more that goes unknown (Toomer, 2018). In addition, 95 percent of women who are raped know the identity of their attacker. Statistics like these pepper Porter's lectures. At a lecture given at Penn State University, Porter stated that abuse goes beyond that of the physical sense, demonstrating the fact that verbal and psychological abuse are just as damaging to women.

Bringing the #MeToo movement into picture, Porter says that the behavior of men that has been the focus of the movement is not surprising to him. He again blames the methods used to raise some men. While he believes that owning up and being accountable for your wrong doings in the past is significant to resolving the issue, he also believes that it would be much more beneficial if men were to move and take steps toward preventing the same issues in the future. Putting an emphasis on the lingering effects of collective socialization on men, Porter wants to provide the right passage for helping men come out of this idea (Toomer, 2018).

A large area of concentration for Porter is single mothers. He states that many of them feel as if it is difficult to raise a son without a father figure in their life. He also points out differences he noticed between single mothers and those who were with their partners while he was a coach for a local basketball team. He noted that the single mother was much more vocal and enthusiastic, while the mother present with her husband was calm and rarely showed interest in what was going on. He says this is because the single mother must take on extra duties because of the fact that she is alone, while the mother who is married does not have to take on this responsibility. Sometimes single mothers can feel at a disadvantage because of their status and feel like they would have to make up for the lack of a fatherly role when it comes to raising a son and teaching him lessons that the father normally would. However, this often leads to them overdoing it or going to the extreme when it was not necessary (Tony Porter Wants Our Boys to Break Out of the "Man Box," 2016).

Tony Porter, author, educator, and activist, is a presence against domestic abuse targeting women. Through his methods, the education and upbringing of men will continue to develop into new notions where women are viewed as equal to men and would have a newfound respect given to them that has been deserved for years.

Lynn Rosenthal

Lynn Rosenthal is one the most active individuals in the United States addressing the issue of domestic violence. She began her career as director of a local domestic violence shelter and rape crisis center and then later served as executive director of state domestic violence coalitions in Florida and New Mexico. In addition, she was a consultant in Florida, aiming to improve housing opportunities for domestic violence survivors. Rosenthal is currently policy director for the Biden Foundation's Violence against Women Initiatives. Prior to holding this meaningful role, she advocated against violence based on gender and served as vice president for Strategic Partnerships at the National Domestic Violence Hotline. Rosenthal was also the first White House advisor on Violence Against Women, a position in which she served from 2009 through 2014.

From 2000 to 2006, Rosenthal served as executive director of the National Network to End Domestic Violence, representing state domestic violence coalitions in Congress and working with corporate leaders to promote funding initiatives to address women abuse.

As senior advisor to Vice President Biden, Rosenthal developed innovative strategies to address sexual assault, reduce domestic violence homicides, and enhance employer's reactions toward abuse against women. She also cochaired the White House Task Force to protect students from sexual abuse. Rosenthal represented the vice president on the White House Council on Women and Girls and cochaired the Federal Interagency Working Group on HIV/AIDS and Violence against Women.

Lynn Rosenthal serves as Cohort 3 in the Move to End Violence organization. Move to End Violence works with dedicated agents and leaders in organizations advocating to end violence against girls and women. They promote a paradigm shift in social perspectives about violence toward girls and women through a variety of training opportunities, counseling, and other resources. The core program elements address areas such as a what they call Beloved Community, which encourages victims to reach their full potential by being themselves, embracing their culture, heritage, strengths, learning lessons, past experiences, and so on, in order to build a strong and new individual rooted in love, kindness, and grace. Other programs include Liberation and Equity, Transformational Leadership Development, Organizational Development, and Movement Building for Social Change. Through approximately nine years of operation, Move to End Violence has positively impacted the lives of several victims, created awareness, and empowered girls and women to reach their full capacity.

Rosenthal currently leads the Biden Foundation's effort to prevent sexual and domestic abuse through cultural change and supports from survivors. It has also made significant achievements since 1994, when the former vice president spearheaded the Violence Against Women Act. It helped shift the public perception that gender-based violence was a family issue, therefore should be handled internally, as opposed to social problems that needed outside intervention. Since teenagers and young adults often encounter highest rates of domestic and sexual abuse, the Biden Foundation developed Youth LEADS (Leverage, Energize, and Define Solutions). This program was aimed at developing young leaders of the community to promote cultural and social awareness about gender-based violence. Through educational youth engagement sessions, they would be able to recognize the symptoms of violence, respond under those circumstances, and educate others, including policymakers and stakeholders, about the matter.

In 2016, Rosenthal received the Alliance for HOPE International's Lifetime Achievement Award at the Sixteenth Annual International Family Justice Center Conference.

"Lynn Rosenthal's work has saved countless lives by providing a greater understanding of domestic violence and sexual assault. Lynn's work is ongoing with the National Domestic Violence Hotline, but we cannot ignore the stunning lifetime of accomplishments she has already amassed," said Gael Strack, chief executive officer of Alliance for HOPE International. "Lynn is a true hero in the domestic violence and sexual assault movements and she continues to set the agenda for our national and international effort to stop violence against women, men, and children" (National Domestic Violence Advocate Wins, 2016).

Susan Schechter

Susan Schechter was a social worker, educator, and one of the early leaders of the anti-domestic violence movement. With others, Schechter helped establish the Abused Women's Coalition, the first domestic violence shelter in Chicago in 1976. Schechter is known for drawing attention to the intersection of domestic violence services and child protection efforts. She noted that most existing battered women's efforts did not extend to hospitals, clinics, and schools, and she was one of the first to call for collaborations between systems and to promote curricula to train workers, health-care professionals, and clinicians about domestic violence. In 1986, Schechter established Advocacy for Women & Kids in Emergencies (WAKE) at Children's Hospital in Boston. It was the first service to assist families experiencing both child abuse and domestic violence. Another contribution Schechter made to the field was the notion that victims who wanted to stay with abusers could develop safety plans for how to do so. Further, Schechter drew attention to the intersections of race and class in the lives of domestic violence victims.

Born and raised in St. Louis, Missouri, Schechter earned a bachelor of arts degree from Washington University and a master's degree in social work from the University of Illinois at Chicago. She began working as a social worker in Chicago shortly thereafter and was routinely asked to give presentations about domestic violence. After founding WAKE in 1986, she served as its program coordinator and then as a consultant until 1993. In 1991, Schechter began working as a clinical professor in the School of Social Work at the University of Iowa. There she partnered with several organizations in an effort to improve the quality of child protection services, and she also served as a research associate at the Injury Prevention Research Center at the university.

Schechter authored many books, articles, and other publications during her career. In 1982 she wrote *Women and Male Violence: The Visions and Struggles of the Battered Women's Movement*, which showcased the history of the movement and the causes of abuse and made recommendations for improvement. Reflecting about this seminal work, Schechter commented, "I hoped to tell a story about feminist, grassroots organizing and about the hard work required to build organizations, change law and social policy, and at the same time sustain a social movement. I wanted to brag about and document the accomplishments but also describe the hard, complicated work almost invisible underneath our new buildings and laws. It felt urgent to preserve this untouted knowledge that I could find nowhere else. I also wanted to extend a feminist explanation of theories about violence against women and open up debates about strategies, tactics and future political directions" (Danis, 2006, p. 337). With Ann Jones, a journalist, Schechter wrote *When Loves Goes Wrong* in 1992, intending it to be a resource for battered women to show how control manifests and emphasizing the unique needs of women of color and poor women. Schechter's (1996) book with Dr. Anne Ganley, *Domestic Violence: A National Curriculum for Children's Protective Services*, provides a curriculum for training child protection workers how *to work with victims of domestic violence and their children.* In 1999, Schechter coauthored *Effective Intervention in Domestic Violence and Child Maltreatment* with Jeff L. Edleson to provide guidelines and tools for assisting families experiencing both child abuse and domestic violence. Having received an endorsement from the National Council of Juvenile and Family Judges, the book has been used widely in the field and has helped shape public policy. In 2004, Schechter authored a paper called "Early Childhood, Domestic Violence, and Poverty: Helping Young Children and Their Families," which also helped share policy and practice on these issues.

Another significant contribution was the development of the Family Violence Prevention Fund's child welfare programming. Further, in 2001 Schechter began working as the director of the National Resource Center on Domestic Violence's project called Building Comprehensive Solutions to Domestic Violence that was designed to help domestic violence organizations collaborate with other organizations, especially those involved in helping poor women. Schechter also served as chair of the Prevention and Early Intervention Task Force of the National Advisory Council on Violence Against Women. Schechter died at age fifty-seven on February 3, 2004, having suffered from endometrial cancer.

Susan Schechter received many awards, and several awards are given in her honor. She received the Distinguished Achievement Award from the University of Iowa in 2002, and in 2003 she won the Leadership in Public Child Welfare Award from the National Association of Public Child Welfare. Former attorney general Janet Reno and former U.S. secretary of health and human services appointed Schechter to the National Advisory Council on Violence Against Women. Schechter was posthumously inducted into the Iowa Women's Hall of Fame in 2005. The Pennsylvania Coalition against Domestic Violence developed the Susan Schechter Legacy Award in her honor in 2006, and the Family Violence Prevention Fund and CONNECT, in San Francisco and New York, respectively, established leadership fellowships to honor Susan Schechter's lifetime work on domestic violence.

Sir Patrick Stewart

Sir Patrick Stewart was born on July 13, 1940, in Mirfield, Yorkshire, England. He was raised in a household of two brothers by an alcoholic army veteran father and a loving and caring mother. His father was a weekend alcoholic, who began abusing Stewart, his siblings, and his mother. His father suffered from combat fatigue, which today is known as PTSD (posttraumatic stress disorder). At the age of fifteen, Patrick Stewart left school to spend more time in the local theater, increasing his participation in acting. Domestic violence was something that Stewart saw almost every day, and it influenced him for the rest of his life. His father's physical attacks on his mother left an effect on him as a child, which, Stewart (2009) says, is, "something a child must not be used to." "The physical harm . . . was shocking pain." "Violence is a choice and is a choice a man makes . . . the lasting impact on my mother . . . and indeed on myself . . . was extreme."

Stewart says that his father had no control over "his emotions, his action, or especially his hands." He left scars and wound that would not heal, many times drawing blood from his mother. But it is not only the physical actions that caused harm and left wounds; it was also the psychological hurt that he inflicted on Patrick and his mother. Patrick felt somewhat

responsible, as he was seeing these actions yet was not able to
do much about it. He did, however, try to disrupt the abuse
many times. There were times where Patrick would stand by
the door where his parents were fighting or arguing, and he
knew exactly when to jump in. When it was going to get physical, he would rush into the room and jump between them to
try to put a stop to the abuse. He says this is something "no
child should be used to doing" (Stewart, 2009). Patrick admits
that his relationships in his past have been difficult because of
what he was used to seeing as a child.

Patrick says that when he was a child, domestic violence
against women or even sometimes men was a "shameful secret." Everyone knew—your neighbors, your family, your
friends—both where and when it was happening, but nobody
did anything. Nobody would take action or call the authorities
about a violent household" (Stewart, 2009). As a result, the
abuse typically continued, and children like Patrick were left to
deal with the consequences without assistance.

Occasionally law enforcement was called to the Stewart residence. Thinking back to when he was a child, Patrick says that
officers and ambulances would come home to see his mother
wounded and many times even passed out on the floor bleeding, but then they would say that his mother probably provoked
the situation and that they could not do anything about it. Patrick remembers going to the doctors with his mother, and the
doctor told his mother that "it takes two to make a fight."

As an adult, Patrick Stewart is a part of a campaign against
domestic violence created by the human rights organization
Amnesty International. Amnesty has long focused on gender-
based violence as one of its issues or campaigns. Stewart's involvement includes recording videos sharing his story, working
with other artists on a project called Freedom Voices using the
app Dubsmash, and speaking at events. He also wrote a book
named *Created Equal* about women's rights.

As he grew older, Stewart admits that it took so much time,
effort, courage, and thinking to admit or even speak of what

happened in his household growing up. To this day, he speaks out, sharing his story and trying to make a difference, just as he does with his work for Amnesty International. He emphasizes what abuse is like from the eyes of a child. Stewart's work also highlights the high percentage of soldiers who had or have a history of domestic violence. Many of these veterans are in prison to this day, and many suffer from PTSD, which today can be treated.

Murray Straus

Murray Straus was an American professor of sociology at the University of New Hampshire. Straus wrote extensively about crime, and especially family violence, including corporal punishment, domestic violence, and other conflicts in the family. He is best known for developing the Conflict Tactics Scale (CTS) in the 1970s. CTS has been used to measure conflict and specifically to assess individuals' propensity to use it in their interpersonal relationships. Further, Straus is known for drawing attention to gender symmetry in domestic violence, using the CTS to find similar rates of aggression by women as by men in intimate partnerships. This is a controversial position that is contested by many researchers. Further, Straus is considered a leader in cross-national research on family violence. In 2008 he earned the Award for Distinguished Lifetime Contributions to Research on Aggression from the International Society for Research on Aggression.

Straus was born in New York on June 18, 1926. He earned his bachelor's, master's, and doctoral degrees from the University of Wisconsin. In 1968 he founded the Family Research Laboratory at the University of New Hampshire and served as codirector until his passing in 2016. Straus is founding editor of *Teaching Sociology* and the *Journal of Family Issues*, as well as the author or coauthor of more than 250 journal articles and more than 20 books.

Straus's CTS, first created in 1979 and later revised (CTS2), has been used in more than 1,000 studies. There is also a parent-child version (CTSPC). CTS2 measures thirty-nine behaviors that are divided into five categories: negotiation, psychological aggression, physical assault, sexual coercion, and injury. Each category is then subdivided, so negotiation includes cognitive and emotional, and the other categories are all divided into minor and severe. Questions on the CTS2 are then focused on how often an individual engaged in each behavior in a specific time period as well as how often that individual experienced the same behavior by a partner in that referent period.

In a 1973 publication, Straus first noted his first findings using the CTS and then again in a 1979 publication. Based on what he referred to as a nationally representative sample of 2,143 couples that involved sixty-minute, in-person interviews, Straus noted that females aggressed approximately as frequently as did males. In a 1980 study with Richard Gelles and Susan Steinmetz, Straus again noted that the CTS found similar rates of violence by gender and, in fact, that females aggressed against male partners with slightly greater frequency. Although he had been identified as a feminist, many feminist activists took issue with Straus's findings, arguing that it misrepresented women's self-defense as aggression. Researchers like Michael Kimmel maintain that women are more likely to report violence, and thus, measures like CTS overrepresent their activity and underrepresent that of males. Kimmel and others have also critiqued the heavy emphasis on cohabitating or married couples and on heterosexual couples. Further, critics like Dobash and Dobash (1992, 2004) maintain that the CTS couples incidents in a problematic fashion, noting that two slaps are counted the same as two knife attacks. Finally, Melton and Belknap (2003) noted that the CTS studies typically interview only one person in the relationship but that a different picture may emerge if the other partner had also been interviewed.

Straus and his defenders countered that his findings were valid and were poorly received not because they were wrong but because they challenged the patriarchal emphasis of feminists. Proponents note that some 200 studies have found similar gender parity in domestic violence cases and that it is the most widely used tool for assessing family violence, even among feminists. In 2004, Straus conducted a cross-cultural assessment using the CTS2. It compared 7,179 students at 33 universities in 17 countries. It not only found high rates of dating violence but served, according to Straus, as further validation of CTS as a tool. Some studies have found CTS2 to be useful but only in conjunction with other measures (Jones, Browne, & Chou, 2017).

The CTSPC measures physical assault, psychological aggression, and nonviolent disciplinary techniques. It has also been revised several times. Straus's work with the CTSPC has also been controversial in that he argued that research has shown that children who have experienced corporal punishment are at greater risk of using violence later in life, including possibly being abusers.

Lenore Walker

Lenore E. A. Walker is a long-time educator, advocate, and licensed psychologist who is most known for developing the concept of battered woman syndrome (BWS). Walker is a regular speaker and trainer on domestic violence who has appeared on many television programs and received numerous accolades.

Walker earned her undergraduate degree in psychology in 1962 from Hunter College of the City University of New York and her master's of science degree in clinical school psychology at CUNY in 1967 and an EdD in school psychology from Rutgers State University of New Jersey in 1972. Walker then completed a postdoctoral master's degree in clinical psychopharmacology in 2004 at Nova Southeastern University (NSU) in Ft. Lauderdale, Florida. She retired from NSU and is Emerita there. She is also a licensed psychologist in three states (Florida, Colorado, and New Jersey) and still conducts research through the Domestic Violence Institute. In addition, Walker is president and CEO of Walker and Associates, Ltd., which provides psychological assessments of victims of domestic violence, assessing the effect of the trauma experienced. In addition, Walker assists police in forensic cases about sexual abuse and other related issues.

As a feminist therapist, Walker began working with victims of domestic violence and their children in the 1970s. Her work then led her to develop the BWS, which theorizes that abuse is a subset of post-traumatic stress disorder and explains that victims of abuse often experience learned helplessness. Victims come to believe they deserve the abuse and thus find it hard to break free. The first high-profile use of BWS was in the case of Francine Hughes in 1977. After decades of abuse, and feeling as though she would definitely be killed by her husband, James Hughes, Francine set his bed on fire and James burned to death. She faced trial, and Walker's work was elevated to the national stage. She has testified in hundreds of cases, especially those in which a wife kills her husband, arguing that the dynamics of abusive relationships are such that victims may feel fearful for their lives even if the threat does not seem imminent, as in the case of Francine Hughes. In another case, Walker testified on behalf of "Roberta," a Colorado woman who endured years of abuse, including the last straw, an attack that included a threat from her husband to tear out her windpipe. At the end of the assault, Roberta loaded her husband's hunting rifle and shot him while he watched television. Roberta was acquitted of his murder when Walker testified that the threat triggered Roberta to flashback to earlier beatings that made her feel imminent threat.

Walker's work is controversial, especially among prosecutors. They argue that the lack of specific imminent threat means these women have many other options besides deadly force, and therefore, they should be prosecuted for murder or at least manslaughter. An attorney in one case argued that allowing Walker to testify would be "open season on killing men."

Historically, many judges did not allow Walker's testimony as they did not see BWS as a recognized topic in psychology. Some argue that the idea of BWS is disempowering to victims and thus potentially harmful. Critics say that research does not support BWS and argue that, while it has been used in court, it is not a specified defense. Rather than individual victims who survive abuse as needed for their specific situation, critics maintain that BWS lumps all survivors together and overemphasizes the degree of learned helplessness many experience.

In 1998, Walker extended her research on BWS, expanding the questionnaire she had developed to assess a more comprehensive version of it, drawing on samples of women in prison and in other countries. She remains one of the staunchest advocates for psychotherapeutic services for victims of domestic violence.

Reese Witherspoon

Reese Witherspoon is an American actress, producer, and entrepreneur. Born in New Orleans, Louisiana, and raised in Tennessee, she began her career as a teenager in her first film *The Man in the Moon*. As an entrepreneur, Witherspoon owns her own production company and a clothing company and is actively involved in children's and women's advocacy organizations. She serves on the board of the Children's Defense Fund and is global ambassador for Avon. Witherspoon acts as spokeswoman for the Avon Foundation, a charitable organization that supports women and focuses on breast cancer research and the prevention of domestic violence.

With the voice of Reese Witherspoon and other advocates, the Avon Foundation for Women has been improving the lives of millions of women around the world. Since 2004, the Avon Foundation's Speak Out against Domestic Violence initiative has been a powerful voice for women, with programs in fifty countries and in almost all fifty U.S. states. The program has served eleven million women, has educated twenty-nine million about domestic violence, and has been able to contribute

$60 million to empowerment programs. The foundation has been able to grow exponentially over the past fourteen years. In 2004, the Avon Foundation launched its Speak Out against Domestic Violence program, and in 2008 Avon created its first global empowerment fund-raising product to support efforts to end violence against women. In 2010, Avon and the Avon Foundation partnered with Vital Voices and the U.S. Department of State to launch the Global Partnership to End Violence against Women, an innovative public-private partnership that fosters cross-sector collaborations with the goal of reducing violence against women. In 2013, #SeeTheSigns social media campaign launched during "16 Days of Activism against Gender Violence." Lastly, from 2014 to the present Avon and the Avon Foundation has contributed more than $1 billion to causes for women (Avon Foundation for Women—History, 2018).

Reese Witherspoon has traveled around the world and spoken on domestic violence. In December 2009, she visited the House of Commons to raise awareness for domestic violence. Witherspoon also signed a petition calling on the government to provide more funding for domestic abuse services so there is complete coverage in the United Kingdom. The Avon Foundation and Refuge launched a campaign that Witherspoon spearheaded to encourage an impact called Four Ways to Speak Out, focusing on encouraging people to sign the funding petition, to speak to friends and family about the campaign, and to put up posters to publicize where to get help (Claire, 2009). In efforts to keep their impact ongoing, Reese Witherspoon and the Avon Foundation have funded many institutions globally, including organizations in Guadalajara, Mexico; Belfast, Northern Ireland; Medellin, Columbia; and Pretoria, South Africa. In 2012, Reese Witherspoon and Avon chairman/CEO Andrea Jung announced ten $60,000 grants to support women's domestic violence shelters and agencies around the world. With these grants, at the time, Avon made a total of twenty-six Global Believe Fund grants in twenty-one countries to support women's domestic violence shelters, and agencies. The Believe Fund is a part of the Avon Speak Out against Domestic Violence program (Avon Foundation for Women and Reese Witherspoon, 2016). In March 2017, the Avon Foundation for Women announced $1 million in new funding for ten new justice institutes in 2017 and 2018. The goal of each institute is to improve victim protection efforts and the criminal justice response to domestic violence through a trauma-informed approach. Long before becoming an advocate, Witherspoon had a personal tie with domestic violence. In a conversation with Oprah Winfrey to promote their film *A Wrinkle in Time*, Witherspoon revealed that she left an abusive relationship at a very young age. She disclosed that the abuse was psychological and verbal and that deciding to leave changed her on a cellular level. When speaking about when she knew she had to leave the relationship, she expressed, "I drew a line in the sand, and it got crossed, and my brain just switched. I could not go any further. I was really young, and it was profound." She also stated: "It changed who I was on a cellular level, the fact that I stood up for myself. It's part of the reason I can stand up and say 'Yes, I'm ambitious,' because someone tried to take that away from me" (Welsh, 2018). Reese feels women using their power is the way to combat gender inequality.

Experiencing abuse firsthand is what also informed Reese Witherspoon's decision to produce and star in the Emmy-winning HBO series *Big Little Lies*, which features a domestic abuse story line. Also starring in *Big Little Lies* are domestic abuse advocates Nicole Kidman and Shailene Woodley. When she and her *Big Little Lies* colleagues shared their stories with each other, Witherspoon said that there wasn't a woman in the room that hadn't been affected by abuse.

In October 2017, amid the sexual harassment scandal involving renowned producer Harvey Weinstein, Witherspoon admitted during a speech at *Elle*'s Women in Hollywood event that at the age of sixteen she was sexually assaulted by a director (Vivinetto, 2018). The familiarity with domestic violence is also a big part of why Witherspoon felt compelled to become a worldwide advocate.

A controversy came about in September 2017 when Witherspoon's ex-husband Ryan Phillippe was accused of physically attacking his then girlfriend, model Elsie Hewitt, during an altercation at his home on July 4. Phillippe was served with a $1 million domestic abuse lawsuit. Hewitt claimed that Phillippe kicked, punched, and threw her down a flight of stairs, causing injuries to her legs, back, arms, shoulder, and face. After a thorough investigation with full cooperation from Phillippe, police dropped all charges against him. Witherspoon stood by her ex-husband's side, and it was reported that she was willing to testify if needed. Witherspoon stated that Phillippe had never displayed any violence toward her or their children.

Organizations

Avon Foundation for Women

The Avon Foundation was founded in 1955 by the cosmetics company, Avon Products, Inc. It has been involved with a number of social issues, most notably breast cancer and domestic violence. The Foundation claims to take "a female-centric approach to break down traditional barriers and build a better future for women. Its ethos is based on the belief that the greater the support, the more empowered women feel to take control of their own safety and health" (Avon Foundation for Women . . ., 2016). Since it began, the Foundation has contributed more than US$1 billion to U.S. and global causes for women.

In 2004, the Avon Foundation launched its Avon Speak Out against Domestic Violence program, which has contributed nearly US$60 million to date. It partners with a number of businesses and organizations to raise funds for these initiatives, including "m.powerment by mark," which raises money through jewelry sales and the National Domestic Violence Hotline. It also utilizes celebrity spokespersons and has sponsored a global app challenge related to dating violence prevention. In 2012, Avon global ambassador and honorary chairman of the Avon Foundation for Women actress Reese Witherspoon, along with Avon chairman and CEO Andrea Jung, announced ten $60,000 grants to support domestic violence shelters in ten countries: Australia, Canada, Chile, Colombia, Ecuador, Ukraine, Romania, Slovakia, Italy, and Greece. That same year, Witherspoon and Jung presented four organizations with Violence against Women awards. One was to Women's Aid of the United Kingdom for its ad and movie campaign called CUT, which featured actress Keira Knightley enduring a brutal attack. As of 2018, the Foundation has a global advisory board that includes women from eight different countries: Argentina, Brazil, Philippines, Romania, Russia, South Africa, the United Kingdom, and the United States.

The Foundation supports the National Network to End Domestic Violence's (NNEDV) National Domestic Violence Counts Report. Each year, NNEDV takes a one-day census of the domestic violence shelters in the United States in order to assess demand for services and unmet needs. It has found a shocking nearly 11,000 unmet requests for services (Avon Foundation Spotlight, n.d.).

The Avon Foundation's website also provides a wealth of information about domestic violence. It includes the results of a global violence against women study that involved 14,400 women in 15 countries (Argentina, Brazil, Chile, Columbia, Ecuador, Italy, Mexico, Peru, Philippines, Poland, Romania, Russia, Turkey, South Africa, and the United Kingdom). It assessed expectations within relationships, beliefs about violence, the degree to which women feel safe in public, expectations about how abuse will be treated by authorities, and understanding of where to go for help. The study found great variance in beliefs regarding whether a woman has a duty to provide sex to her partner if he wants it, with only 2 percent of Argentinian women believing so compared to 38 percent of women in the Philippines. While most women feel safe in public, 21 percent do not, including 47 percent in South Africa and 51 percent in Turkey. Women do not generally trust the justice system to take abuse seriously, with 59 percent and 60 percent, respectively, saying they do not have such trust. Only 62 percent of women globally say they know where to go for help, with lower rates in some countries (40 percent in the United Kingdom and 32 percent in Russia, respectively). In all, 56 percent of women surveyed had some experience with abuse, be it psychological, physical, or sexual (Global Women's Survey, n.d.).

Along with many organizations, the Avon Foundation is using Twitter and other social media to share its work and to garner support. Its primary hashtag on such sites is #embracethechange, and there is a separate website for that effort. In addition, the Foundation's website features resources for families, campuses, and corporations.

New steps for the Avon Foundation for Women are underway. In February 2018, Avon and the Avon Foundation announced its recommitment to the cause of domestic violence by launching the Avon Promise to End Violence against Women and Girls. The new program is committing its resources, people, and energy to encourage conversation, provide information, and improve support. When encouraging conversation, the new program will use its global voice to shed light on the many forms of violence against women and girls and discuss what needs to change. When providing information, it will make sure that its network of representatives, employees, customers, and partners has the knowledge and information it needs to recognize and respond to violence safely and on its own terms. It will ensure that it knows what support is available and how to access these resources so it can make informed choices. Finally, to improve support, it will work with local organizations to ensure women and girls have access to the support they need. It will convene global leaders and change makers to help make sure women and girls are understood, supported, and fairly treated when they seek help or report abuse (Avon Foundation for Women—Violence against Women, 2018).

Break the Cycle

Los Angeles–based Break the Cycle is a nonprofit organization focused on ending dating violence through empowering young people. It emphasizes that knowledge is key to ending abuse and sees dating violence as a "silent epidemic." In addition to educational programs for youth, educators, and administrators, Break the Cycle lobbies for legal and policy changes and provides legal services to teen victims.

Founded in 1996, Break the Cycle was one of the first organizations specifically focused on dating violence. After eight years, Break the Cycle's work expanded to the national stage, and an office was added in Washington, D.C.

One of Break the Cycle's primary initiatives is to train young people to transform their schools and communities by speaking out about dating violence. Let's Be Real is a nationwide program that operates in real life and online. It is an attempt to help youth below the age of twenty-four engage in honest conversations about relationships. Love Is Not Abuse is targeted at people aged twenty-four and above.

Futures without Violence

Futures without Violence, formerly the Family Violence Prevention Fund, is a nonprofit organization aiding children and women on health and social justice issues. The organization's work ranges from working to prevent bullying, sexual assault, and domestic violence to advocating for public and political action. Futures without Violence also provides resources for people seeking information about or in need of assistance for these situations. This organization does extensive work to not only help women and children but also advocate for change.

Futures without Violence was founded more than thirty years ago by Esta Soler. Its headquarters are in San Francisco, California, and it has locations in Washington, D.C., and Boston, Massachusetts. Over the past thirty years, Futures without Violence has earned a numbers of awards for its dedication and unwavering work for victims. These awards include America's 100 Best Charities, FBI Directors Community Leadership Award, and Charity Navigator Four Star Charity Award.

Futures without Violence works on many different initiatives related to domestic, dating, and sexual violence and, more broadly, childhood trauma. It works with every age group from children to young adults to parents. The organization offers resources and guides for parents to address childhood trauma and healing, for themselves if they grew up with abuse, and for their children who may have witnessed it. For those children who do not have parents, the organization conducts research on how to improve child welfare agencies and domestic violence programs. For children around middle school age, it offers resources to help with bullying and the trials and tribulations of adolescence. For high school–age students, it offers advice and programs for individuals suffering from pressure of relationships and from psychological, physical, and sexual abuse. Futures without Violence provides resources related to technology and abuse, as teens frequently use cell phones, social media, and other technology as tools to control their victims.

One of the most important players in ending domestic violence is men. Futures without Violence works to engage men in the process. Athletic coaches are very influential in the lives of young men: the organization's website explains that "coaches are the #1 influence on youth." This organization gives advice and tips to coaches to help establish a healthy sense of what being masculine or feminine is. Futures without Violence also has a link to a blog that encourages fathers who have honest conversations about dating violence and consent and to give their kids a positive example of what kind of relationships are healthy and unhealthy. The author of the blog is a father, and he emphasizes that it is critical to treat daughters and sons equivalently. This is something more fathers should do as they often aim to toughen sons up and treat daughters more delicately.

Futures without Violence notes the importance of changing the way we look at domestic violence and argues that it must start with younger generations. By creating safe environments on college campuses, students are able to address the pressing issues of gender-based violence. It is true that many women find themselves experiencing sexual assault during their college years. Futures without Violence helps victims of sexual assault navigate the proper channels to get justice and protect other students by reaching out to colleges and really doing the legwork for victims by working with college presidents and directors. For those colleges, Futures without Violence offers webinars and workshops to help prevent gender-based violence on college campuses.

In addition, Futures without Violence offers leadership and professional development courses available for those in the workplace. The main goal is to build strong communities and ambassadors through education programs. Futures without Violence helps companies build their executive boards and strategize for other nonprofits. They have so much knowledge to offer because Futures without Violence has been so successful.

One of the most admirable aspects of Futures without Violence is that it addresses these issues internationally. The United States is not the only place where sexually violent acts occur. In fact, it's much more widespread in other countries, and Futures without Violence understands the importance of global collaboration. This nonprofit organization has been working with ChildFund, Save the Children, and World Vision to seek a partnership with the United Nations and change the trends in child violence across the globe. On its website, the global violence prevention page offers reports on efforts in Africa impacting the ending of gender-based violence. Futures without Violence also stands with two Nobel Peace Prize winners, Dr. Denis Mukwege and Nadia Murad, for their advocacy against sexual violence.

Another focus of Futures without Violence is health, both physical and mental. Futures without Violence provides training to health-care providers so that they can identify abuse and survivors can get the best care possible. The organization offers online resources, so anyone can access these helpful tools and tips. It encourages a more holistic approach to care as well.

Futures without Violence not only educates about abuse but also engages in political lobbying for legislative change. It advocates for legitimate policy changes and encourages state and federal legislatures to help end domestic and dating violence and to provide ample resources for victims. The organization was involved in the passage of the Violence Against Women Act. Futures without Violence has written letters and briefs to the U.S. Senate recommending tips to the Trump administration related to violence extremism and women, peace, and security.

INCITE! Women, Gender Non-Conforming, and Trans People of Color against Violence

INCITE! Women of Color against Violence, today identified as INCITE! Women, Gender Non-Conforming, and Trans People of Color against Violence, is a national activist organization founded in the United States. It was formed by and is run by a group of progressive feminists advancing a movement to cease violence against their own and their communities. INCITE! was founded in Santa Cruz, California, in April 2000 by Andrea Smith and now has active chapters and affiliations across the United States, including Washington, New Mexico, Michigan, New York, Massachusetts, and Pennsylvania, and a chapter in Canada.

INCITE! began after a small conference called "The Color of Violence: Violence against Women of Color" held at the University of Santa Cruz was well attended and well received. The conference addressed issues such as homophobia, heterosexism, militarism, the proliferation of women, economic neocolonialism, immigration rights, and sexual violence. When more than 2,000 people in attendance had to be turned away because of space restrictions, Andrea Smith and conference organizers knew this was a huge issue in the world. As a result of the well-attended conference, INCITE! was founded to share more ideas and to enact much-needed change. Cofounder Andrea Smith wrote, "The overwhelming response to this initial effort suggests that women of color and their allies are hungry for a new approach toward ending violence" (INCITE! Explained, n.d.). It is clear that women of color, lesbians, bisexual women, and gender nonconforming individuals suffer from abuse at higher rates than do cisgender, white women, making the work of INCITE! critically important.

INCITE! recognizes "violence against women of color" as a combination of "violence directed at communities," such as police violence, war, and colonialism, and "violence within communities," such as rape and domestic violence (INCITE! Women of Color against Violence, 2006). INCITE! attracts women of color who are living in the perilous crossing points of sexism and prejudice and any other maltreatment. Women of color who survive sexual or domestic violence are often told that they must tackle their experiences of violence against their communities. In the meantime, communities of color often argue that women should keep silent about sexual and domestic violence so as not to encourage involvement with the racist criminal justice system. INCITE! recognizes that it is impossible to address seriously sexual/domestic violence in communities of color without addressing these broader structures of violence, such as militarism, attacks on the rights of immigrants and the rights of Indian treaties, the proliferation of prisons, economic neocolonialism, and the medical sector. The organization works by building collective organizing power to tackle the unique ways in which violence occurs in everyday life.

Chapters and affiliates engage in strategies and projects that address both personal and state violence, acknowledging the ways that oppressions intersect in our lives. Some of those projects include producing a women-of-color radio show, challenging the nonprofitization of anti-violence and other social justice movements, organizing rallies on street harassment, training women of color on self-defense, organizing mothers on welfare, building and running a grassroots clinic, and supporting communities to engage in community accountability strategies.

This organization works on a number of local and national campaigns, including organizing against police violence against women and transsexual people of color, and community-based strategies to hold people responsible for abusive behavior, such as domestic and sexual violence. INCITE! assisted in establishing the Boarding School Healing Project, a project that organizes Native Americans to hold the U.S. government liable for compelling over 100,000 Native children to go to Christian boarding schools where they were often raped and abused.

The grassroots chapters of INCITE! also organize projects to address multiple kinds of violence against women of color. After Hurricane Katrina, the New Orleans chapter of INCITE! started a women's health clinic to help low-income, uninsured women of color meet their health needs and organize for racial, gender, economic, and environmental justice. The Philadelphia chapter of INCITE! has worked on housing and gentrification issues. The affiliate of INCITE!, Sista II Sista, organized campaigns against sexual harassment by police officers in Brooklyn, New York, against young women of color.

One innovative aspect about INCITE! is that it has disavowed nonprofit status. Its members have expressed concern that with 501(c)3 nonprofit status comes a bureaucratization of services and an ever-increasing quest for funding that can stand in the way of true social change. Instead, INCITE! raises funds through grassroots efforts.

National Network to End Domestic Violence (NNEDV)

The National Network to End Domestic Violence (NNEDV) is an organization that was founded in 1990 in Washington, D.C., and successfully works in different directions, including the prevention of violence against women, gun violence, strengthening of violence advocacy, and other social and political aspects of this global issue. The organization was formerly known as the Domestic Violence Coalition on Public Policy, which "was formed in 1990 when a small group of domestic violence victim advocates came together to promote federal legislation related to domestic violence" (Our History, n.d.). Over the years, it has developed into an organization uniting different shelter programs and groups aimed to stop violence around the country. One of the most significant contributions made by the Domestic Violence Coalition on Public Policy was the development of the famous Violence Against Women Act in 1994 (Our History, n.d.). This Act was one of the first federal efforts regulating the issues of domestic violence in the United States. As the organization was renamed and became the National Network to End Domestic Violence, it spread its influence on different aspects of prevention of domestic violence, including support for victims and promotion of education on violence prevention and advocacy.

Today, the organization follows its original mission and strives to decrease the level of cases involving domestic violence and help people defend their rights. More precisely, the NNEDV, being a social change organization, "is dedicated to creating a social, political, and economic environment in which violence against women no longer exists" (Mission + Vision, n.d.). According to this, the main objectives of the organization include the development of the issue of domestic violence into a national priority and transforming people's perception of and responses to domestic violence. Besides that, "NNEDV is the leading voice for domestic violence victims and their advocates" (Mission + Vision, n.d.). With regard to that, it is apparent that the members of this organization work closely with victims of domestic violence helping them overcome psychological issues and build new lives.

The organization offers an array of programs and initiatives to address the complex causes and far-reaching consequences of domestic violence. The members of the organization across the country cooperate with each other and establish corporate partnerships in order to realize the needs of the victims and address all the aspects of domestic violence comprehensively. Another direction of the organization's activity involves special training for law enforcement officers, advocates, prosecutors, and other community members focused on how to respond properly to domestic violence while addressing the needs of survivors.

One of the issues addressed by the NNEDV is the intersection of technology and violence. The main controversy in this sphere lies in the fact that "the government has argued that encrypted devices and new technologies make it more difficult for law enforcement to investigate crimes while technology companies claimed that weakening encryption weakens security for everyone" (Smartphone Encryption: Protecting Victim Privacy While Holding Offenders Accountable, 2016). This issue is directly connected to domestic violence and its prevention. As data security is inevitably related to overall safety, it shows how new technologies can be misused and how this can reinforce domestic violence, sexual assault, and other issues. Thus, it is important to find a balance between victim privacy and offender accountability while using smartphones and other gadgets, and the NNEDV is working on this issue to propose effective solutions.

Annual statistics and surveys released by the NNEDV prove the efficiency of the organization's activity as well as document the need for increased domestic violence services. Each year, NNEDV conducts a twenty-four-hour census in which it relies on domestic violence agencies to report, for a given twenty-four-hour period, how many people reached out for help and how many were helped and in what ways. It also addresses those who were not provided assistance, which helps identify areas in need of more resources. The eleventh Annual Census reveals that more and more people are turning to specialized organizations and advocates to defend themselves against domestic violence. At the same time, it reveals some negative tendencies and limitations of the existing programs and resources.

In particular, it is mentioned that "most survivors with children often face a significant hurdle when it comes to finding afford-able childcare for their children" (Domestic Violence Counts: 11th Annual Census Report, 2016, p. 13). Generally, the most significant limitation lies in the lack of resources for victims. As the director of one of the local organizations for defense against domestic violence confesses, "Victims are turned away every day because our shelters are full and understaffed and we know they are either going back to live with their abusive part-ner or are forced into homelessness" (National Network to End Domestic Violence Releases Annual Statistics, 2015).

In sum, the NNEDV as a social change organization is ef-fectively working to prevent cases involving domestic violence and inform people about their rights and opportunities for de-fense and support. Annual surveys and reports show that the organization is transforming the way people respond to do-mestic violence, and it is a considerable step toward the main mission of the organization. While working with victims of domestic violence and empowering them to start new lives, the organization is also focused on protecting people at the state level through the introduction of changes in legislature and other initiatives. At the same time, there still exist certain limitations and controversies that need to be further explored and addressed to improve the modern state of the issue across the country. The main limitation lies in the lack of available resources that should be used for helping survivors of domestic violence.

NO MORE

NO MORE is a nonprofit organization that is "dedicated to ending domestic violence and sexual assault by increasing awareness, inspiring action and fueling culture change" (Our Mission, 2019). It started in 2013 as a coalition of diverse communities that brings together stakeholders in the private and public sectors around a common brand and unifying symbol. NO MORE operates on five unifying values: unity and collaboration, impact, inclusion, innovation, and transparency. "Unity and collaboration" refers to "forging innovative public-private partnerships and collaborative efforts that unite domestic violence and sexual assault organizations that share our vision" (Our Mission, 2019). Impact emphasizes the need for continual evaluation and measurement of the work's effectiveness. Inclusion emphasizes the importance of recruiting and working with diverse groups. Innovation refers to the utilization of cutting-edge tools and approaches to ending domestic and sexual violence. Transparency addresses the need to build trust and public support through openness and communication.

The four main pillars of NO MORE's work are large-scale media campaigns, education and community engagement, grassroots activism and fund-raising, and outreach and technical assistance. Its large-scale media campaigns focus on public service announcements (PSAs) from celebrities, athletes, and everyday people. NFL players, actors, and others have contributed PSAs and a special PSA aired during the 2015 Super Bowl.

Through its education and community involvement, NO MORE provides a hub for information and for inspiring action. One action NO MORE encourages people to take is their pledge, which is a commitment to knowing more, standing with survivors, speaking up, and donating to the cause. The organization's website says 28,320 people have taken the pledge (Take the Pledge, 2019). NO MORE's website also features a gallery of more than 7,000 survivors and allies who spoke out about abuse. NO MORE also offers a toolkit that provides resources and handouts, its logo (in both English and Spanish, No Mas), digital graphics, posters and signs, research, case studies, and organizing tips. Infographics focuses on the degree to which certain groups are victims and specific types of abuse, including financial abuse. Further, NO MORE provides materials for Domestic Violence Awareness Month and Sexual

Assault Awareness Month. Finally, NO MORE also promotes the No Mas campaign to focus on abuse among Latinos/Latinas and that community's efforts to end it.

NO MORE's grassroots activism and fund-raising efforts include an online shop, fund-raising competitions with small grants to small, under-resourced programs, and materials for NO MORE WEEK. This includes social media campaigns, television marathons, and local events.

Outreach, support, and media training are provided to individuals who agree to become NO MORE ambassadors. This includes educators, students, community organizations, and corporations. Trained individuals are then encouraged to share the work with their groups or schools.

NO MORE measures its effectiveness by assessing the number of people it has reached. According to the organization's website, "In just a few years, NO MORE has become largest and most successful public awareness campaign on domestic violence and sexual assault in history. Nearly 1,200 organizations and 75,000 individuals have joined NO MORE. Hundreds of schools created NO MORE groups, and another 30 local city-wide, state-wide and international NO MORE programs have been born. Thanks to our partners, our PSAs have gotten more than 4.4 billion impressions." Further, the NO MORE campaign helped lobby for the Campus Sexual Violence Elimination Act, which requires prevention and training programs on college campuses. NO MORE also supported the Obama administration's "It's on Us" sexual assault campaign and efforts to clarify what campuses must do to be in compliance with Title IX regulations about sexual misconduct and gender discrimination. NO MORE supported the Sexual Assault Survivors' Rights Bill that was signed into law by President Obama in 2016 (Pauly, 2016).

The organization's website also features a blog and materials for individuals seeking to conduct bystander intervention trainings. Finally, one innovative collaboration NO MORE has made is with the driving service Uber.

No More Tears

No More Tears (NMT) deals with domestic violence and the growing issue of human trafficking, largely in South Florida but also in other states and occasionally globally. NMT was founded by Somy Ali, who is also a sexual assault and survivor. Ali also grew up in an abusive household. While growing up in Pakistan, she was exposed to violence and injustices in her home and among women in the community. She has stated that women were told this was normal. She also witnessed abuse during her career as an actress in Bollywood and experienced sexual violence as a teen. She started NMT in hopes of helping those who are brought to the United States to be abused, although today the organization works with victims from the United States as well. NMT provides survivors with food, legal counsel such as immigration and family attorneys, and therapy and helps them look for housing and start obtaining an education, medical support, and all the basic needs that are required for them to better themselves. What sets NMT apart from other nonprofit organizations is that it does not have a waiting list. It always provides the victim/survivor with immediate assistance.

When it comes to high numbers of human trafficking, Miami has become number three. NMT increasingly gets calls about human trafficking and has collaborated with local trafficking coalitions and state and federal agencies to assist victims. While trafficking shares many characteristics in common with domestic violence, victims have unique needs that NMT seeks to address.

The money donated to NMT is all used toward the victims it aids. Given that NMT is entirely volunteer based—no one makes a salary, not even Ali—and the organization has no overhead costs as it has no shelter or office spaces, all donations directly support services. Money is generally raised via monthly donors, philanthropists, and events.

NMT is well known in the South Florida area. Somy Ali has appeared on multiple news stations as a human trafficking expert in the attempt to get people more aware of the growing issue. Since 2007, NMT has helped over 30,000 men, women, and children. In addition, the organization, Ali, and some supporters have received various local, state, and national accolades for their work.

Rape, Abuse, and Incest National Network (RAINN)

Founded in 1994 by Scott Berkowitz, the Rape, Abuse, and Incest National Network (RAINN) is the nation's largest nonprofit anti-sexual violence organization. It has helped over 2.7 million people since its inception.

In 1994, Scott Berkowitz first launched RAINN as a National Sexual Assault Hotline, which became the nation's first decentralized hotline that connected those in need with help in their local communities. In 2006, RAINN launched the Online Hotline, which was the first online crisis intervention service in the United States. Today, RAINN is in partnership with more than 1,000 local sexual assault service providers across the country and operates the Safe Helpline for the Department of Defense.

RAINN has created programs and organized experts in victim services, public education, public policy, consulting services, and technology to prevent sexual violence, help survivors, and ensure that perpetrators are brought to justice. Since launching, RAINN has educated more than 130 million Americans each year about sexual assault.

Within the victim services program, victim service experts at RAINN take a victim-centered, trauma-informed approach to developing programs and services that support survivors of sexual violence and their loved ones in all stages of recovery. Some of these programs and services include offering innovative technology and services for partners in the field, including organizations, universities, and government agencies; providing training services for companies and organizations, as well as staff and volunteers at more than 1,000 local sexual assault service provider partners; and working with volunteers across the country to make a difference in the lives of survivors.

In the public education program and services, RAINN's communications experts raise the visibility of sexual violence and increase the public's understanding of the crime. RAINN achieves this by working with the media, entertainment industry, and colleges across the country to provide accurate information about sexual violence prevention, prosecution, and recovery. To attain this goal, RAINN maintains an active social media presence, reacting to current events and ensuring that people who need support can find it through the National Sexual Assault Hotline; it operates the Speakers Bureau, which is a network of more than 1,500 survivors who volunteer to share their stories with local communities and the media; and it also operates the Prevention Navigator, which is a free, online resource to help colleges find the right sexual assault program for their campus.

RAINN's public policy program features a policy team that works at the federal and state levels to improve the criminal justice system, prevent sexual assault, and ensure justice for survivors. The policy team helps to create and advocate for laws and regulations that make communities safer and support survivors. RAINN leads the national effort to end the rape kit backlog, while collaborating with allies to promote state action through the Rape Kit Action Project. Rape kits are the physical evidence taken after a sexual assault, and across the nation, owing to a shortage of analysts and a lack of prioritization by law enforcement and prosecutors, rape kits remain untested. The result of this is that victims must wait long periods of time for trials and, consequently, for any sense of justice, and offenders are free to continue perpetrating assaults with impunity. RAINN also maintains the Laws in Your State database, which is the most up-to-date source of information for students, lawmakers, and others seeking to understand sexual violence laws across the nation.

In addition, in the consulting services program, RAINN's consulting and subject-matter experts work with clients across the public, private, and nonprofit areas to develop effective sexual violence education and response programs. RAINN's services prepare organizations to effectively provide education about sexual violence and to respond to incidents in a way that facilitates healing and promotes safe and healthy communities. They do this by offering a variety of specialized consulting services that meet each organization's unique needs, such as hotline services, consulting, program assessments, and education and training. In order to achieve these goals, RAINN provides tailored consulting to help organizations that are at any point in the process, whether this is the first conversation an organization has had on the topic or there have been policies in place for years, and provides educational content and training that engages, educates, and prepares adult learners to support and help survivors of sexual assault. RAINN also offers both the technology infrastructure and the victim service expertise to provide quality, anonymous, and confidential crisis intervention services via telephone or online hotline in English and Spanish.

U.S. Department of Justice Office on Violence Against Women (OVW)

The OVW's mission is to "federal leadership in developing the national capacity to reduce violence against women and administer justice for and strengthen services to victims of domestic violence, dating violence, sexual assault, and stalking." It was launched in 1995, after the 1994 passage of the Violence Against Women Act (VAWA). It is the only federal office specifically devoted to gender-based violence.

OVW administers financial and technical assistance to organizations around the country that offer programs, policies, and practices related to dating violence, domestic violence, sexual violence, and stalking. It provides both formula grants and discretionary grants that are authorized through VAWA or other legislation. The four formula grants include STOP (services, training, officers, prosecutors), SASP (Sexual Assault Services Program), state coalitions, and tribal coalitions. The discretionary programs support programs that serve victims and hold perpetrators accountable via coordinated community responses. According to OVW's website, "Funding is awarded to local, state and tribal governments, courts, non-profit organizations, community-based organizations, secondary schools, institutions of higher education, and state and tribal coalitions. Grants are used to develop effective responses to violence against women through activities that include direct services, crisis intervention, transitional housing, legal assistance to victims, court improvement, and training for law enforcement and courts. Since its inception, OVW has awarded over $8.1 billion in grants and cooperative agreements and has launched a multifaceted approach to implementing VAWA" (About the Office, 2019).

OVW's website provides information for grant-seekers and grantees. It also features relevant regulations and legislation, including OVW's own regulations as well as the 2013 reauthorization of VAWA, the 2005 and 2000 reauthorizations, the original VAWA of 1994, and analysis and research on violence against Indian women.

Further, OVW's website offers definitions of domestic violence, sexual assault, dating violence, and stalking. These definitions are used in OVW's grant process. For each, there are links to additional resources.

> The term "domestic violence" includes felony or misdemeanor crimes of violence committed by a current or former spouse or intimate partner of the victim, by a person with whom the victim shares a child in common, by a person who is cohabiting with or has cohabited with the victim as a spouse or intimate partner, by a person similarly situated to a spouse of the victim under the domestic or family violence laws of the jurisdiction receiving grant monies, or by any other person against an adult or youth victim who is protected from that person's acts under the domestic or family violence laws of the jurisdiction. (Domestic Violence, 2019)

Sexual assault "means any nonconsensual sexual act proscribed by Federal, tribal, or State law, including when the victim lacks capacity to consent" (Sexual Assault, 2019). Dating violence "means violence committed by a person who is or has been in a social relationship of a romantic or intimate nature with the victim and where the existence of such a relationship shall be determined based on a consideration of the following factors: the length of the relationship; the type of relationship; and the frequency of interaction between the persons involved in the relationship" (Dating Violence, 2019). Finally, stalking "means engaging in a course of conduct directed at a specific person that would cause a reasonable person to fear for his or her safety or the safety of others or suffer substantial emotional distress" (Stalking, 2019).

In addition, OVW provides a wealth of information about violence against women in Indian country, including research, publications, reports to Congress, and specific grants.

Katherine (Katie) Sullivan is acting director of OVW as of May 2019. She is a former state trial court judge in Eagle County, Colorado. Prior to that, Sullivan was deputy district attorney for Colorado's Ninth Judicial Circuit. Sullivan holds a JD from George Washington University.

Under President Trump, OVW made changes to the definitions of sexual assault and domestic violence. The previous definitions had been approved by the Obama administration and were first vetted by domestic violence groups. The new definition narrows the scope of what is considered abuse to physical harm that warrants prosecution. The new definition of sexual assault says that it is any nonconsensual sexual act proscribed by federal, tribal, or state law, including when the victim lacks capacity to consent. Critics have expressed concern that these definitions will result in fewer people receiving help, as they fail to fully encompass all that abuse and sexual assault entail. It might also result in restrictions on grant funds that are needed to support services for victims (Derysh, 2019).

References

About Jackson. (2018). JacksonKatz.com. Retrieved November 12, 2018, from http://www.jacksonkatz.com/about-jackson/

About the Office. (2019, March 22). U.S. Department of Justice Office of Violence on Women. Retrieved May 28, 2019, from https://www.justice.gov/ovw/about-office

About UN Women. (n.d.). *UN Women*. Retrieved September 5, 2019, from https://www.unwomen.org/en/about-us/about-un-women

Anderson, K., Botton, S., Gest, E., & Ogunnaike, L. (2002, June 24). Hayek's "wedding" march targets abuse. *Daily News*. Retrieved November 2, 2018, from http://www.nydailynews.com/archives/gossip/hayel-wedding-march-targets-abuse-article-1.488375

Associated Press. (2016, November 17). Nicole Kidman speaks out on violence against women in UN fundraiser. *Hollywood Reporter*. Retrieved September 6, 2019, from https://www.hollywoodreporter.com/news/nicole-kidman-speaks-violence-women-at-fundraiser-948523

Avon Foundation for Women and Reese Witherspoon Announce New Domestic Violence Grants on International Women's Day. (2016, May 10). Retrieved September 10, 2019, from https://grantpros2011.wordpress.com/2012/03/08/avon-foundation-for-women-reese-witherspoon-announce-new-domestic-violence-grants/

Avon Foundation Spotlight: Addressing Domestic Violence in a Digital Era. (n.d.). Avon.com. Retrieved January 6, 2019, from https://www.avon.com/blog/empowerment/cindy-southworth-nnedv

Burleigh, N. (2014, July 24). Meet the ex-football star on a mission to end sexual violence. *Elle*. Retrieved November 12, 2018, from https://www.elle.com/culture/career-politics/news/a14677/jackson-katz-the-macho-paradox/

Cartner-Morley, J. (2015, March 4). Salma Hayek: "I am feminist because a lot of amazing women have made me who I am today." *Guardian.* Retrieved November 2, 2018, from https://www.theguardian.com/lifeandstyle/2015/mar/04/salma-hayek-feminist-women-the-prophet-interview

Cissner, A. (2009). Evaluating the Mentors in Violence Prevention program. Court Innovation. Retrieved June 13, 2019, from http://www.courtinnovation.org/sites/default/files/MVP_evaluation.pdf

Claire, M. (2009, December 3). Reese Witherspoon's stand against domestic violence. Marie Claire. Retrieved December 1, 2018, from https://www.marieclaire.co.uk/news/reese-witherspoon-s-stand-against-domestic-violence-172659

Danis, F. (2006). A tribute to Susan Schechter: The vision and struggles of the battered women's movement. *Journal of Women and Social Work, 21*(3), 336–341.

Dating Violence. (2019, March 22). U.S. Department of Justice Office of Violence on Women. Retrieved May 28, 2019, from https://www.justice.gov/ovw/dating-violence

Deer, S. (2015). *Tribal criminal law and procedure.* Louisville, CO: Rowman & Littlefield.

Derysh, I. (2019, January 23). Trump administration quietly changes definition of "domestic violence" and "sexual assault." *Salon.* Retrieved June 13, 2019, from https://www.salon.com/2019/01/23/trump-administration-quietly-changes-definition-of-domestic-violence-and-sexual-assault/

Dobash, R. E., & Dobash, R. (1992). *Women, violence and social change.* Routledge: London.

Dobash, R. E., & Dobash, R. E. (2004). Women's violence to men in intimate relationships. *British Journal of Criminology, 44,* 324–349.

Domestic Violence. (2019, March 22). U.S. Department of Justice Office of Violence on Women. Retrieved May 28, 2019, from https://www.justice.gov/ovw/domestic-violence

Domestic Violence Counts: 11th Annual Census Report. (2016). NNEDV. Retrieved November 7, 2018, from https://nnedv.org/content/domestic-violence-counts-11th-annual-census-report/

Dressler, J. (2005). Battered women and sleeping abusers: Some reflections. *Ohio State Journal of Criminal Law, 3,* 457–471.

Ellis, L. (2002, October). *Nicole Kidman: The biography.* London: Aurum.

Esmey, D. (2012, December 19). Refuting 40 years of lies about domestic violence [interview transcript]. A Voice for Men. Retrieved September 10, 2019, from https://www.avoiceformen.com/mens-rights/domestic-violence-industry/refuting-40-years-of-lies-about-violence/

Fessler, L. (2018, October 31). Tony Porter makes the case for re-socializing boys and men. QZ. Retrieved November 28, 2018, from https://qz.com/work/1415245/this-ceo-makes-a-strong-case-for-how-feminism-liberates-men/

Flaherty, C. (2018, August 10). More than rumors. Inside Higher Ed. Retrieved January 3, 2019, from https://www.insidehighered.com/news/2018/08/10/michael-kimmels-former-student-putting-name-and-details-those-harassment-rumors

Global Women's Survey. (n.d.). Avon Foundation. Retrieved January 6, 2019, from https://www.avonworldwide.com/supporting-women/violence-against-women-and-girls.html

Hayek, Salma. (2018, May 14). Biography. Retrieved November 2, 2018, from https://www.biography.com/people/salma-hayek-14514423

Hayes, D. (2018, February 8). Salma Hayek tells Oprah Winfrey why she decided to share her #MeToo Story. Deadline. Retrieved November 2, 2018, from https://deadline.com/2018/02/salma-hayek-tells-oprah-winfrey-how-she-decided-to-tell-her-metoo-story-1202281044/

INCITE! Explained. (n.d.). Everything Explained. Retrieved June 11, 2019, from https://everything.explained.today/ Incite!/

INCITE! Women of Color against Violence (2006). *Color of violence: The INCITE! anthology.* Cambridge, MA: South End Press.

IVAWA Summary. (n.d.). Futures without Violence. Retrieved September 5, 2019, from https://www .futureswithoutviolence.org/wp-content/uploads/IVAWA-Summary-20141.pdf

Jones, R., Browne, K., & Chou, S. (2017). A critique of the revised Conflict Tactics Scale-2 (CTS2). *Aggression and Violent Behavior, 37,* 83–90.

Katz, J. (2006. October 13). Coverage of "school shootings" avoids the central issue. JacksonKatz.com. Retrieved June 11, 2019, from http://www.jacksonkatz.com/publication/ pub_coverage/

Kimmel, M. (2015). Why gender equality is good for everyone. TEDWomen. Retrieved January 3, 2019, from https://www.ted.com/talks/michael_kimmel_ why_gender_equality_is_good_for_everyone_men_ included?language=en

Kivel, P. (2002). Jewish men and Jewish male violence. *Journal of Religion & Abuse, 4*(3), 5–13.

Kristof, N. (2014, March 8). To end the abuse, she grabbed a knife. *New York Times.* Retrieved January 6, 2019, from https://www.nytimes.com/2014/03/09/opinion/ sunday/kristof-to-end-the-abuse-she-grabbed-a-knife .html

Kristof, N., & WuDunn, S. (2009). *Half the sky: Turning oppression into opportunity for women worldwide.* New York, NY: Alfred A. Knopf.

Li, S. (2017, September 18). *Big Little Lies* stars make plea for "more great roles for women" in Emmys speech. *Time.*

Retrieved September 6, 2019, from https://time
.com/4945732/emmys-2017-reese-witherspoon-nicole-
kidman-big-little-lies/

McNulty, F. (1980). *The burning bed.* New York, NY:
Harcourt Brace Jovanovich.

Melton, H. C., & Belknap, J. (2003) He hits, she hits:
Assessing gender differences and similarities in officially
reported intimate partner violence. *Violence against Women,
30,* 323–334.

Mission + Vision. (n.d.). NNEDV. Retrieved November 7,
2018, from https://nnedv.org/content/mission-vision/

National Domestic Violence Advocate Wins Lifetime
Achievement Award: A Lifetime of Work Recognized by
Domestic Violence Professionals. (2016). Alliance for Hope
International, San Diego, CA. Retrieved September 10,
2019, from https://www.allianceforhope.com/lynn-rosenthal-
lifetime-achievement-award/

National Network to End Domestic Violence Releases
Annual Statistics. (2015). NNEDV. Retrieved November 7,
2018, from http://www.cawsnorthdakota.org/index
.php/national-network-to-end-domestic-violence-releases-
annual-statistics/

Our History. (n.d.). NNEDV. Retrieved November 7, 2018,
from https://nnedv.org/content/our-history/

Our Mission. (2019). NO MORE. Retrieved May 29, 2019,
from https://nomore.org/about/our-story/

Pauly, M. (2016, October 7). Obama just signed a
bill of rights for sexual assault survivors. Mother
Jones. Retrieved June 13, 2019, from https://
www.motherjones.com/politics/2016/10/
obama-signs-sexual-assault-survivor-bill-rights/

Porter, T. (2010a, December 2). A call to men. TED.
Retrieved December 2, 2018, from https://www.ted.com/
talks/tony_porter_a_call_to_men?

Porter, T. (2010b). Tony Porter. TED. Retrieved November 29, 2018, from https://www.ted.com/speakers/tony_porter

Producer, Actress, and Activist Salma Hayek Pinault to Receive Award for Individual Achievement. (2015, April 29). Amnesty International. Retrieved November 2, 2018, from http://www.aaiusa.org/producer-actress-and-activist-salma-hayek-pinault-to-receive-award-for-indi

Rabinovitch, D. (2001, November 26). Domestic violence can't be a gender issue. *Guardian.* Retrieved September 10, 2019, from https://www.theguardian.com/world/2001/nov/26/gender.uk1

Rose, E. (2017). Sarah Deer, the beginning and end of rape: Confronting sexual violence in Native America [reviews]. *Law & Society Review, 51*(1), 209.

Salma Hayek Delivers Anti-Domestic Violence Speech. (2013, March 8). Express. Retrieved November 2, 2018, from https://www.express.co.uk/celebrity-news/382915/Salma-Hayek-delivers-anti-domestic-violence-speech

Salma Hayek Pinault and Avon CEO Sheri McCoy Announce Winners of 2nd Avon Global Communications Awards for Speaking Out about Violence against Women in Recognition of International Women's Day. (2016, June 8). Avon Foundation. Retrieved November 1, 2018, from https://www.looktothestars.org/news/9837-salma-hayek-pinault-speaks-out-against-violence-against-women-with-avon-foundation

Schechter, S. (2004). Early childhood, domestic violence, and poverty: Helping young children and their families. NCDSV. Retrieved January 2, 2018, from http://www.ncdsv.org/images/UI-SSW_EarlyChildhoodDVandPoverty_1-2004.pdf

Sexual Assault (2019, March 22). U.S. Department of Justice Office of Violence on Women. Retrieved May 28, 2019, from https://www.justice.gov/ovw/sexual-assault

Smartphone Encryption: Protecting Victim Privacy While Holding Offenders Accountable. (2016, April 12). TechSafety. Retrieved November 7, 2018, from https://www.techsafety.org/blog/2016/4/12/smartphone-encryption-protecting-victim-privacy-while-holding-offenders-accountable

Stalking. (2019, March 22). U.S. Department of Justice Office of Violence on Women. Retrieved May 28, 2019, from https://www.justice.gov/ovw/stalking

Stewart, P. (2009, November 26). Patrick Stewart: The legacy of domestic violence. *The Guardian.* Retrieved September 6, 2019, from https://www.theguardian.com/society/2009/nov/27/patrick-stewart-domestic-violence

Take the Pledge. (2019). NO MORE. Retrieved May 29, 2019, from https://nomore.org/take-action/pledge-driving-change-original/

Toomer, L. (2018, September 20). Tony Porter's "A CALL TO MEN" comes to Penn State, encourages healthy masculinity. *Penn State Collegian.* Retrieved from December 1, 2019, https://www.collegian.psu.edu/news/campus/article_07b76e4e-bc92-11e8-aaf2-276e968f01dd.html

Villines, Z. (2015, June 4). Rising above violence against women: An interview with Paul Kivel. GoodTherapy. Retrieved November 1, 2018, from https://www.goodtherapy.org/blog/how-men-can-stop-violence-against-women-1101127?replytocom=77465#respondForm

Vivinetto, G. (2018, February 6). Reese Witherspoon shares how leaving an abusive relationship changed her life. *Today.* Retrieved from https://www.today.com/popculture/reese-witherspoon-leaving-abusive-relationship-changed-my-life-t122424

Wagmeister, E. (2017). Nicole Kidman speaks out against "abuse and misuse of power" amid Harvey Weinstein scandal. *Celebrity Nine.* Retrieved

September 5, 2019, from https://celebrity.nine.com
.au/latest/nicole-kidman-speaks-out-against-abuse-
and-misuse-of-power-amid-harvey-weinstein-scandal/
ae256f75-6c53-4d1c-9a6e-c6c94400787c

Warner, K. (2016, November 3). How Salma Hayek is
fighting for women's rights around the world. Retrieved
October 17, 2018, from https://people.com/movies/how-
salma-hayek-is-fighting-for-womens-rights-around-the-
world/

Welsh, D. (2018, February 7). Reese Witherspoon opens
up about her experiences of domestic abuse. *Huffington
Post*. Retrieved from https://www.huffingtonpost.com
.au/2018/02/07/reese-witherspoon-opens-up-about-her-
experiences-of-domestic-abuse_a_23355782/

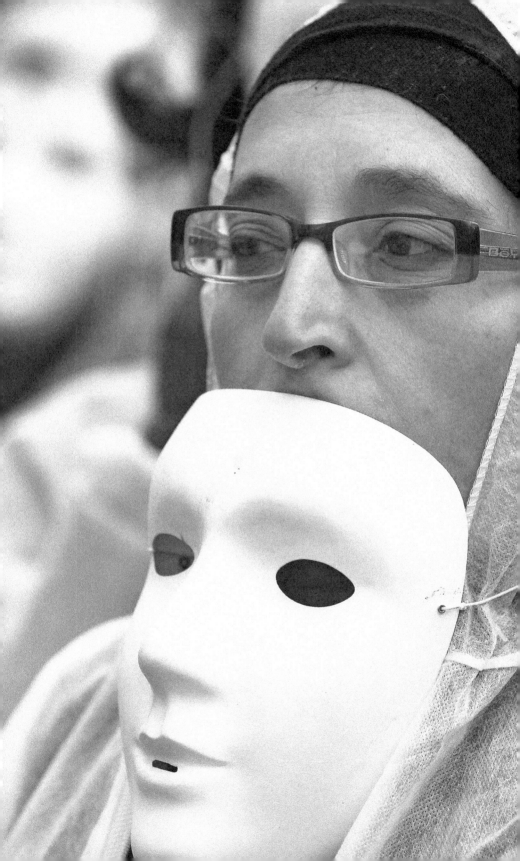

5 Data and Documents

The tables and figures provide statistical evidence about the most frequent types of abuse, who is most likely to be affected, and the impact of abuse. These data show differences by age and gender. Following the data, a selection of primary documents is included. The first document is the transcript from the Interamerican Commission on Human Rights in the case of Jessica Lenahan (Gonzales), which addresses the responsibility of police to enforce restraining orders. Next is the 2013 reauthorization of the Violence Against Women Act, followed by the United Nations Convention on the Elimination of All Forms of Discrimination against Women (CEDAW) (1979) and concluding with the decisions for three Supreme Court cases related to domestic violence.

Data

Table 5.1 shows that women experience more domestic violence than men. This includes both physical and sexual violence as well as stalking.

French women protest gender violence on the International Day for the Elimination of Violence against Women. (Joel Saget/AFP/Getty Images)

Table 5.1   Lifetime Prevalence of Contact Sexual Violence, Physical Violence, or Stalking Victimization by an Intimate Partner, 2015

	Women		Men	
	Percentage	Estimated Number of Victims	Percentage	Estimated Number of Victims
Any contact sexual violence, physical violence, and/or stalking	36.4	43,579,000	33.6	37,342,000
Contact sexual violence	18.3	21,897,000	8.2	9,082,000
Physical violence	30.6	36,632,000	31.0	34,436,000
Slapped, pushed, shoved	29.1	34,828,000	28.8	31,983,000
Any severe physical violence	21.4	25,570,000	14.9	16,556,000
Stalking	10.4	12,499,000	2.2	2,485,000
Any contact sexual violence, physical violence, and/or stalking with intimate partner violence–related impact	25.1	30,025,000	10.8	12,118,000

Source: National Intimate Partner and Sexual Violence Survey: 2015 Data Brief, Updated Release. Available at https://www.cdc.gov/violenceprevention/pdf/2015data-brief508.pdf

Women endure unwanted sexual contact at higher rates than do men in the course of their lifetimes. Figure 5.1 shows that women are almost ten times as likely to endure an attempted or completed rape.

As Figure 5.2 shows, various forms of psychological abuse are common within intimate partner relationships. Both men and women endure these forms of abuse, with women experiencing them at slightly higher rates.

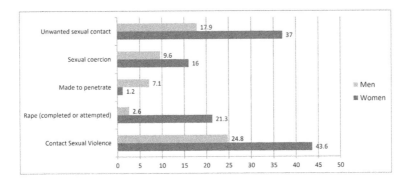

Figure 5.1   Lifetime Prevalence of Sexual Violence Victimization (Percentage), 2015

Source: National Intimate Partner and Sexual Violence Survey: 2015 Data Brief, Updated Release. Available at https://www.cdc.gov/violenceprevention/pdf/2015data-brief508.pdf

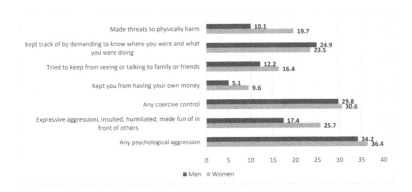

Figure 5.2   Lifetime Prevalence of Psychological Aggression by an Intimate Partner, 2015

Source: National Intimate Partner and Sexual Violence Survey, 2015 Data Brief, Updated Release. Available at https://www.cdc.gov/violenceprevention/pdf/2015data-brief508.pdf

Table 5.2 shows that domestic violence often results in injuries. Many times, those injuries go untreated.

Table 5.2 Violent Victimization Resulting in Injury and Medical Treatment, by Victim–Offender Relationship, 2003–2012

Type of Injury and Treatment	Domestic Violence					Well-Known/Casual Acquaintance (%)	Stranger (%)
	Total (%)	Intimate Partner (%)	Immediate Family (%)	Other Relative (%)			
Injury							
Not injured	55.4	51.9	62.6	63.5		78.3	78.7
Injured	44.6	48.1	37.4	36.5		21.7	21.3
Serious injuries	8.9	111	4.1	4.2		3.8	4.4
Bruises or cuts	39.6	43.2	32.1	31.3		17.3	17.7
Other injuries	4.1	3.3	7.3	3.1		3.1	2.5
Treatment for injury							
No treatment	6.4	66.1	89.1	49.5		63.0	52.6
Any treatment	36.6	33.9	40.6	50.5		37.0	47.4
Treatment setting							
At the scene/home of victim, neighbor, or friend/other location	47.0	51.4	46.2	24.3		38.5	36.1
In the doctor's office/hospital emergency room/overnight at hospital	53.0	48.63	53.8	75.7		61.5	60.9
Average number of annual violent victimizations	1,411,330	967,710	284,670	158,950		2,103,240	2,548,860

Source: Truman, Jennifer L., and Morgan, Rachel E. Nonfatal Domestic Violence, 2003–2012. U.S. Department of Justice, Bureau of Justice Statistics, NCJ244697, April 2014. Available at https://www.bjs.gov/content/pub/pdf/ndv0312.pdf

As Figure 5.3 shows, abuse occurs most often within dating relationships, followed by marital partnerships. It is clear from the figure that abuse occurs within other relationships as well, however.

Table 5.3 highlights the fact that people aged eighteen to twenty-four are at greatest risk f or experiencing domestic violence. It also shows that women of color experience abuse at higher rates than do Caucasian women.

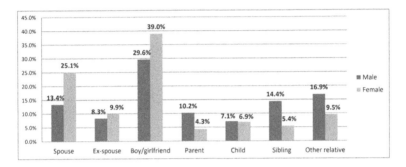

Figure 5.3   Composition of Victim–Offender Relationships in Domestic Violence Victimizations, by Victim's Sex, 2003–2012

Source: Truman, Jennifer L., and Morgan, Rachel E. Nonfatal Domestic Violence, 2003–2012. U.S. Department of Justice, Bureau of Justice Statistics, NCJ244697, April 2014. Available at https://www.bjs.gov/content/pub/pdf/ndv0312.pdf

Table 5.3   Rate of Violent Victimization, by Victim Characteristics and Victim–Offender Relationship, 2003–2012

Demographic Characteristic	Domestic Violence				Well-Known/ Casual Acquaintance (%)	Stranger (%)
	Total (%)	Intimate Partner (%)	Immediate Family (%)	Other Relative (%)		
Total	5.6	3.9	1.1	0.6	8.4	10.2
Sex						
Male	2.8	1.4	0.9	0.5	8.9	14.2
Female	8.4	6.2	1.4	0.8	7.9	6.4

(Continued)

Table 5.3   (Continued)

Demographic Characteristic	Domestic Violence					
	Total (%)	Intimate Partner (%)	Immediate Family (%)	Other Relative (%)	Well-Known/ Casual Acquaintance (%)	Stranger (%)
Age						
12–17	5.0	1.1	2.6	1.2	26.9	15.2
18–24	11.6	8.7	1.8	1.2	14.0	19.9
25–34	8.7	7.3	0.7	0.7	7.5	14.5
35–49	6.4	4.7	1.2	0.5	6.4	9.7
50–64	2.9	1.5	1.0	0.5	4.8	5.9
65 or older	0.6	0.2	0.2	0.1	1.3	1.6
Race/Hispanic Origin						
White	5.7	3.9	1.2	0.6	8.6	9.7
Black	6.7	4.7	0.7	1.2	10.1	12.3
Hispanic/ Latino	4.0	2.8	0.6	0.6	6.3	10.4
Other race	3.7	2.3	1.3	0.2!	4.6	8.4
Two or more races	22.5	16.5	4.4	1.6	24.6	26.7
Marital Status						
Never married	7.0	4.4	1.7	0.9	15.6	17.1
Married	2.0	1.0	0.6	0.4	3.7	5.9
Widowed	2.3	0.6	1.5	0.2*	2.2	2.3
Divorced	13.8	11.4	1.5	0.9	11.4	12.9
Separated	49.1	44.7	2.8	1.6	13.9	16.0

Source: Truman, Jennifer L., and Morgan, Rachel E. Nonfatal Domestic Violence, 2003–2012. U.S. Department of Justice, Bureau of Justice Statistics, NCJ244697, April 2014. Available at https://www.bjs.gov/content/pub/pdf/ndv0312.pdf

*Interpret with caution. Estimate based on ten or fewer sample cases, or coefficient of variation is greater than 50 percent.

Documents

The Jessica Gonzales Case (2011)

The first document is the report issued by the Inter-American Commission on Human Rights about the case filed on behalf of

Jessica Lenahan, formerly Gonzales. Gonzales had obtained a restraining order prohibiting her ex-husband, Simon Gonzales, from coming near their three daughters except during specified times. He took the girls in violation of the order, and Jessica contacted the Castle Rock, Colorado, police multiple times, but they refused to follow up. Simon ended up killing the girls and then being shot and killed by the police when he pulled his truck into the station and opened fire. Jessica filed a lawsuit, asserting that the police were culpable for failing to enforce the restraining order. The case ended up before the Supreme Court, which in 2005 ruled that the wording of Colorado law meant police "shall" but were not "required" to enforce the order. Jessica and her attorneys then appeared before the Inter-American Commission, which determined in 2011 that Jessica's human rights had been violated and called on the United States to better train police and to make a number of changes to keep people safe from domestic violence.

Report No. 80/11 Case 12.626 Merits Jessica Lenahan (Gonzales) et al. United States July 21, 2011

I. Summary

1. This report concerns a petition presented to the Inter-American Commission on Human Rights (hereinafter the "Commission" or "IACHR") against the Government of the United States (hereinafter the "State" or the "United States") on December 27, 2005, by Caroline Bettinger-Lopez, Emily J. Martin, Lenora Lapidus, Stephen Mcpherson Watt, and Ann Beeson, attorneys-at-law with the American Civil Liberties Union. The petition was presented on behalf of Ms. Jessica Lenahan, formerly Jessica Gonzales and her deceased daughters Leslie (7), Katheryn (8) and Rebecca (10) Gonzales.

2. The claimants assert in their petition that the United States violated Articles I, II, V, VI, VII, IX, XVIII and XXIV of

the American Declaration by failing to exercise due diligence to protect Jessica Lenahan and her daughters from acts of domestic violence perpetrated by the ex-husband of the former and the father of the latter, even though Ms. Lenahan held a restraining order against him. They specifically allege that the police failed to adequately respond to Jessica Lenahan's repeated and urgent calls over several hours reporting that her estranged husband had taken their three minor daughters (ages 7, 8 and 10) in violation of the restraining order, and asking for help. The three girls were found shot to death in the back of their father's truck after the exchange of gunfire that resulted in the death of their father. The petitioners further contend that the State never duly investigated and clarified the circumstances of the death of Jessica Lenahan's daughters, and never provided her with an adequate remedy for the failures of the police. According to the petition, eleven years have passed and Jessica Lenahan still does not know the cause, time and place of her daughters' death.

3. The United States recognizes that the murders of Jessica Lenahan's daughters are "unmistakable tragedies."

The State, however, asserts that any petition must be assessed on its merits, based on the evidentiary record and a cognizable basis in the American Declaration. The State claims that its authorities responded as required by law, and that the facts alleged by the petitioners are not supported by the evidentiary record and the information available to the Castle Rock Police Department at the time the events occurred. The State moreover claims that the petitioners cite no provision of the American Declaration that imposes on the United States an affirmative duty, such as the exercise of due diligence, to prevent the commission of individual crimes by private actors, such as the tragic and criminal murders of Jessica Lenahan's daughters.

4. In Report No 52/07, adopted on July 24, 2007 during its 128th regular period of sessions, the Commission decided to admit the claims advanced by the petitioners under Articles I, II, V, VI, VII, XVIII and XXIV of the American Declaration, and to proceed with consideration of the merits of the petition. At the merits stage, the petitioners added to their allegations that the failures of the United States to conduct a thorough investigation into the circumstances surrounding Leslie, Katheryn and Rebecca's deaths also breached Jessica Lenahan's and her family's right to truth in violation of Article IV of the American Declaration.

5. In the present report, having examined the evidence and arguments presented by the parties during the proceedings, the Commission concludes that the State failed to act with due diligence to protect Jessica Lenahan and Leslie, Katheryn and Rebecca Gonzales from domestic violence, which violated the State's obligation not to discriminate and to provide for equal protection before the law under Article II of the American Declaration. The State also failed to undertake reasonable measures to protect the life of Leslie, Katheryn and Rebecca Gonzales in violation of their right to life under Article I of the American Declaration, in conjunction with their right to special protection as girl-children under Article VII of the American Declaration. Finally, the Commission finds that the State violated the right to judicial protection of Jessica Lenahan and her next-of kin, under Article XVIII of the American Declaration. The Commission does not consider that it has sufficient information to find violations of articles V and VI of the American Declaration. As to Articles XXIV and IV of the American Declaration, it considers the claims related to these articles to have been addressed under Article XVIII of the American Declaration.

V. Conclusions

1. Based on the foregoing considerations of fact and law, and having examined the evidence and arguments presented by the parties during the proceedings, the Commission concludes that the State failed to act with due diligence to protect Jessica Lenahan and Leslie, Katheryn and Rebecca Gonzales from domestic violence, which violated the State's obligation not to discriminate and to provide for equal protection before the law under Article II of the American Declaration. The State also failed to undertake reasonable measures to prevent the death of Leslie, Katheryn and Rebecca Gonzales in violation of their right to life under Article I of the American Declaration, in conjunction with their right to special protection as girl-children under Article VII of the American Declaration. Finally, the Commission concludes that the State violated the right to judicial protection of Jessica Lenahan and her next-of kin, under Article XVIII of the American Declaration.

2. The Commission does not find that it has sufficient information to find violations of articles V and VI. As to Articles XXIV and IV of the American Declaration, it considers the claims related to these articles to have been addressed under Article XVIII of the American Declaration.

VI. Recommendations

3. Based on the analysis and conclusions pertaining to the instant case, the Inter-American Commission on Human Rights recommends to the United States:

   1. To undertake a serious, impartial and exhaustive investigation with the objective of ascertaining the cause, time and place of the deaths of Leslie, Katheryn and Rebecca Gonzales, and to duly inform their next-of kin of the course of the investigation.

2. To conduct a serious, impartial and exhaustive investigation into systemic failures that took place related to the enforcement of Jessica Lenahan's protection order as a guarantee of their non-repetition, including performing an inquiry to determine the responsibilities of public officials for violating state and/or federal laws, and holding those responsible accountable.

3. To offer full reparations to Jessica Lenahan and her next-of-kin considering their perspective and specific needs.

4. To adopt multifaceted legislation at the federal and state levels, or to reform existing legislation, making mandatory the enforcement of protection orders and other precautionary measures to protect women from imminent acts of violence, and to create effective implementation mechanisms. These measures should be accompanied by adequate resources destined to foster their implementation; regulations to ensure their enforcement; training programs for the law enforcement and justice system officials who will participate in their execution; and the design of model protocols and directives that can be followed by police departments throughout the country.

5. To adopt multifaceted legislation at the federal and state levels, or reform existing legislation, including protection measures for children in the context of domestic violence. Such measures should be accompanied by adequate resources destined to foster their implementation; regulations to ensure their enforcement; training programs for the law enforcement and justice system officials who will participate in their execution; and the design of model protocols and directives that can be followed by police departments throughout the country.

6. To continue adopting public policies and institutional programs aimed at restructuring the stereotypes of

domestic violence victims, and to promote the eradication of discriminatory socio-cultural patterns that impede women and children's full protection from domestic violence acts, including programs to train public officials in all branches of the administration of justice and police, and comprehensive prevention programs.

7. To design protocols at the federal and state levels specifying the proper components of the investigation by law enforcement officials of a report of missing children in the context of a report of a restraining order violation.

Source: *Jessica Lenahan (Gonzales) et al. v. United States.* Report No. 80/11, Case 12.626. Merits. July 21, 2011. Available at https://www.law.columbia.edu/sites/default/files/microsites/human-rights-institute/files/gonzales%20decision.pdf

Reauthorization of the Violence Against Women Act (2013)

Congress was deeply divided about several of the provisions in this reauthorization, including extending protection to Native Americans; undocumented immigrants; and lesbian, gay, bisexual, and transgender individuals. Republican opposition resulted in VAWA briefly in 2012 before the reauthorization was passed in 2013. This summary reviews the major components of the reauthorization.

Violence Against Women Reauthorization Act of 2013—(Sec. 3) Amends the Violence Against Women Act of 1994 (VAWA) to add or expand definitions of several terms used in such Act, including: (1) "culturally specific services" to mean community-based services that offer culturally relevant and linguistically specific services and resources to culturally specific communities; (2) "personally identifying information or personal information" with respect to a victim of domestic violence, dating violence, sexual assault, or stalking; (3) "underserved populations" as populations that face barriers in accessing and using victim services because of geographic location, religion, sexual orientation or gender identity; and (4) "youth" to mean a person who is 11 to 24 years old.

Modifies or expands grant conditions under such Act, including requirements relating to: (1) nondisclosure of personally identifying information or other client information, (2) information sharing between grantees and subgrantees, (3) civil rights and nondiscrimination, (4) audit requirements for grants, and (5) nonprofit organizations.

Requires the Office on Violence Against Women of the Department of Justice (DOJ) to establish a biennial conferral process with state and tribal coalitions, technical assistance providers, and other key stakeholders on the administration of grants and related matters.

. . .

Title I: Enhancing Judicial and Law Enforcement Tools to Combat Violence against Women—(Sec. 101) Amends the Omnibus Crime Control and Safe Streets Act of 1968 to authorize appropriations for FY2014-FY2018 for grants to combat violent crime against women (STOP grants). Expands the purposes for which STOP grants may be used to include training of law enforcement personnel and prosecutors, addressing backlogs of sexual assault evidence collection kits, and providing protections for male victims of sexual assault crimes. Revises the application process for STOP grants. . . .

(Sec. 102) Amends the Omnibus Crime Control and Safe Streets Act of 1968 to expand the grant program to encourage governmental entities to implement policies, training programs, and best practices for recognizing, investigating, and prosecuting instances of domestic violence and violent sex crimes. Requires such entities to use grant funds for: (1) training programs with respect to domestic violence and sexual assaults against women; (2) developing best practices for responding to domestic violence and sexual assault crimes; (3) developing, implementing, or enhancing sexual assault nurse examiner programs and Sexual Assault Response Teams; (4) providing human immunodeficiency virus testing programs; and (5) identifying and inventorying backlogs of sexual assault evidence collection kits. Requires not less than 25% of grant funding to be used for projects that address sexual assault. Authorizes appropriations for such grant program for FY2014-FY2018, and requires the allotment of not less than 5% of such funding for Indian tribal governments.

(Sec. 103) Amends the Violence Against Women Act of 2000 to expand the availability of competent pro bono legal assistance to victims of domestic violence, dating violence, sexual assault, or stalking and to authorize appropriations for FY2014-FY2018.

(Sec. 104) Revises the grant programs for supporting families with a history of domestic violence, dating violence, sexual assault, or stalking to authorize the Attorney General to make grants to improve the response of the civil and criminal justice system to such families and to train court personnel in assisting such families. Authorizes appropriations for FY2014-FY2018.

(Sec. 105) Extends through FY2018 the authorization of appropriations for: (1) the training of probation and parole officers to manage sex offenders, and (2) the Court-Appointed Special Advocate program.

(Sec. 107) Amends the federal criminal code with respect to the crime of stalking to prohibit the use of any interactive computer or electronic communication service to stalk victims.

(Sec. 108) Revises and reauthorizes through FY2018 the grant program for outreach strategies targeted at adult or youth victims of domestic violence, dating violence, sexual assault, or stalking in underserved populations.

(Sec. 109) Eliminates the requirement that recipients of grants to combat violent sex crimes against women include linguistically specific services in administering such grants.

Title II: Improving Services for Victims of Domestic Violence, Dating Violence, Sexual Assault, and Stalking— (Sec. 201) Amends VAWA to authorize appropriations for

FY2014-FY2018 for grants to: (1) assist states, Indian tribes, and U.S. territories to establish, maintain, and expand rape crisis centers and other nongovernmental or tribal programs to assist victims of sexual assault; and (2) assist victims of domestic violence and other sexual assault crimes in rural areas.

(Sec. 203) Amends the Victims of Trafficking and Violence Protection Act of 2000 to authorize appropriations for FY2014-FY2018 for grants to end violence against women with disabilities.

(Sec. 204) Amends VAWA to authorize appropriations for FY2014-FY2018 for the grant program to end elder abuse, including domestic violence, dating violence, sexual assault, stalking, exploitation, and neglect, and to provide training for law enforcement agencies to better serve victims of abuse in later life (i.e., individuals who are 50 years of age or older). Directs the Attorney General in awarding grants to end elder abuse to give priority to proposals for serving culturally specific and underserved populations.

Title III: Services, Protection, and Justice for Young Victims of Violence—(Sec. 301) Amends the Public Health Service Act to: (1) include territorial or tribal sexual assault coalitions in the grant program for rape prevention and education, and (2) authorize appropriations for FY2014-FY2018 for grants for rape prevention and education programs conducted by rape crisis centers. Establishes a minimum allocation of grant funding for states, the District of Columbia, Puerto Rico, and each U.S. Territory.

(Sec. 302) Amends VAWA to replace certain grant programs for the protection of young victims of violent crimes with a program requiring the Attorney General, in collaboration with the Secretary of Health and Human Services (HHS) and the Secretary of Education, to award grants to enhance the safety of youth and children who are victims of, or exposed to, domestic violence, dating violence, sexual assault, or stalking and to prevent future violence. Authorizes appropriations for FY2014-FY2018.

(Sec. 303) Amends the Violence against Women and Department of Justice Reauthorization Act of 2005 to expand the grant program for combating violent crimes on college campuses by providing for educational materials to address prevention and intervention in domestic violence, dating violence, sexual violence, and stalking and to develop or adapt population specific strategies for victims of domestic violence and violent sex crimes for underserved populations on campus. Authorizes appropriations for FY2014-FY2018.

(Sec. 304) Amends the Higher Education Act of 1965 to expand requirements for the disclosure of campus security policy and crime statistics by institutions of higher education to require education programs to: (1) promote the awareness of rape and other violent sex crimes, (2) require disclosure of disciplinary proceedings involving rape and other violent sex crimes and the standard of evidence that will govern such proceedings, and (3) establish procedures for the protection of the rights of accusers and the accused in disciplinary proceedings and the confidentiality of crime victims.

Title IV: Violence Reduction Practices—(Sec. 401) Amends the Violence against Women and Department of Justice Reauthorization Act of 2005 to authorize appropriations for FY2014-FY2018 for grants from the Centers for Disease Control and Prevention (CDC) to academic institutions and organizations to support research that examines best practices for reducing and preventing violence against women and children. Reduces the amount of such funding by 50% of the level for FY2007-FY2011.

(Sec. 402) Amends VAWA to authorize the Attorney General, in consultation with the HHS Secretary and the Secretary of Education, to award grants to prevent domestic violence, dating violence, sexual assault, and stalking by taking a comprehensive approach that focuses on youth, children exposed to violence, and men as leaders and influencers of social norms (SMART Prevention grants). Authorizes appropriations for FY2014-FY2018.

Repeals grant programs for: (1) training home visitation service providers, (2) engaging men and youth in preventing domestic violence and violent sex crimes, and (3) increasing public awareness of issues regarding domestic violence against pregnant women.

Title V: Strengthening the Healthcare System's Response to Domestic Violence, Dating Violence, Sexual Assault, and Stalking—(Sec. 501) Amends the Public Health Service Act to revise, and consolidate grant programs that address domestic violence, dating violence, sexual assault, and stalking by developing or enhancing and implementing: (1) interdisciplinary training for health professionals, public health staff, and allied health professionals; (2) education programs for health profession students to prevent and respond to domestic violence, dating violence, sexual assault, and stalking; and (3) comprehensive statewide strategies to improve the response of clinics, public health facilities, hospitals, and other health settings to domestic violence, dating violence, sexual assault, and stalking.

Permits grant funds to be used for the development, expansion, and implementation of sexual assault forensic medical examination or sexual assault nurse examiner programs. . . .

Title VI: Safe Homes for Victims of Domestic Violence, Dating Violence, Sexual Assault, and Stalking—(Sec. 601) Amends VAWA with respect to housing rights of victims of domestic violence, dating violence, sexual assault, and stalking.

Prohibits denial or termination of housing assistance on the basis of being such a victim under specified federal housing programs (covered programs), including the low-income housing tax credit program, if the applicant or tenant otherwise qualifies for admission, assistance, participation, or occupancy under such programs.

Prohibits denial of assistance, tenancy, or occupancy rights to assisted housing based solely on certain criminal activity directly related to domestic violence engaged in by a member of the individual's household or by any guest or other person under the individual's control, if the tenant or an affiliated individual is the victim or threatened victim.

Defines "affiliated individual" as: (1) a spouse, parent, brother, sister, or child of that individual, or someone to whom such individual stands in loco parentis; or (2) any other individual, tenant, or lawful occupant living in the individual's household.

Allows a public housing agency (PHA) or an owner or manager of assisted housing to bifurcate a housing lease in order to evict, remove, or terminate assistance to any tenant or lawful occupant who engages in criminal activity directly relating to domestic violence, dating violence, sexual assault, or stalking against an affiliated individual or other individual, without evicting or otherwise penalizing a victim of such criminal activity who is also a tenant or lawful occupant. Requires specified accommodation of any tenants remaining after the eviction of the sole tenant eligible to receive assistance under a covered housing program. . . .

Title VIII: Protection of Battered Immigrants—(Sec. 801) Amends the Immigration and Nationality Act (INA) to expand the definition of nonimmigrant U-visa (aliens who are victims of certain crimes) to include victims of stalking.

(Sec. 802) Directs the Secretary of Homeland Security (DHS) to report annually to the Judiciary Committees of Congress on the number of aliens: (1) applying for and granted or not granted nonimmigrant status based upon being victims of trafficking or other criminal activities such as domestic violence or sexual exploitation, and (2) granted continued U.S. presence. Requires such report to include a description of actions being taken to reduce the adjudication and processing time for U visas. . . .

(Sec. 805) Amends INA to: (1) provide that an unmarried alien who seeks to accompany or follow to join a parent granted U-visa status who was under 21 years of age on the date on which the parent petitioned for such status shall continue to be classified as a child if the alien attains 21 years of age after the parent's petition was filed but while it was pending, (2) extend the conditions under which the waiver of the two-year waiting period for a permanent resident status application may be granted to a battered alien spouse, and (3) expand the scope of criminal-related information that must be disclosed by a U.S. citizen petitioning for a nonimmigrant K-visa (alien fiancee or fiance).

Title IX: Safety for Indian Women—(Sec. 901) Amends the Omnibus Crime Control and Safe Streets Act of 1968 to include sex trafficking as a target of the grants to Indian tribal governments to combat violent crime against Indian women. Allows such grants to be used to: (1) address the needs of youth who are victims of, or exposed to, domestic violence, dating violence, sexual assault, sex trafficking, or stalking; and (2) develop and promote best practices for responding to domestic violence, dating violence, sexual assault, sex trafficking, and stalking.

(Sec. 902) Allows tribal coalition grants to be used to develop and promote state, local, and tribal legislation and policies that enhance best practices for responding to violent crimes against Indian women. . . .

(Sec. 904) Gives Indian tribes jurisdiction over domestic violence, dating violence, and violations of protective orders that occur on their lands. Makes that jurisdiction concurrent with federal and state jurisdiction. Requires Indian tribes prosecuting crimes of violence to: (1) prove that a defendant has requisite ties to the Indian tribe; (2) provide defendants the right to an impartial jury trial; and (3) notify defendants of their rights, including the right to file a writ of habeas corpus in federal court. . . .

(Sec. 905) Grants courts of an Indian tribe full civil jurisdiction to issue and enforce protection orders in matters arising anywhere in the Indian country of the Indian tribe or otherwise within the authority of the tribe.

(Sec. 906) Amends the federal criminal code to include sexual abuse crimes under the 20-year criminal penalty for assault.

Imposes enhanced criminal penalties on individuals who: (1) commit an assault resulting in substantial bodily injury to a spouse, intimate partner, or a dating partner who has not attained age 16; and (2) assault a spouse, intimate partner, or dating partner by strangling, suffocating, or attempting to strangle or suffocate.

Makes federal felony assault penalties and enhanced penalties for prior domestic violence or stalking offenses applicable to Indians and Indian tribes.

(Sec. 907) Amends the Violence against Women and Department of Justice Reauthorization Act of 2005 to require the National Institute of Justice to include women in Alaska Native Villages and sex trafficking in its study of violence against Indian women. Reauthorizes appropriations for the study for FY2014-FY2015. . . .

Title X: Safer Act—Sexual Assault Forensic Evidence Reporting Act of 2013 or the SAFER Act of 2013—(Sec. 1002) Amends the DNA Analysis Backlog Elimination Act of 2000 to authorize the Attorney General to make Debbie Smith grants under such Act to states or local governments to: (1) conduct audits of samples of sexual assault evidence that are awaiting testing, provided such governments submit an audit plan that includes a good-faith estimate of the number of such samples; and (2) ensure that the collection and processing of DNA evidence by law enforcement agencies from crimes is carried out in an appropriate and timely manner and in accordance with specified protocols and practices.

Source: Violence Against Women Reauthorization Act of 2013. Public Law 113-4. Available at https://www.congress.gov/bill/113th-congress/senate-bill/47

United Nations Convention on the Elimination of All Forms of Discrimination against Women (CEDAW) (1979)

CEDAW is the only international human rights treaty devoted specifically to promoting gender equality. While it does not specifically mention domestic violence, CEDAW does include a number of provisions related to ending discrimination that would be helpful in reducing abuse. President Jimmy Carter was one of the earliest signatories to CEDAW, but Congress has never ratified it, leaving the United States as one of only a few countries that have not.

The States Parties to the present Convention,

Noting that the Charter of the United Nations reaffirms faith in fundamental human rights, in the dignity and worth of the human person and in the equal rights of men and women,

Noting that the Universal Declaration of Human Rights affirms the principle of the inadmissibility of discrimination and proclaims that all human beings are born free and equal in dignity and rights and that everyone is entitled to all the rights and freedoms set forth therein, without distinction of any kind, including distinction based on sex,

Noting that the States Parties to the International Covenants on Human Rights have the obligation to ensure the equal rights of men and women to enjoy all economic, social, cultural, civil and political rights,

Considering the international conventions concluded under the auspices of the United Nations and the specialized agencies promoting equality of rights of men and women,

Noting also the resolutions, declarations and recommendations adopted by the United Nations and the specialized agencies promoting equality of rights of men and women,

Concerned, however, that despite these various instruments extensive discrimination against women continues to exist,

Recalling that discrimination against women violates the principles of equality of rights and respect for human dignity, is an obstacle to the participation of women, on equal terms with men, in the political, social, economic and cultural life of their countries, hampers the growth of the prosperity of society and the family and makes more difficult the full development of the potentialities of women in the service of their countries and of humanity,

Concerned that in situations of poverty women have the least access to food, health, education, training and opportunities for employment and other needs,

Convinced that the establishment of the new international economic order based on equity and justice will contribute significantly towards the promotion of equality between men and women,

Emphasizing that the eradication of apartheid, all forms of racism, racial discrimination, colonialism, neo-colonialism, aggression, foreign occupation and domination and interference in the internal affairs of States is essential to the full enjoyment of the rights of men and women,

Affirming that the strengthening of international peace and security, the relaxation of international tension, mutual co-operation among all States irrespective of their social and economic systems, general and complete disarmament, in particular nuclear disarmament under strict and effective international control, the affirmation of the principles of justice, equality and mutual benefit in relations among countries and the realization of the right of peoples under alien and colonial domination and foreign occupation to self-determination and independence, as well as respect for national sovereignty and territorial integrity, will promote social progress and development and as a consequence will contribute to the attainment of full equality between men and women,

Convinced that the full and complete development of a country, the welfare of the world and the cause of peace require the maximum participation of women on equal terms with men in all fields,

Bearing in mind the great contribution of women to the welfare of the family and to the development of society, so far not fully recognized, the social significance of maternity and the role of both parents in the family and in the upbringing of children, and aware that the role of women in procreation should not be a basis for discrimination but that the upbringing of children requires a sharing of responsibility between men and women and society as a whole,

Aware that a change in the traditional role of men as well as the role of women in society and in the family is needed to achieve full equality between men and women,

Determined to implement the principles set forth in the Declaration on the Elimination of Discrimination against Women and, for that purpose, to adopt the measures required for the elimination of such discrimination in all its forms and manifestations,

Have agreed on the following:

Part I

Article 1

For the purposes of the present Convention, the term "discrimination against women" shall mean any distinction, exclusion or restriction made on the basis of sex which has the effect or purpose of impairing or nullifying the recognition, enjoyment or exercise by women, irrespective of their marital status, on a basis of equality of men and women, of human rights and fundamental freedoms in the political, economic, social, cultural, civil or any other field.

Article 2

States Parties condemn discrimination against women in all its forms, agree to pursue by all appropriate means and without delay a policy of eliminating discrimination against women and, to this end, undertake:

(a) To embody the principle of the equality of men and women in their national constitutions or other appropriate legislation if not yet incorporated therein and to ensure, through law and other appropriate means, the practical realization of this principle;

(b) To adopt appropriate legislative and other measures, including sanctions where appropriate, prohibiting all discrimination against women;

(c) To establish legal protection of the rights of women on an equal basis with men and to ensure through competent national tribunals and other public institutions the effective protection of women against any act of discrimination;

(d) To refrain from engaging in any act or practice of discrimination against women and to ensure that public authorities and institutions shall act in conformity with this obligation;

(e) To take all appropriate measures to eliminate discrimination against women by any person, organization or enterprise;

(f) To take all appropriate measures, including legislation, to modify or abolish existing laws, regulations, customs and practices which constitute discrimination against women;

(g) To repeal all national penal provisions which constitute discrimination against women.

Article 3

States Parties shall take in all fields, in particular in the political, social, economic and cultural fields, all appropriate measures, including legislation, to ensure the full development and advancement of women, for the purpose of guaranteeing them the exercise and enjoyment of human rights and fundamental freedoms on a basis of equality with men.

Article 4

1. Adoption by States Parties of temporary special measures aimed at accelerating de facto equality between men and women shall not be considered discrimination as defined in the present Convention, but shall in no way entail as a consequence the maintenance of unequal or separate

standards; these measures shall be discontinued when the objectives of equality of opportunity and treatment have been achieved.

2. Adoption by States Parties of special measures, including those measures contained in the present Convention, aimed at protecting maternity shall not be considered discriminatory.

Article 5

States Parties shall take all appropriate measures:

(a) To modify the social and cultural patterns of conduct of men and women, with a view to achieving the elimination of prejudices and customary and all other practices which are based on the idea of the inferiority or the superiority of either of the sexes or on stereotyped roles for men and women;

(b) To ensure that family education includes a proper understanding of maternity as a social function and the recognition of the common responsibility of men and women in the upbringing and development of their children, it being understood that the interest of the children is the primordial consideration in all cases.

Article 6

States Parties shall take all appropriate measures, including legislation, to suppress all forms of traffic in women and exploitation of prostitution of women.

Part II

Article 7

States Parties shall take all appropriate measures to eliminate discrimination against women in the political and public life of the country and, in particular, shall ensure to women, on equal terms with men, the right:

(a) To vote in all elections and public referenda and to be eligible for election to all publicly elected bodies;

(b) To participate in the formulation of government policy and the implementation thereof and to hold public office and perform all public functions at all levels of government;

(c) To participate in non-governmental organizations and associations concerned with the public and political life of the country.

Article 8

States Parties shall take all appropriate measures to ensure to women, on equal terms with men and without any discrimination, the opportunity to represent their Governments at the international level and to participate in the work of international organizations.

Article 9

1. States Parties shall grant women equal rights with men to acquire, change or retain their nationality. They shall ensure in particular that neither marriage to an alien nor change of nationality by the husband during marriage shall automatically change the nationality of the wife, render her stateless or force upon her the nationality of the husband.

2. States Parties shall grant women equal rights with men with respect to the nationality of their children.

Part III

Article 10

States Parties shall take all appropriate measures to eliminate discrimination against women in order to ensure to them equal rights with men in the field of education and in particular to ensure, on a basis of equality of men and women:

(a) The same conditions for career and vocational guidance, for access to studies and for the achievement of diplomas in educational establishments of all categories in rural as well as in urban areas; this equality shall be ensured in pre-school, general, technical, professional and higher technical education, as well as in all types of vocational training;

(b) Access to the same curricula, the same examinations, teaching staff with qualifications of the same standard and school premises and equipment of the same quality;

(c) The elimination of any stereotyped concept of the roles of men and women at all levels and in all forms of education by encouraging coeducation and other types of education which will help to achieve this aim and, in particular, by the revision of textbooks and school programmes and the adaptation of teaching methods;

(d) The same opportunities to benefit from scholarships and other study grants;

(e) The same opportunities for access to programmes of continuing education, including adult and functional literacy programmes, [particularly] those aimed at reducing, at the earliest possible time, any gap in education existing between men and women;

(f) The reduction of female student drop-out rates and the organization of programmes for girls and women who have left school prematurely;

(g) The same Opportunities to participate actively in sports and physical education;

(h) Access to specific educational information to help to ensure the health and well-being of families, including information and advice on family planning.

Article 11

1. States Parties shall take all appropriate measures to eliminate discrimination against women in the field of employment in order to ensure, on a basis of equality of men and women, the same rights, in particular:

   (a) The right to work as an inalienable right of all human beings;

   (b) The right to the same employment opportunities, including the application of the same criteria for selection in matters of employment;

   (c) The right to free choice of profession and employment, the right to promotion, job security and all benefits and conditions of service and the right to receive vocational training and retraining, including apprenticeships, advanced vocational training and recurrent training;

   (d) The right to equal remuneration, including benefits, and to equal treatment in respect of work of equal value, as well as equality of treatment in the evaluation of the quality of work;

   (e) The right to social security, particularly in cases of retirement, unemployment, sickness, invalidity and old age and other incapacity to work, as well as the right to paid leave;

   (f) The right to protection of health and to safety in working conditions, including the safeguarding of the function of reproduction.

2. In order to prevent discrimination against women on the grounds of marriage or maternity and to ensure their effective right to work, States Parties shall take appropriate measures:

   (a) To prohibit, subject to the imposition of sanctions, dismissal on the grounds of pregnancy or of maternity leave and discrimination in dismissals on the basis of marital status;

(b) To introduce maternity leave with pay or with comparable social benefits without loss of former employment, seniority or social allowances;

(c) To encourage the provision of the necessary supporting social services to enable parents to combine family obligations with work responsibilities and participation in public life, in particular through promoting the establishment and development of a network of childcare facilities;

(d) To provide special protection to women during pregnancy in types of work proved to be harmful to them.

3. Protective legislation relating to matters covered in this article shall be reviewed periodically in the light of scientific and technological knowledge and shall be revised, repealed or extended as necessary.

Article 12

1. States Parties shall take all appropriate measures to eliminate discrimination against women in the field of health care in order to ensure, on a basis of equality of men and women, access to health care services, including those related to family planning.

2. Notwithstanding the provisions of paragraph I of this article, States Parties shall ensure to women appropriate services in connection with pregnancy, confinement and the post-natal period, granting free services where necessary, as well as adequate nutrition during pregnancy and lactation.

Article 13

States Parties shall take all appropriate measures to eliminate discrimination against women in other areas of economic and social life in order to ensure, on a basis of equality of men and women, the same rights, in particular:

(a) The right to family benefits;

(b) The right to bank loans, mortgages and other forms of financial credit;

(c) The right to participate in recreational activities, sports and all aspects of cultural life.

Article 14

1. States Parties shall take into account the particular problems faced by rural women and the significant roles which rural women play in the economic survival of their families, including their work in the non-monetized sectors of the economy, and shall take all appropriate measures to ensure the application of the provisions of the present Convention to women in rural areas.

2. States Parties shall take all appropriate measures to eliminate discrimination against women in rural areas in order to ensure, on a basis of equality of men and women, that they participate in and benefit from rural development and, in particular, shall ensure to such women the right:

   (a) To participate in the elaboration and implementation of development planning at all levels;

   (b) To have access to adequate health care facilities, including information, counselling and services in family planning;

   (c) To benefit directly from social security programmes;

   (d) To obtain all types of training and education, formal and non-formal, including that relating to functional literacy, as well as, inter alia, the benefit of all community and extension services, in order to increase their technical proficiency;

(e) To organize self-help groups and co-operatives in order to obtain equal access to economic opportunities through employment or self employment;

(f) To participate in all community activities;

(g) To have access to agricultural credit and loans, marketing facilities, appropriate technology and equal treatment in land and agrarian reform as well as in land resettlement schemes;

(h) To enjoy adequate living conditions, particularly in relation to housing, sanitation, electricity and water supply, transport and communications.

Part IV

Article 15

1. States Parties shall accord to women equality with men before the law.

2. States Parties shall accord to women, in civil matters, a legal capacity identical to that of men and the same opportunities to exercise that capacity. In particular, they shall give women equal rights to conclude contracts and to administer property and shall treat them equally in all stages of procedure in courts and tribunals.

3. States Parties agree that all contracts and all other private instruments of any kind with a legal effect which is directed at restricting the legal capacity of women shall be deemed null and void.

4. States Parties shall accord to men and women the same rights with regard to the law relating to the movement of persons and the freedom to choose their residence and domicile.

Article 16

1. States Parties shall take all appropriate measures to eliminate discrimination against women in all matters relating

to marriage and family relations and in particular shall ensure, on a basis of equality of men and women:

(a) The same right to enter into marriage;

(b) The same right freely to choose a spouse and to enter into marriage only with their free and full consent;

(c) The same rights and responsibilities during marriage and at its dissolution;

(d) The same rights and responsibilities as parents, irrespective of their marital status, in matters relating to their children; in all cases the interests of the children shall be paramount;

(e) The same rights to decide freely and responsibly on the number and spacing of their children and to have access to the information, education and means to enable them to exercise these rights;

(f) The same rights and responsibilities with regard to guardianship, wardship, trusteeship and adoption of children, or similar institutions where these concepts exist in national legislation; in all cases the interests of the children shall be paramount;

(g) The same personal rights as husband and wife, including the right to choose a family name, a profession and an occupation;

(h) The same rights for both spouses in respect of the ownership, acquisition, management, administration, enjoyment and disposition of property, whether free of charge or for a valuable consideration.

2. The betrothal and the marriage of a child shall have no legal effect, and all necessary action, including legislation, shall be taken to specify a minimum age for marriage and to make the registration of marriages in an official registry compulsory.

Source: United Nations. Convention on the Elimination of All Forms of Discrimination against Women. Available at https://www.ohchr.org/Documents/ProfessionalInterest/cedaw.pdf

United States v. Hayes (2009)

In this case the Supreme Court held that firearms prohibitions still apply in cases of misdemeanor offenses of a nondomestic nature when someone previously had been convicted of misdemeanor domestic violence.

Syllabus

In 1996, Congress extended the federal Gun Control Act of 1968's prohibition on possession of a firearm by convicted felons to include persons convicted of "a misdemeanor crime of domestic violence." Responding to a 911 call reporting domestic violence, police officers discovered a rifle in respondent Hayes's home. Based on this and other evidence, Hayes was charged under §§922(g)(9) and 924(a)(2) with possessing firearms after having been convicted of a misdemeanor crime of domestic violence. The indictment identified as the predicate misdemeanor offense Hayes's 1994 conviction for battery against his then-wife, in violation of West Virginia law. Hayes moved to dismiss the indictment on the ground that his 1994 conviction did not qualify as a predicate offense under §922(g)(9) because West Virginia's generic battery law did not designate a domestic relationship between aggressor and victim as an element of the offense. When the District Court denied the motion, Hayes entered a conditional guilty plea and appealed. The Fourth Circuit reversed, holding that a §922(g)(9) predicate offense must have as an element a domestic relationship between offender and victim. Held: A domestic relationship, although it must be established beyond a reasonable doubt in a §922(g)(9) firearms possession prosecution, need not be a defining element of the predicate offense. (a) The definition of "misdemeanor crime of domestic violence," contained in §921(a)(33)(A), imposes two requirements. First, the crime must have, "as an element, the use or attempted use of physical force, or the threatened use of a deadly weapon." Second, it must be "committed by" a person who has a specified domestic relationship with the victim. The definition does not, however, require the predicate-offense statute to include, as an element, the existence of that domestic relationship. Instead, it suffices for the Government to charge and prove a prior conviction that was, in fact, for "an offense . . . committed by" the defendant against a spouse or other domestic victim. As an initial matter, §921(a)(33)(A)'s use of the singular word "element" suggests that Congress intended to describe only one required element, the use of force. Had Congress also meant to make the specified relationship a predicate-offense element, it likely would have used the plural "elements," as it has done in other offense-defining provisions. Treating the specified relationship as a predicate-offense element is also awkward as a matter of syntax. It requires the reader to regard "the use or attempted use of physical force, or the threatened use of a deadly weapon" as an expression modified by the relative clause "committed by." It is more natural, however, to say a person "commit[s]" an "offense" than to say one "commit[s]" a "use." The Fourth Circuit's textual arguments to the contrary are unpersuasive. First, that court noted, clause (ii) is separated from clause (i)—which defines "misdemeanor"—by a line break and a semicolon, while clause (ii)'s components—force and domestic relationship—are joined in an unbroken word flow. Such less-than meticulous drafting hardly shows that Congress meant to exclude from §922(g)(9)'s prohibition domestic abusers convicted under generic assault or battery laws. As structured, §921(a)(33)(A) defines "misdemeanor crime of domestic violence" by addressing in clause (i) the meaning of "misdemeanor," and in clause (ii) "crime of domestic violence." Because a "crime of domestic violence" involves both a use of force and a domestic relationship, joining these features together in clause (ii) would make sense even if Congress had no design to confine laws qualifying under §921(a)(33)(A) to those designating as elements both use of force and domestic relationship. A related statutory provision, 25 U.S.C. §2803(3)(C), indicates that Congress did not ascribe substantive significance to the placement of line breaks and semicolons in 18 U.S.C. §921(a)(33)(A). Second, the Fourth Circuit relied on the "rule of the last antecedent" to read "committed by" as modifying the immediately preceding use-of-force phrase rather than the earlier word "offense." The last-antecedent rule, however, "is not an absolute and can assuredly be overcome by other indicia of meaning." Applying the rule here would require the Court to accept the unlikely premises that Congress employed the singular "element" to encompass two distinct concepts, and that it adopted the awkward construction "commi[t]" a use. The rule, moreover, would render the word "committed" superfluous, for Congress could have conveyed the same meaning by referring simply to "the use . . . of physical force . . . by a current or former spouse. . . ." Practical considerations strongly support this Court's reading of §921(a)(33)(A). By extending the federal firearm prohibition to persons convicted of misdemeanor crimes of domestic violence, §922(g)(9)'s proponents sought to close a loophole: Existing felon-in-possession laws often failed to keep firearms out of the hands of domestic abusers, for such offenders generally were not charged with, or convicted of, felonies. Construing §922(g)(9) to exclude the domestic abuser convicted under a generic use-of-force statute would frustrate Congress' manifest purpose. The statute would have been a dead letter in some two-thirds of the States because, in 1996, only about one-third of them had criminal statutes specifically proscribing domestic violence. Hayes argues that the measure that became §§922(g)(9) and 921(a)(33)(A), though it initially may have had a broadly remedial purpose, was revised and narrowed during the legislative process, but his argument is not corroborated by the revisions he identifies. Indeed, §922(g)(9)'s Senate sponsor observed that a domestic relationship often would not be a designated element of the predicate offense. Such remarks are "not controlling," but the legislative record is otherwise silent. The rule of lenity, on which Hayes also relies, applies only when a statute is ambiguous. Section 921(a)(33)(A)'s definition, though not a model of the careful drafter's art, is also not "grievous[ly] ambigu[ous]." The text, context, purpose, and what little drafting history there is all point in the same direction: Congress defined "misdemeanor crime of domestic violence" to include an offense "committed by" a person who had a specified domestic relationship with the victim, whether or not the misdemeanor statute itself designates the domestic relationship as an element of the crime. 482 F. 3d 749, reversed and remanded.

Source: *United States v. Hayes*, 555 U.S. 415 (2009)

United States v. Castleman (2014)

In United States v. Castleman *(2014), the Supreme Court reversed its position from* United States v. Hayes, *holding that misdemeanor convictions for assault did not disqualify someone from having firearms under federal law.*

Syllabus

Respondent Castleman moved to dismiss his indictment under 18 U.S.C. §922(g)(9), which forbids the possession of firearms by anyone convicted of a "misdemeanor crime of domestic violence." He argued that his previous conviction for "intentionally or knowingly caus[ing] bodily injury to" the mother of his child, App. 27, did not qualify as a "misdemeanor crime of domestic violence" because it did not involve "the use or attempted use of physical force." The District Court agreed, reasoning that "physical force" must entail violent contact and that one can cause bodily injury without violent contact, e.g., by poisoning. The Sixth Circuit affirmed on a different rationale. It held that the degree of physical force required for a conviction to constitute a "misdemeanor crime of domestic violence" is the same as that required for a "violent felony" under the Armed Career Criminal Act (ACCA)—namely, violent force—and that Castleman could have been convicted for causing slight injury by nonviolent conduct. Held: Castleman's conviction qualifies as a "misdemeanor crime of domestic violence." (a) Section 922(g)(9)'s "physical force" requirement is satisfied by the degree of force that supports a common-law battery conviction—namely, offensive touching. Congress presumably intends to incorporate the common-law meaning of terms that it uses, and nothing suggests Congress intended otherwise here. The Sixth Circuit relied upon *Johnson v. United States*, 559 U.S. 133, in which the common-law meaning of "force" was found to be a "comical misfit," when read into ACCA's "violent felony" definition. But Johnson resolves this case in the Government's favor: The very reasons for rejecting the common-law meaning in Johnson are reasons to embrace it here. First, whereas it was "unlikely" that Congress meant to incorporate in ACCA's "violent felony" definition "a phrase that the common law gave peculiar meaning only in its definition of a misdemeanor," it is likely that Congress meant to incorporate the misdemeanor-specific meaning of "force" in defining a "misdemeanor crime of domestic violence." Second, whereas the word "violent" or "violence" standing alone "connotes a substantial degree of force," that is not true of "domestic violence," which is a term of art encompassing acts that one might not characterize as "violent" in a nondomestic context. Third, whereas this Court has hesitated to apply ACCA to "crimes which, though dangerous, are not typically committed by those whom one normally labels 'armed career criminals,' " there is no anomaly in grouping domestic abusers convicted of generic assault or battery offenses together with others whom §922(g) disqualifies from gun ownership. In addition, a contrary reading would have made §922(g)(9) inoperative in at least ten States when it was enacted. (b) Under this definition of "physical force," Castleman's conviction qualifies as a "misdemeanor crime of domestic violence." The application of the modified categorical approach—consulting Castleman's state indictment to determine whether his conviction entailed the elements necessary to constitute the generic federal offense—is straightforward. Castleman pleaded guilty to "intentionally or knowingly caus[ing] bodily injury to" the mother of his child, and the knowing or intentional causation of bodily injury necessarily involves the use of physical force. First, a "bodily injury" must result from "physical force." The common-law concept of "force" encompasses even its indirect application, making it impossible to cause bodily injury without applying force in the common-law sense. Second, the knowing or intentional application of force is a "use" of force. (c) Castleman claims that legislative history, the rule of lenity, and the canon of constitutional avoidance weigh against this Court's interpretation of §922(g)(9), but his arguments are unpersuasive. 695 F. 3d 582, reversed and remanded.

Source: *United States v. Castleman*, 572 U.S. _157_ (2014), Available at https://supreme.justia.com/cases/federal/us/572/12-1371/

Voisine v. United States (2016)

In Voisine v. United States *(2016), the Supreme Court ruled that the federal firearm ban applies to those convicted of reckless domestic violence.*

In an effort to "close [a] dangerous loophole" in the gun control laws, *United States v. Castleman*, 572 U.S. ___, ___, Congress extended the federal prohibition on firearms possession by convicted felons to persons convicted of a "misdemeanor crime of domestic violence." Section 921(a)(33)(A) defines that phrase to include a misdemeanor under federal, state, or tribal law, committed against a domestic relation that necessarily involves the "use . . . of physical force." In *Castleman*, this Court held that a knowing or intentional assault qualifies as such a crime, but left open whether the same was true of a reckless assault. Petitioner Stephen Voisine pleaded guilty to assaulting his girlfriend in violation of §207 of the Maine Criminal Code, which makes it a misdemeanor to "intentionally, knowingly or recklessly cause[ ] bodily injury" to another. When law enforcement officials later investigated Voisine for killing a bald eagle, they learned that he owned a rifle. After a background check turned up Voisine's prior conviction under §207, the Government charged him with violating §922(g)(9). Petitioner William Armstrong pleaded guilty to assaulting his wife in violation of a Maine domestic violence law making it a misdemeanor to commit an assault prohibited by §207 against a family or household member. While searching Armstrong's home as part of a narcotics investigation a few years later, law enforcement officers discovered six guns and a large quantity of ammunition. Armstrong was also charged under §922(g)(9). Both men argued that they were not subject to §922(g)(9)'s prohibition because their prior convictions could have been based on reckless, rather than knowing or intentional, conduct and thus did not quality as misdemeanor crimes of domestic violence. The District Court rejected those claims, and each petitioner pleaded guilty. The First Circuit affirmed, holding that "an offense with a *mens rea* of recklessness may qualify as a 'misdemeanor crime of violence' under §922(g)(9)." Voisine and Armstrong filed a joint petition for certiorari, and their case was remanded for further consideration in light of *Castleman*. The First Circuit again upheld the convictions on the same ground. Held: A reckless domestic assault qualifies as a "misdemeanor crime of domestic violence" under §922(g)(9). (a) That conclusion follows from the statutory text. Nothing in the phrase "use . . . of physical force" indicates that §922(g)(9) distinguishes between domestic assaults committed knowingly or intentionally and those committed recklessly. Dictionaries consistently define the word "use" to mean the "act of employing" something. Accordingly, the force involved in a qualifying assault must be volitional; an involuntary motion, even a powerful one, is not naturally described as an active employment of force. But nothing about the definition of "use" demands that the person applying force have the purpose or practical certainty that it will cause harm, as compared with the understanding that it is substantially likely to do so. Nor does *Leocal v. Ashcroft*, 543 U.S. 1, which held that the "use" of force excludes accidents. Reckless conduct, which requires the conscious disregard of a known risk, is not an accident: It involves a deliberate decision to endanger another. The relevant text thus supports prohibiting petitioners, and others with similar criminal records, from possessing firearms. (b) So too does the relevant history. Congress enacted §922(g) (9) in 1996 to bar those domestic abusers convicted of garden-variety assault or battery misdemeanors—just like those convicted of felonies—from owning guns. Then, as now, a significant majority of jurisdictions—34 States plus the District of Columbia—defined such misdemeanor offenses to include the reckless infliction of bodily harm. In targeting those laws, Congress thus must have known it was sweeping in some persons who had engaged in reckless conduct. Indeed, that was part of the point: to apply the federal firearms restriction to those abusers, along with all others, covered by the States' ordinary misdemeanor assault laws. Petitioners' reading risks rendering §922(g)(9) broadly inoperative in the 35 jurisdictions with assault laws extending to recklessness. Consider Maine's law, which criminalizes "intentionally, knowingly or recklessly" injuring another. Assuming that statute defines a single crime, petitioners' view that §921(a)(33)(A) requires at least a knowing *mens rea* would mean that no conviction obtained under that law could qualify as a "misdemeanor crime of domestic violence."

In *Castleman*, the Court declined to construe §921(a)(33)(A) so as to render §922(g)(9) ineffective in 10 States. All the more so here, where petitioners' view would jeopardize §922(g)(9)'s force in several times that many. 778 F. 3d 176, affirmed.

Source: *Voisine v. United States*, 579 U.S. ___ (2016). Available at https://supreme.justia.com/cases/federal/us/579/14-10154/

6 Resources

This chapter suggests reports, books, websites, curricula, and videos to help the reader continue their research into the topic of domestic violence. It also includes descriptions of organizations and coalitions that address abuse.

Reports, Studies, and Articles

Alejo, K. (2014). Long-term physical and mental health effects of domestic violence. *Themis: Research Journal of Justice Studies and Forensic Science, 2*(5), 82–98. Available at https://scholarworks.sjsu.edu/themis/vol2/iss1/5

> This research, published by San Jose State University, studied the effects of domestic violence on physical and mental health. The study compared short-term and long-term effects in both heterosexual and homosexual relationships and determined whether men or women suffer more from their experience with domestic violence. The author, Kavita Alejo, concludes that women suffer more long-term health problems from domestic violence than men because they are the more targeted group.

Alhusen, J. L., Ray, E., Sharps, P., & Bullock, L. (2015). Intimate partner violence during pregnancy: Maternal and

The Women's March in San Francisco in 2018, on the anniversary of President Donald Trump's inauguration. (Andrei Gabriel Stanescu/Dreamstime.com)

neonatal outcomes. *Journal of Women's Health, 24*(1), 100–106. doi:10.1089/jwh.2014.4872

The *Journal of Women's Health* presented a feature on intimate partner violence and the effect that it has on pregnancies. The authors argue that the damaging results from domestic violence on pregnant women are largely preventable through medical support programs. There is also discussion of whether the pregnancy period is a protective one for battered women or one that brings more violence and terror. The report discussed several relevant topics, including health behaviors of depressed mothers, maternal mental health, perinatal death, and clinical implications. It provides a holistic view of all the aspects of health that come into play when a pregnant woman experiences stress and abuse. The final portion of the research explains the importance of collaboration between all disciplines to come to a final solution to the problem of domestic violence.

Cesur, R., & Sabia, J. J. (2016). When war comes home: The effect of combat service on domestic violence. *Review of Economics and Statistics, 98*(2), 209–225. doi:10.1162/rest_a_00541

The *Review of Economics and Statistics* issued an article on military families and the rate of domestic violence that occurs within them. Cesur and Sabia state that women in these families are in need of the most protection due to the behavior that their husbands demonstrate after coming back from their service. The study in this report examines how active servicemen in the global war on terror manage their familial relationships. The findings conclude that combat instincts do play a role in the increase of domestic violence and child abuse in these families.

The report utilized extensive calculations of a representative sample to investigate the conclusion that domestic violence is rising in military families. Charts were also added to provide visual representation of the data found among this population.

Dank, M., Love, H., Esthappan, S., & Zweig, J. (2018, January). Exploratory research into the intersection of forced marriage, intimate partner violence, and sexual violence. Available at https://www.ncjrs.gov/pdffiles1/nij/grants/251485.pdf

> The objective of the study by the National Criminal Justice Reference Service was to understand the impact and experiences of women forced into marriage. According to the study, the most apparent pressure on individuals to marry was their family members because of various factors, including age of the victim, distaste in the victim's partner choice, and cultural and religious traditions. There were various cases where victims stated that they were abused by either their proposed partners or their future in-laws and were forced into intercourse before marriage. The study also includes the short-term and long-term effects that the victims acquire after being pressured into forced marriages.

Dotson, R., & Frydman, L. (2017). Neither security nor justice: Sexual and gender-based violence in El Salvador, Honduras, and Guatemala. Kids in Need of Defense. Available at https://supportkind.org/wp-content/uploads/2017/05/Neither-Security-nor-Justice_SGBV-Gang-Report-FINAL.pdf

> Kids in Need of Defense has sponsored a report to research the gender-based violence in Honduras, El Salvador, and Guatemala. The study included as participants migrant children as well as government officials who work for human rights initiatives. The main focus of the report is on the intersection between gang violence and gender-based violence. Research shows the girls that live in gang-controlled neighborhoods are told that their bodies belong to the gangs. Gangs in these three nations use sexual assault to control girls and manipulate men by threatening their female relatives. It gives various accounts

of female victims who have escaped to the United States because of this violence.

Dutton, D., & Painter, S. (1981). Traumatic bonding: The development of emotional attachments in battered women and other relationships of intermittent abuse. *Victimology: An International Journal* 6(1–4): 139–155.

Huang, G. (2018, June 30). How to make sure immigrant women aren't left out of #MeToo. Huffington Post. Available at https://www.huffpost.com/entry/opinion-huang-immigrant-women-me-too_n_5b33f9dee4b0b5e692f3f7e6
This article ties to the recent #MeToo movement that has spread across the United States. The article argues that more than 7 percent of the labor force of the United States consists of immigrant women working predominantly in service industry positions, with a large percentage of them having been sexually harassed or assaulted. The article also sheds light on the U-visas meant to help integrate immigrants to the workforce and the struggles and fears that these groups of people face daily when looking for employment opportunities.

Grace Huang, the author of this work, is director of the Asian Pacific Institute on Gender-Based Violence and focuses on bringing awareness to domestic violence, human trafficking, and other issues affecting women of the Asian and Pacific Islander communities.

Katz, J. (2017, October 24). How men can address sexual harassment. *Time* magazine. Available at http://time.com/4993854/men-roles-sexual-harassment/
In this *Time* article, Katz argues that men have a role in changing the social paradigm of domestic violence. Through the simple act of listening and being understanding, men can demonstrate support for women and their experiences. He states that by standing together and

creating encouraging movements like #HowIWillChange
to support #MeToo, men are taking steps in the positive
direction toward spreading awareness to men all around
the world that there is a grave misunderstanding that
needs to be addressed.

Jackson Katz is an educator and cofounder of the Mentors in Violence Prevention program. His article is inspiring and relevant to the social movements that affect
society today. It provides a solid case for the involvement
of men in breaking the silence that has trapped many domestic violence victims.

Swegman, C. (2016, February). The intersectionality of forced
marriage with other forms of abuse in the United States. Ta-
hirih Justice Center Forced Marriage Initiative. National Resource Center on Domestic Violence, Harrisburg, PA. Available
at https://vawnet.org/sites/default/files/materials/files/2016-09/
AR_ForcedMarriage.pdf

Casey Swegman in the article "The Intersectionality
of Forced Marriage with Other Forms of Abuse in the
United States" focuses on the effect of forced marriages
and other abuses on children. She touches upon several
forms of abuse that children worldwide go through and
then specifically speaks of the legislation that the United
States has created to fight against these issues. Her research shows that with today's technology, stalking still
remains a prevalent issue and that domestic violence is
common among forced childhood marriages.

The report includes various surveys and statistics on child
marriage in both the United States and Canada as well as
informs on various topics, including human trafficking,
female genital mutilation, stalking, and sexual harassment. The article also provides a final sheet that contains
the key findings of the report and summarizes the main
ideas discussed. The data is pulled from multiple established world organizations as well as government legal

documents from the mid-twentieth century onward, making it an updated, relevant source.

2011 College Dating Violence and Abuse Poll. (2011, June 9). Retrieved December 19, 2018, from Knowledge Networks website: http://www.loveisrespect.org/pdf/College_Dating_And_Abuse_Final_Study.pdf

Knowledge Network conducted a survey on dating violence among the college student population. Its findings show that white women are the primary targets of violence by their partners and they themselves do not realize the warning signs until later in the relationship. When friends and victims were asked why there was no action taken in these situations, the common response was that they simply did not know how to help or they did not want to get into any further trouble.

The sampling methodology for this report is representative of most college campuses in the United States. The company was able to reach a large-enough sample to find significant results. It also added the factors of age and living accommodations to further explain the attitudes and the frequency at which these abuse cases happen.

Wihbey, J. (2015, August 17). Domestic violence and abusive relationships: Research review. Available at https://journalistsresource.org/studies/society/gender-society/domestic-violence-abusive-relationships-research-review/

In this research review, John Wihbey brings awareness to the fact that domestic violence is a prevalent issue that has progressively gained media attention over the years. Using statistics from renowned global institutions like the World Health Organization, he argues that the rate of domestic violence has been decreasing as more legislation is put in place to solve the problem.

In addition, he refers to a representative study conducted in 2013 that speaks about the factors that encourage women to leave abusive relationships. This study stands out from those previously mentioned, in that it examines the relationship between higher education and divorce rates. The findings concluded that women with greater education degrees were more likely to file for divorce than those who did not. This report helps inform on a new approach toward domestic violence by using research sources that support the idea of education being a catalyst for action.

Journals and Magazines

Contemporary Justice Review

Everyday Sexism

Feministing

Gender & Society

Good Men Project

Jezebel

Journal of Interpersonal Violence

Men's Voices

Violence against Women: An International and Interdisciplinary Journal

Violence and Victims

The Voice: A Journal of the Battered Women's Movement

Women's Enews

Books

Abrahams, H. (2007). *Supporting women after domestic violence: Loss, trauma and recovery.* Philadelphia, PA: Jessica Kingsley Publishers.

Provides help for those who love someone who has endured abuse; discusses the trauma the victim endured and how loved ones can understand and support.

Aldarondo, E., & Mederos, F. (Eds.). (2002). *Programs for men who batter.* Kingston, NJ: Civic Research Institute.
  Discusses batterer intervention programs and other efforts to change the behavior of abusive men.

Anderson, K. (2009). *Enhancing resilience in survivors of family violence.* New York, NY: Springer Publishing Company.
  Assists survivors in understanding that abuse is never their fault and provides strategies for hope and resilience.

Bales, K. (2007). *Ending slavery: How we free today's slaves.* Berkeley: University of California Press.
  Includes data and descriptions of human trafficking and offers strategies for ending it.

Bales, K., & Sudalter, R. (2010). *The slave next door: Human trafficking and slavery in America today.* Berkeley: University of California Press.
  Emphasizes that human trafficking also occurs in the United States and provides resources for understanding it.

Banaszak, L. (2005). *The U.S. women's movement in global perspective.* Lanham, MD: Rowman & Littlefield.
  An historical overview of the women's movement in the United States and includes comparisons to other efforts toward gender equality globally.

Bancroft, L. (2002). *The batterer as parent: Addressing the impact of domestic violence on family dynamics.* Thousand Oaks, CA: Sage.
  Focuses on the effect of domestic violence on children.

Bancroft, L. (2003). *Why does he do that?: Inside the minds of angry and controlling men.* New York, NY: Berkley Trade.
  Classic in the field focused on understanding abusers.

Bancroft, L. (2005). *When dad hurts mom: Helping your children heal the wounds of witnessing abuse*. New York, NY: Berkley Trade.
> Offers strategies to assist children who have witnessed abuse in the home. Useful for parents as well as advocates.

Barnett, O., Miller-Perrin, C., & Perrin, R. (2011). *Family violence across the lifespan: An introduction* (3rd ed.). Thousand Oaks, CA: Sage.
> Used in college classes largely; offers a description of various forms of abuse and emphasizes how it may be experienced differently across the lifespan.

Batstone, D. (2007). *Not for sale*. New York: HarperCollins.
> Addresses the scope and extent of human trafficking and sexual slavery.

Baumgardner. J., & Richards, A. (2005). *Grassroots: A field guide for feminist activism*. New York: Farrar, Straus, & Giroux.
> Offers stories and strategies for feminist activism.

Benedict, J. (1997). *Public heroes, private felons*. Boston, MA: Northeastern University Press.
> Addresses the overrepresentation of some collegiate athletes in cases of domestic violence and sexual assault.

Benedict, J. (1998). *Athletes and acquaintance rape*. Boston, MA: Northeastern University Press.
> Provides data and descriptions of cases of acquaintance rape involving athletes.

Benedict, J. (2001). *Out of bounds: Inside the NBA's culture of rape, violence and crime*. Boston, MA: Northeastern University Press.
> Study of crime committed by NBA players in the 1990s, including domestic violence and sexual assault.

Bentovim, A. (2009). *Safeguarding children living with trauma and family violence: Evidence-based assessment, analysis and planning interventions.* Philadelphia, PA: Jessica Kingsley Publishers.
Focuses on tools and strategies for assisting children who have witnessed abuse.

Berns, N. (2004). *Framing the victim: Domestic violence, media, and social problems.* Piscataway, NJ: Aldine.
Discusses concerns about how media covers domestic violence.

Betancourt, M. (1997). *What to do when love turns violent: A practical resource for women in abusive relationships.* New York: HarperResource.
Useful in advocacy settings with victims; focuses on understanding abusers and healing victims.

Boyle, K. (2004). *Media violence: Gendering the debates.* London, England: Sage.
Addresses how media depicts violence, focusing largely on gender issues.

Brewster, S. (1997). *To be an anchor in the storm.* New York: Ballantine Books.
Helpful to those offering support to a victim of abuse.

Brewster, S. (2005). *Helping her get free: A guide for families and friends of abused women.* New York, NY: Seal Press.
Useful tool for family and friends who want to assist someone in an abusive relationship.

Brownridge, D. (2009). *Violence against women: Vulnerable populations.* New York: Routledge.
Examines the demographic characteristics that make some women more vulnerable to abuse.

Bumiller, K. (2008). *In an abusive state: How neoliberalism appropriated the feminist movement against sexual violence.* Durham, NC: Duke University Press.
>   Critique of the nonprofit model of assistance for victims in the United States.

Buzzawa, E., & Buzzawa, C. (2002). *Domestic violence: The criminal justice response.* Thousand Oaks, CA: Sage.
>   Tool for criminal justice students, professors, and practitioners emphasizing the best law enforcement responses to domestic violence.

Ching-In, C., Dulani, J., & Piepzna-Samarasinha, L. (Eds.). (2011). *The revolution starts at home: Confronting intimate violence within activist networks.* Boston, MA: South End Press.
>   Addresses the scope, manner, frequency, and response when abuse occurs within progressive communities.

Chu, J. (2011). *Rebuilding shattered lives* (2nd ed.). New York: Wiley.
>   Focuses on how victims of abuse can heal and move on.

Cloitre, M., Cohen, L., & Koenen, K. (2006). *Treating survivors of childhood abuse: Psychotherapy for the interrupted life.* New York: Guilford.
>   Helpful for practitioners working with victims of abuse.

Cook, P. (2009). *Abused men: The hidden side of domestic violence.* Westport, CT: Praeger.
>   Discusses the scope, types, and dynamics of abuse perpetrated against men as well as resources for them.

Dalpiaz, C. (2008). *Breaking free, starting over: Parenting in the aftermath of family violence.* Santa Barbara, CA: Praeger.
>   Offers advice to survivors who have to parent with abusers and to those who have no contact with them.

Day, A. (2009). *Domestic violence—working with men: Research, practice experiences and integrated responses.* Alexandria, Australia: Federation Press.
>   Practitioner guide for working with men, both as perpetrators and as victims.

Douglas, K. (1997). *Invisible wounds: A self-help guide for women in destructive relationships.* London, England: Trafalgar Square Publishing.
>   Tool for survivors who want to understand and heal from abuse.

Dugan, M. (2000). *It's my life now: Starting over after an abusive relationship or domestic violence.* New York: Routledge.
>   Personal story about abuse and healing.

Dutton, D. (2007). *Rethinking domestic violence.* Vancouver, Canada: UBC Press.
>   Review of research about domestic violence; emphasizes that abuse is bilateral.

Dworkin, A. (1997). *Life and death.* New York: Free Press.
>   Collection of essays by Dworkin sharing her political opinions on feminist issues.

Edleson, J. (2006). *Parenting by men who batter: New directions for assessment and intervention.* Cambridge, MA: Oxford University Press.
>   Advocate tool for working with male abusers, specifically emphasizing parenting skills.

Faludi, S. (1991). *Backlash: The undeclared war against American women.* New York, NY: Doubleday.
>   Feminist classic discussing the backlash against the 1970s' women's rights movement in the 1980s.

Finley, L. (Ed.). (2013). *Encyclopedia of domestic violence and abuse.* Santa Barbara, CA: ABC-CLIO.
>   Reference tool addressing abuse and sexual assault.

Finley, L. (2016). *Domestic abuse and sexual assault in popular culture.* Santa Barbara, CA: ABC-CLIO.
 Focuses on how TV, film, music, radio, and video games depict abuse.

Finley, L., & Stringer, E. (Eds.). (2010). *Beyond burning bras: Feminist activism for everyone.* Santa Barbara, CA: Praeger.
 Stories from educators, advocates, and activists for gender equality.

Freedman, E. (2002). *No turning back: The history of feminism and the future of women.* New York, NY: Ballantine Books.
 Comprehensive history of the feminist movement.

Geffner, R. (2009). *Children exposed to violence: Current issues, interventions and research.* New York: Routledge.
 Focuses on helping heal children who have been exposed to violence in the home.

Goodman, L. (2007). *Listening to battered women: A survivor-centered approach to advocacy, mental health, and justice.* Washington, DC: American Psychological Association.
 Tool for advocates, social workers, and clinicians working with victims of abuse.

Gordon, L. (1989). *Heroes of their own lives: The politics and history of family violence.* New York: Penguin.
 Detailed history of violence in the home.

Haaken, J. (2010). *What does storytelling tell us about domestic violence? Hand knocks: Domestic violence and the psychology of storytelling.* London, England: Routledge.
 Emphasizes the importance of victims' stories in their healing and in ending abuse.

Harne, L. (2008). *Tackling domestic violence.* Bloomington, ID: Open Universe Publishing.
 Focuses on efforts to help victims and hold abusers accountable.

Herman, J. (1997). *Trauma and recovery: The aftermath of violence—from domestic abuse to political terror.* New York: Basic Books.
    Classic text for understanding the trauma victims endure.

Herman, J. (2015). *Trauma and recovery: The aftermath of violence—from domestic abuse to political terror* (2nd ed.). New York: Basic Books.
    Updated version of Herman's classic text.

Hertica, M. (2001). *Growing free: A manual for survivors of domestic violence.* New York: Routledge.
    Guide to use with survivors focusing on healing and moving forward.

Hester, M. (2007). *Making an impact: Children and domestic violence: A reader.* Philadelphia, PA: Jessica Kingsley Publishers.
    Compendium of research and strategies for working with child victims.

Holland, J. (2006). *Misogyny: The world's oldest prejudice.* New York, NY: Carroll & Graf.
    History of misogyny, globally and in the United States.

Humphreys, C. (2006a). *Domestic violence and child protection: Directions for good practice.* Philadelphia, PA: Jessica Kingsley Publisher.
    Emphasizes best practices in keeping children safe when there is domestic violence in their homes.

Humphreys, C. (2006b). *Talking about domestic abuse: A photo activity workbook to develop communication between mothers and young people.* Philadelphia, PA: Jessica Kingsley Publishers.
    Guide for parents to address abuse with their teens.

Humphreys, C. (2006c). *Talking to my mum: A picture workbook for workers, mothers and children affected by domestic abuse.* Philadelphia, PA: Jessica Kingsley Publishers.
    Guide for parents to discuss abuse with their children.

INCITE! Women of Color against Violence. (Eds.). (2007). *The revolution will not be funded: Beyond the non-profit industrial complex.* Boston, MA: South End Press.
> Stresses the concerns about nonprofit status and suggests other models of community activism.

Johnson, M., & Finley, L. (Eds.). (2018). *Trumpism.* Cambridge: Cambridge Scholars Press.
> Collection focuses on gender and the Trump election/presidency.

Kaschak, E. (2002). *Intimate betrayal: Domestic violence in lesbian relationships.* New York: Routledge.
> Addresses the scope, extent, and types of abuse in lesbian relationships as well as police response.

Katz, J. (2006). *The macho paradox.* Naperville, IL: Sourcebooks.
> Emphasizes that gender role norms contribute to poor health outcomes for both women and men.

Kilbourne, J. (2000). *Can't buy my love: How advertising changes the way we think and feel.* New York, NY: Free Press.
> Classic text focusing on how advertisements depict women.

Kimmel, M. (2006). *Manhood in America* (2nd ed.). New York, NY: Oxford University Press.
> History of manhood and how gender role norms are shaped over time.

Kimmel, M. (2008). *Guyland: The perilous world where boys become men.* New York, NY: Harper.
> Looks at the culture of college-age men and their hyper-masculine bonding.

Kimmel, M. (2013). *Angry white men.* New York, NY: Harper.
> Addresses why white men are so angry by advancements in gender equality and, in particular, their use of firearms.

Kristof, N., & WuDunn, S. (2009). *Half the sky: Turning oppression into opportunity for women worldwide.* New York: NY: Alfred A. Knopf.
  Shows the extent of global gender inequalities as well as stories of resilience and activism.

Kristof, N., & WuDunn, S. (2014). *A path emerges: Transforming lives, creating opportunity.* New York: NY: Vintage House.
  Emphasizes how people can work in community to address gender inequality and other social issues.

Kubany, E. (2004). *Healing the trauma of domestic violence: A workbook for women.* Oakland, CA: New Harbinger.
  Workbook for use with or by female victims of abuse.

Kubany, E. (2008). *Treating PTSD in battered women: A step-by-step manual for therapists & counselors.* Oakland, CA: New Harbinger.
  Tool for practitioners to help victims suffering from PTSD.

LaViolette, A. (2000). *It could happen to anyone: Why battered women stay.* Thousand Oaks, CA: Sage.
  Addresses the complex and unique reasons why victims stay with abusers.

Leonard, E. (2002). *Convicted survivors: The imprisonment of battered women who kill.* New York, NY: SUNY Press.
  Detailed research on women's self-defense and related legal issues.

Lockhart, L., & Danis, F. (2010). *Domestic violence: Intersectionality and culturally competent practice.* New York: Columbia University Press.
  Focuses on understanding abuse as it is experienced by victims of color and other demographic characteristics.

Mahmoody, M. (2017). *My name is Mahtob: A daring escape, a life of fear, and the forgiveness that set me free.* New York: Thomas Nelson.
> Story of a girl whose mother had to escape her abuser in Iran to keep herself and her daughter safe.

McNulty, F. (1989). *The burning bed.* New York, NY: Avon.
> True story of Francine Hughes, who was acquitted of setting fire to her abusive husband while he slept.

Muhammad, M. (2009). *Scared silent: The Mildred Muhammad story.* New York, NY: Strebor Books.
> Personal story of abuse and escape.

Murray, A. (2008). *From outrage to courage: Women taking action for health and justice.* Monroe, ME: Common Courage.
> Global examination of efforts to address abuse and other gender inequalities.

Penfold, R. (2006). *Dragonslippers: This is what an abusive relationship looks like.* New York, NY: Grove Press.
> Detailed look at the many forms of abuse.

Pleck, E. (1989). *Domestic tyranny: The making of American social policy against family violence from colonial times to the present.* New York, NY: Oxford.
> Historical examination of domestic violence and other forms of family violence in the United States.

Radford, L. (2006). *Mothering through domestic violence.* Philadelphia, PA: Jessica Kingsley Publishers.
> Discusses how abuse affects mothers and children.

Richie, B. (1995). *Compelled to crime: The gender entrapment of battered, black women.* New York: Taylor & Francis.
> Focuses on self-defense by black women.

Rowland, D. (2004). *The boundaries of her body: The troubling history of women's rights in America*. Naperville, IL: Sphinx.
Comprehensive history of women's rights in the United States.

Russell, B. (2010). *Battered woman syndrome as a legal defense: History, effectiveness, and implications*. Jefferson, NC: McFarland.
Detailed examination of battered woman syndrome in court.

Sanderson, C. (2008). *Counselling survivors of domestic abuse*. Philadelphia, PA: Jessica Kingsley Publishers.
Tool for practitioners who work with victims of abuse.

Sanderson, C. (2009). *Introduction to counselling survivors of interpersonal trauma*. Philadelphia, PA: Jessica Kingsley Publishers.
Resource for practitioners helping victims of domestic violence and other traumas.

Smith, A. (2005). *Conquest: Sexual violence and American Indian genocide*. Boston, MA: South End Press.
Focuses on sexual assault and domestic violence affecting Native women.

Snyder, R. (2019). *No visible bruises: What we don't know about domestic violence can kill us*. London: Bloomsbury.
Examines psychological abuse and its effect.

Sterne, A. (2009). *Domestic violence and children: A handbook for schools and early years settings*. London: Routledge.
Handbook for working with school-age youth.

Straus, M., Gelles, R., & Steinmetz, S. (2009). *Behind closed doors: Violence in the American family*. New Brunswick, NJ: Transaction.
Research-based examination of domestic violence and other forms of family violence.

Sundahl, S., & Raab, J. (2019). *Stalker poison: A safety guide for women experiencing domestic violence and stalking.* Independently published. Available on Amazon.com
> Guidance for females who want to obtain safety from abuse or stalking.

Weiss, E. (2003). *Family and friends' guide to domestic violence: How to listen, talk and take action when someone you care about is being abused.* Volcano, CA: Volcano Press.
> Helps family members and friends understand abuse.

Weitzman, S. (2001). *"Not to people like us": Hidden abuse in upscale marriages.* New York: Basic Books.
> Therapists' observations about abuse among wealthier women.

Wiehe, V. (1997). *Sibling abuse: Hidden physical, emotional and sexual trauma* (2nd ed.). Thousand Oaks, CA: Sage.
> Focuses on sibling-on-sibling abuse.

Wilson, K. (2005). *When violence begins at home: A comprehensive guide to understanding and ending domestic violence.* New York: Hunter House.
> Detailed discussion and research about domestic violence.

Wolfe, D., & Temple, J. (2018). *Adolescent dating violence: Theory, research and prevention.* Cambridge, MA: Academic Press.
> Presents research about dating violence and appropriate interventions.

Curricula, Manuals, and Handbooks

Be Strong from the Inside Out. N.d. From Peace over Violence. Available at www.youthoverviolence.org
> Focuses on encouraging young people to take action for peace in their relationships, schools, and communities.

Choose Respect. 2007. Centers for Disease Control. Available at https://www.cdc.gov/careerpaths/scienceambassador/documents/choose-respect-respect-data.pdf
Widely used dating violence curriculum.

Creighton, A., & Kivel, P. (1993). *Helping teens stop violence: A practical guide for counselors, educators, and parents* (2nd ed.). Alameda, CA: Hunter House.
Guide for adults working with teens to stop violence in many forms.

Creighton, A., & Kivel, P. (1998). *Young men's work: Stopping violence and building community: A multi-session group program.* Center City, MN: Hazelden.
Tool for working with young men who have committed violence.

Expect Respect. 1989. The Safe Alliance. Available for order at https://www.safeaustin.org/our-services/prevention-and-education/expect-respect/program-manuals-and-one-day-training/
Widely used dating violence curriculum.

Fortune, M. (1991). *Violence in the family: A workshop curriculum for clergy and other helpers.* Cleveland, OH: Pilgrim House.
Faith-based tool for addressing abuse.

Foshee, V., & Langwick, F. 2010. Safe Dates. Available at http://www.violencepreventionworks.org/public/safe_dates.page
Curriculum for addressing abuse and sexual assault.

The Fourth "R." 2009. Youth.gov. Available at https://youthrelationships.org/fourth-r-programs
Dating violence curriculum emphasizing respect in relationships.

Goodman, M., & Fallon, B. (1995). *Pattern changing for abused women: An educational program.* Thousand Oaks, CA: Sage.
Tool for working with victims of abuse.

Kivel, P. (1993). *Men's work: Comprehensive violence treatment.* Center City, MN: Hazelden.
Guide for working with male abusers.

Kivel, P., & Creighton, A. (2002). *Making the peace: A 15-session violence prevention curriculum for young people.* Alameda, CA: Hunter House.
Curriculum for teens on violence prevention.

Love—All That and More. N.d. Faith Trust Institute. Available for purchase at https://store.faithtrustinstitute.org/products/love-all-that-and-more-a-dvd-curriculum-on-healthy-teen-relationships
Christian-focused curriculum on healthy relationships.

Love Is Not Abuse. 2014. Break the Cycle. Available at https://www.breakthecycle.org/sites/default/files/pdf/lina-curriculum-high-school.pdf
Guide for working with teens; emphasizes healthy boundaries.

Mentors in Violence Prevention. 1993. Center for the Study of Sport in Society. Available for order at https://www.mvpstrat.com/training-materials/order-mvp-playbooks
Emphasizes the empowerment of bystanders to disrupt abuse and assault.

MOST Clubs. 2000. Men Can Stop Rape. Available at https://mcsr.org/men-of-strength-most-club
Empowers men to work with one another and with women to stop sexual assault.

Patterson, S. (2002). *I wish the hitting would stop.* Fargo, ND: Green Flag.
Tool for helping people understand why abuse occurs.

Strong Girls, Healthy Relationships. N.d. Jewish Women International. Available at https://www.jwi.org/tools
Jewish-focused curriculum about dating violence.

Vasquez, H., Myhand. N., & Creighton, A. (2003). *Making allies, making friends: A curriculum for making the peace in middle school communities.* Alameda, CA: Hunter House.
    Middle school curriculum for violence prevention.

Documentaries

The Bro Code: How Contemporary Culture Creates Sexist Men. (2011). Media Education Foundation. Available for purchase at www.mediaed.org
    Addresses misogynistic male bonding.

City of Shelter: A Coordinated Community Response to Domestic Violence. (2006). Global Village Communications. Available for purchase at www.cityofshelter.org
    Showcases the power of an effective community response to abuse.

Domestic Violence: What Churches Can Do. (2002). Faith Trust Institute. Available for purchase at www.faithtrustinstitute.org
    Provides suggestions for Christians and churches seeking to address domestic violence.

Dreamworlds 3: Desire, Sex & Power in Music Video. (2007). Media Education Foundation. Available for purchase at www.mediaed.org
    Examines the depiction of gender in music videos.

Flirting with Danger. (2012). Media Education Foundation. Available for purchase at www.mediaed.org
    Looks at the line between consent and coercion for young women.

Generation M: Misogyny in Media and Culture. (2008). Media Education Foundation. Available for purchase at www.mediaed.org
    Addresses how media promotes misogyny.

Half the Sky: Turning Oppression into Opportunity for Women. (2012). Show of Force and Half the Sky Foundation. Available for purchase at http://www.pbs.org/independentlens/half-the-sky/video/

> Starring many celebrities; shows global efforts to address human trafficking and other forms of gender-based violence.

Hip Hop: Beyond Beats and Rhymes. (2006). Media Education Foundation. Available for purchase at www.mediaed.org

> Focuses on sexism and violence in rap music.

Killing Us Softly 4. (2010). Media Education Foundation. Available for purchase at www.mediaed.org

> Addresses how advertising depicts women.

Not Just a Game: Power, Politics & American Sports. (2010). Media Education Foundation. Available for purchase at www.mediaed.org

> Examination of gender inequalities in U.S. sports.

Power and Control: Domestic Violence in America. (n.d.). Available for purchase at https://www.powerandcontrolfilm.com/

> Documentary about the dynamics of abuse.

Private Violence. (2014). Available for purchase at http://www.privateviolence.com/

> Shows the scope, extent, and dynamics of abuse.

Something My Father Would Do. (n.d.). Futures without Violence. Available for purchase at www.futureswithoutviolence.org

> Addresses the way abuse affects kids.

There's No Fear like Home: Growing Up with Family Violence. (n.d.). Intermedia. Available for purchase at www.intermedia-inc.com

> Shows how abuse affects kids in the short- and long term.

Tough Guise 2. (2013). Media Education Foundation. Available for purchase at www.mediaed.org
  Follow-up to the original showing how traditional gender roles harm both women and men.

Toxic Relationships: The Next Generation Speaks out about Dating Violence. (2000). Insight Media. Available for purchase at www.insight-media.com
  Focuses on teen dating violence from a teen perspective.

Voices of Survivors. (n.d.). Futures without Violence. Available for purchase at www.futureswithoutviolence.org
  Shares stories of survivors to show the dynamics of abuse.

When Injuries Speak, Who Will Listen? A Healthcare Response to Domestic Violence. (n.d.). Intermedia. Available for purchase at www.intermedia-inc.com
  Focused on how health-care providers can screen for and respond to abuse.

Wrestling with Manhood: Boys, Bullying and Battering. (2002). Media Education Foundation. Available for purchase at www .mediaed.org
  Addresses how world wrestling utilizes story lines that promote abuse.

Short Videos

Daumit, A. (2017). Rolling with the punches: Be the change that knocks out domestic violence. TED. Available at https:// www.youtube.com/watch?v=Y28N0BwyMEI
  Personal story of abuse and resilience.

Harris, N. (2014). How childhood trauma affects health across a lifetime. TED. Available at https://www.ted.com/talks/nadine_ burke_harris_how_childhood_trauma_affects_health_across_ a_lifetime

Emphasizes findings from the Adverse Child Experiences Studies and how pediatricians can help address violence.

Judd, A. (2016). How online abuse of women has spiraled out of control. TED. Available at https://www.ted.com/talks/ash ley_judd_how_online_abuse_of_women_has_spiraled_out_ of_control
   Actress Ashley Judd shares her experiences with online abuse.

Katz, J. (2013). Violence against women: It's a men's issue. TED. Available at https://www.youtube.com/watch?v=KTvSfeCRxe8
   Focuses on how men must take action to end gender-based violence.

Neben, B. Preventing teen dating violence from the inside out. TED. Available at https://www.youtube.com/watch?v=iwuy5 UZy3Gw
   Addresses how to build strong teen relationships.

Parekh, A. (2016). Understanding relationship abuse in the digital age. TED. Available at https://www.youtube.com/watch?v=5e 61e3arayM
   Description of how technology affects abuse.

Reeay, H. (2016). Domestic violence: I choose to be her voice. TED. Available at https://www.youtube.com/watch?v=A5Adq-jVQ1s
   Focuses on supporting survivors of abuse.

Soler, S. (2014). How we turned the tide on domestic violence. TED. Available at https://www.youtube.com/watch?v=Li4-1y yrsTI
   Emphasizes improvements in the response to abuse.

Steiner, L. (2013). Why domestic violence victims don't leave. TED. Available at https://www.ted.com/talks/leslie_morgan_ steiner_why_domestic_violence_victims_don_t_leave
   Survivor explains why it was difficult to leave her abuser.

State and National Coalitions

State and national coalitions work to address abuse via the following strategies: lobbying legislatures for the improvement of protection of order laws; helping to set standards for care and service for member organizations; seeking and distributing funding from state and other sources; developing training materials and information for state officials; advocating for housing and public housing policies; and working with media to raise awareness.

ACTION OHIO
Website: www.actionohio.org
E-mail: actionohio@wowway.biz

Alabama Coalition against Domestic Violence
Website: www.acadv.org
E-mail: info@acadv.org

Alaska Network on Domestic and Sexual Violence
Website: www.andvsa.org
E-mail: andvsa@andvsa.org

America Samoa Alliance against Domestic and Sexual Violence
Website: www.asalliance.co
E-mail: asadsv@gmail.com

Arizona Coalition to End Sexual & Domestic Violence
Website: www.acesdv.org
E-mail: info@acesdv.org

Arkansas Coalition against Domestic Violence
Website: www.domesticpeace.com
E-mail: info@domesticpeace.com

California Partnership to End Domestic Violence
Website: www.cpedv.org
E-mail: info@cpedv.org

Connecticut Coalition against Domestic Violence
Website: www.ctcadv.org
E-mail: contactus@ctcadv.org

DC Coalition against Domestic Violence
Website: www.dccadv.org
E-mail: info@dccadv.org

Delaware Coalition against Domestic Violence
Website: www.dcadv.org
E-mail: dcadvadmin@dcadv.org

Florida Coalition against Domestic Violence
Website: www.fcadv.org

Georgia Coalition against Domestic Violence
Website: www.gcadv.org
E-mail: info@gcadv.org

Guam Coalition against Sexual Assault and Family Violence
Website: www.guamcoalition.org

Hawaii State Coalition against Domestic Violence
Website: www.hscadv.org
E-mail: admin@hscadv.org

Idaho Coalition against Sexual and Domestic Violence
Website: www.idvsa.org
E-mail: info@engagingvoices.org

Illinois Coalition against Domestic Violence
Website: www.ilcadv.org
E-mail: ilcadv@ilcadv.org

Indiana Coalition against Domestic Violence
Website: www.icadvinc.org
E-mail: icadv@icadvinc.org

Iowa Coalition against Domestic Violence
Website: www.icadv.org
E-mail: admin@icadv.org

Jane Doe, Inc./Massachusetts Coalition against Sexual Assault and Domestic Violence
Website: www.janedoe.org
E-mail: info@janedoe.org

Kansas Coalition against Sexual and Domestic Violence
Website: www.kcsdv.org
E-mail: coalition@kcsdv.org

Kentucky Domestic Violence Association
Website: www.kcadv.org
E-mail: info@kcadv.org

Louisiana Coalition against Domestic Violence
Website: www.lcadv.org
E-mail: sheila@lcadv.org

Maine Coalition to End Domestic Violence
Website: www.mcedv.org
E-mail: info@mcedv.org

Maryland Network against Domestic Violence
Website: www.mnadv.org
E-mail: info@mnadv.org

Michigan Coalition against Domestic and Sexual Violence
Website: www.mcadsv.org
E-mail: general@mcadsv.org

Minnesota Coalition for Battered Women
Website: www.mcbw.org
E-mail: mcbw@mcbw.org

Mississippi Coalition against Domestic Violence
Website: www.mcadv.org
E-mail: support@mcadv.org

Missouri Coalition against Domestic and Sexual Violence
Website: www.mocadsv.org
E-mail: mocadsv@mocadsv.org

Montana Coalition against Domestic & Sexual Violence
Website: www.mcadsv.com
E-mail: mtcoalition@mcadsv.com

Nebraska Domestic Violence Sexual Assault Coalition
Website: www.nebraskacoalition.org
E-mail: help@ndvsac.org

Nevada Network against Domestic Violence
Website: www.nnadv.org
Email: info@nnadv.org

New Hampshire Coalition against Domestic and Sexual Violence
Website: www.nhcadsv.org
E-mail: info@nhcadsv.org

New Jersey Coalition against Domestic Violence
Website: www.njcedv.org
E-mail: info@njcedv.org

New Mexico Coalition against Domestic Violence
Website: www.nmcadv.org
E-mail: info@nmcadv.org

New York State Coalition against Domestic Violence
Website: www.nyscadv.org
E-mail: nyscadv@nyscadv.org

North Carolina Coalition against Domestic Violence
Website: www.nccadv.org
Email: info@nccadv.org

North Dakota Council on Abused Women's Services
Website: www.ndcaws.org
E-mail: ndcaws@ndcaws.org

Northern Marianas Coalition against Domestic and Sexual Violence
E-mail: info@endviolencenmi.org

Ohio Domestic Violence Network
Website: www.odvn.org
E-mail: info@odvn.org

Oklahoma Coalition against Domestic Violence and Sexual Assault
Website: www.ocadvsa.org
Email: info@ocadvsa.org

Oregon Coalition against Domestic and Sexual Violence
Website: www.ocadsv.com
E-mail: adminasst@ocadsv.com

Pennsylvania Coalition against Domestic Violence
Website: www.pcadv.org
Email: info@pcadv.org

Puerto Rico Coalition against Domestic Violence and Sexual Assault: Coordinadora Paz para la Mujer
Website: http://www.pazparalamujer.org/
E-mail: info@pazparalamujer.org

Rhode Island Coalition against Domestic Violence
Website: www.ricadv.org
E-mail: ricadv@ricadv.org

South Carolina Coalition against Domestic Violence and Sexual Assault
Website: www.sccadvasa.org
E-mail: info@sccadvasa.org

South Dakota Coalition Ending Domestic & Sexual Violence
Website: http://www.sdcedsv.org/
E-mail: chris@sdcedsv.org

South Dakota Network against Family Violence & Sexual Assault

Website: https://sdnafvsa.com/home/

E-mail: krista@sdnafvsa.org

Tennessee Coalition to End Domestic and Sexual Violence

Website: https://www.tncoalition.org/

Email: info@tncoalition.org

Texas Council on Family Violence

Website: www.tcfv.org

E-mail: info@tcfv.org

Utah Domestic Violence Council

Website: www.udvac.org

E-mail: admin@udvc.org

Vermont Network against Domestic Violence and Sexual Assault

Website: www.vtnetwork.org

E-mail: info@vtnetwork.org

Violence Free Colorado

Website: www.violencefreecolorado.org/

E-mail: info@violencefreeco.org

Virginia Sexual & Domestic Violence Action Alliance

Website: www.vsdvalliance.org

E-mail: info@vsdvalliance.org

Virgin Islands Domestic Violence & Sexual Assault Council

Website: www.vidvsac.org

E-mail: info@vidvsac.org

Washington State Coalition against Domestic Violence
Website: www.wscadv.org
E-mail: wscadv@wscadv.org

Washington State Native American Coalition against Domestic and Sexual Assault
Website: www.womenspirit.net
Email: Info@womenspirit.net

West Virginia Coalition against Domestic Violence
Website: www.wvcadv.org
Email: info@wcadv.org

Wisconsin Coalition against Domestic Violence
Website: www.endabusewi.org
E-mail: wcadv@wcadv.org

Women's Coalition of St. Croix
Website: www.wcstx.org
E-mail: wcsc@pennswoods.net

Wyoming Coalition against Domestic Violence and Sexual Assault
Website: www.wyomingdvsa.org
E-mail: info@wyomingdvsa.org

Organizations

Abused Deaf Women's Advocacy Services

The Abused Deaf Women's Advocacy Services (ADWAS) provides a variety of services for the deaf, most notably in its partnership with National Domestic Violence Hotline in providing U.S. nationwide helpline services to the nonhearing via video phone calls, instant messaging, and e-mail. Contact 1-800-812-1001 or nationaldeafhotline@adwas.org.

Alianza: National Latino Alliance for the Elimination of Domestic Violence

This organization focuses on the unique needs of Latino/Latina victims of domestic violence, providing information and resources.

American Bar Association Commission on Domestic Violence

The ABA Commission on Domestic Violence seeks to increase access to justice for victims of domestic violence, sexual assault, and stalking by mobilizing the legal profession. The Commission helps increase the number of well-trained and supported attorneys providing representation to victims by providing creative training opportunities for lawyers, law students, and other legal advocates.

American Civil Liberties Union

The American Civil Liberties Union promotes civil rights on a number of issues, including gender-based violence, provides resources as well as legal advocacy, and promotes policy changes.

American Humane Association

The American Humane Association provides information related to the correlation between pet abuse and domestic violence.

American Medical Association

The American Medical Association (AMA) provides information and resources for health-care professionals about domestic violence, including screening tools and protocols once abuse is identified.

Amnesty International

Amnesty International (AI) is a global human rights watchdog. Gender-based violence is one of its many campaigns. AI uses the power of the masses through letter-writing, events, and advocacy to effect social change.

Asian & Pacific Islander Institute on Domestic Violence

The Asian & Pacific Islander Institute on Domestic Violence is a national resource center and clearinghouse on gender violence in Asian American, Native Hawaiian, and Pacific Islander communities. It serves a national network of community-based organizations; advocates and professionals in legal, health, mental health, and social services; government agencies; state coalitions; national domestic and sexual violence organizations; and activists from communities and social justice organizations working to eliminate violence against women. Its goals are to strengthen advocacy, promote community organizing, and influence systems change. It identifies and addresses critical issues, provides technical assistance and training, conducts research, and engages in policy advocacy.

Asian Task Force against Domestic Violence

The Asian Task Force against Domestic Violence (ATASK) primarily serves Asian families and individuals in Massachusetts and New England who suffer from or are at risk of suffering from domestic violence. Its clients include a range of Asian ethnic populations. ATASK embraces and represents all ages, cultures, abilities, and sexual preferences.

Asista

Asista works to centralize, enhance, and expand immigration assistance to frontline advocates and attorneys who provide legal assistance to immigrant victims.

The Audre Lorde Project

The Audre Lorde Project promotes community wellness and economic and social justice for all.

Ayuda

Ayuda provides information and resources for immigrant victims of domestic violence.

Battered Women's Justice Project

The Battered Women's Justice Project (BWJP) provides training and technical assistance on civil, legal, and criminal justice system issues related to violence against women, including survivors who have been charged with crimes. For assistance, call 1-800-903-0111 and follow the prompts to access assistance on the issues on which you have questions.

Break the Cycle

Break the Cycle provides comprehensive dating abuse programs exclusively to young people aged twelve to twenty-four. From the classroom to the courtroom to the floor of Congress, it works to give young people, and those who care about them, the tools they need to live safer, healthier lives. Its website offers national resources as well as legal resources to those who live in the Washington, D.C., area.

Bureau of Justice Statistics Clearinghouse

The Bureau of Justice Statistics Clearinghouse provides statistics and research on various crime topics, including domestic violence, sexual assault, and stalking.

A Call to Men

A Call to Men works to create a world where men and boys are loving and respectful and all women and girls are valued and safe. It provides training, seminars, workshops, and campus initiatives that have reached more than 100,000 individuals and 3,000 organizations since its origin in 2002.

Camp Hope

First nationwide camping and mentoring initiative in the United States for kids exposed to domestic violence, Camp Hope operates in collaboration with Family Justice Centers, Multi-Agency Centers, and community-based domestic violence and child advocacy agencies across the United States at no cost to campers or their families.

The Center for Survivor Agency and Justice

The Center for Survivor Agency and Justice (CSAJ) is a national organization dedicated to enhancing advocacy for survivors of oppression-based intimate partner violence. CSAJ seeks to promote survivor-centered advocacy by enhancing the work of attorneys, by organizing communities, and by offering leadership on critical issues facing survivors and advocates throughout the nation. CSAJ strives to enhance advocacy by cultivating a community of attorneys and advocates who are skilled in survivor-centered advocacy and capable of meeting the entire spectrum of civil legal assistance needs of survivors through their own advocacy and in partnership with others.

The Center on Domestic Violence—University of Colorado Denver

Founded in 2000, the Center on Domestic Violence is an academic, research, and service center based at the University of Colorado Denver. The Center established the first graduate-level academic program in the nation to address the serious social issue of domestic violence through leadership development. The Center's programs prepare individuals, organizations, and communities with the knowledge and ability to reduce, treat, intervene and prevent interpersonal violence.

The Center has three primary goals: (1) develop skilled and informed leaders across the country for the movement to end interpersonal violence; (2) inform and empower service providers, advocates, and policymakers through original research; and (3) serve the community through direct services, capacity-building initiatives, training, and advocacy.

These combined efforts are reflected in the center's mission: to end domestic violence by fostering institutional and social change through leadership development, education, research, and community collaboration.

Centre for Research & Education on Violence against Women & Children

This resourceful Canadian group offers an array of resources, including studies on workplace violence and a website for hair-care professionals and those in the beauty industry (Cut It Out). The organization also offers trainings on safe schools, media literacy, and more.

Childhelp USA

Childhelp USA provides information and resources related to child abuse and neglect as well as child victims of domestic violence.

Childhood Domestic Violence Association

The Childhood Domestic Violence Association offers a number of groundbreaking tools and resources, including books, articles, and documentaries related to childhood exposure to domestic violence.

Child Welfare League of America

The Child Welfare League of America (CWLA) is a powerful coalition of hundreds of private and public agencies serving children and families that are vulnerable since 1920. CWLA's expertise, leadership, and innovation on policies, programs, and practices help improve the lives of millions of children across the country. CWLA offers trainings, webinars, and conferences as well.

Children's Defense Fund

The Children's Defense Fund serves as a voice for children, promoting their health, safety, and overall well-being. Information and legal resources are available.

Code Pink for Peace

Code Pink for Peace focuses on ending war and militarism as well as the promotion of peace more broadly, including the end of gender-based violence.

College Brides Walk

College Brides Walk (CBW) emerged in 2011 as a subset of the Brides' Marches, which were first sponsored in 2002 to pay tribute to Gladys Ricart. Ricart was murdered by her abusive ex-boyfriend on September 26, 2011, just minutes before she was to head to the chapel to wed her fiancé. CBW brings the idea of the Brides' March to college campuses, educating young people about abuse and inspiring them to take action in their communities.

Communities against Violence Network

Communities against Violence Network (CAVNET) provides resources on a variety of topics related to violence.

Community United against Violence

Community United against Violence (CUAV) is the nation's first LGBTQ (lesbian, gay, bisexual, transgender, queer, and questioning) anti-violence organization. Its mission is to prevent and respond to violence against and within diverse LGBTQ communities. CUAV accomplishes this through peer-based counseling, direct assistance, education and outreach, grassroots organizing, and policy advocacy.

Corporate Alliance to End Partner Violence

The Corporate Alliance to End Partner Violence (CAEPV) is a national nonprofit organization dedicated to reducing the costs and consequences of partner violence at work—and eliminating it altogether. From policy and programs to legal issues and legislation, CAEPV is a credible source for information, materials, and advice.

Cyber Civil Rights Initiative

The Cyber Civil Rights Initiative promotes education and advocacy related to rights in the cyber world, including those related to stalking and online abuse.

Do Something

This teen-focused organization provides information on a number of social issues. It is intended to inspire action for community betterment.

FaithTrust Institute

FaithTrust Institute is an international, multifaith organization working to end sexual and domestic violence. It provides communities and advocates with tools to address the religious and cultural issues related to abuse. The FaithTrust website contains many resources that can be ordered to assist with these efforts. FaithTrust Institute works with many communities, including Asian and Pacific Islander, Buddhist, Jewish, Latino/Latina, Muslim, black, Anglo, indigenous, Protestant, and Roman Catholic.

The Feminist Majority and the Feminist Majority Foundation

This organization promotes gender equality through information, resources, and legal advocacy.

Futures without Violence

Futures without Violence, formerly Family Violence Prevention Fund, has worked to prevent and end violence against women and children around the world for more than thirty years. In 1994, Futures without Violence was instrumental in developing the landmark Violence Against Women Act passed by the U.S. Congress. Striving to reach new audiences and transform social norms, Futures without Violence trains professionals such as doctors, nurses, athletic coaches, and judges on improving responses to violence and abuse. The organization works with advocates, policymakers, and others to build sustainable community leadership and educate people everywhere about the importance of respect and healthy relationships—the relationships that all individuals, families, and communities need and deserve.

Gay Men's Domestic Violence Project

The Gay Men's Domestic Violence Project is a grassroots, nonprofit organization founded by a gay male survivor of domestic violence and developed through the strength, contributions, and participation of the community. It supports victims and survivors through education, advocacy, and direct services.

Give Back a Smile

The American Academy of Cosmetic Dentistry Charitable Foundation's Give Back a Smile program heals some of the most devastating effects of domestic and sexual violence by restoring the smiles of adult women and men who have suffered dental injuries to the front eight teeth from a former intimate partner or spouse or family member or due to sexual assault.

Go Ask Rose

Through its Operation: Safe Escape program, Go Ask Rose helps victims safely get out of an abusive relationship when technology is being used to prevent escape. It applies the same security principles used by the military, law enforcement, and other personnel security environments to make sure survivors have the information and resources needed to safely leave abusers.

Good Men Project

Good Men Project provides educational resources about current issues focused on gender and gender equality.

Health Resource Center on Domestic Violence

For more than a decade, the National Health Resource Center on Domestic Violence has supported health-care practitioners, administrators and systems, domestic violence experts, survivors, and policymakers at all levels as they improve health care's response to domestic violence. The Center develops educational resources, training materials, and model protocols on domestic violence and screening to help health-care providers better serve survivors of domestic violence.

Hot Peach Pages

This Canadian-based site offers a global list of 10,000 abuse hotlines, shelters, refuges, crisis centers, and women's organizations in 110 languages in nearly 200 countries.

Human Rights Watch

Human Rights Watch is a global human rights watchdog focused on myriad issues, including gender-based violence.

INCITE! Women of Color against Violence

INCITE! Women of Color against Violence is a national activist organization of radical feminists of color advancing a movement to end violence against women of color and their communities through direct action, critical dialogue, and grassroots organizing.

Indigenous Women's Network

The Indigenous Women's Network provides information, resources, and support for indigenous women broadly, as well as for victims of domestic violence and sexual assault.

Institute on Domestic Violence in the African American Community

The Institute on Domestic Violence in the African American Community (IDVAAC) is an organization focused on the unique circumstances of African Americans as they face issues related to domestic violence, including intimate partner violence, child abuse, elder maltreatment, and community violence. IDVAAC's mission is to enhance society's understanding of and ability to end violence in the African American community.

Jewish Women International—Domestic Violence in the Jewish Community

Jewish Women International is the leading Jewish organization empowering women and girls—through economic literacy, community training, healthy relationship education, and the proliferation of women's leadership. Its innovative programs, advocacy, and philanthropic initiatives protect the fundamental rights of all girls and women to live in safe homes, thrive in healthy relationships, and realize the full potential of their personal strength.

Joyful Heart Foundation

Founded by Law & Order: Special Victims Unit actress Mariska Hargitay, Joyful Heart's mission is to heal, educate, and empower survivors of sexual assault, domestic violence, and child abuse and to shed light into the darkness that surrounds these issues. Further, Joyful Heart engages in education and advocacy to close the backlog on analysis of rape kits.

LAMBDA GLBT Community Services

LAMBDA GLBT Community Services supports GLBT individuals, including victims of domestic violence and sexual assault.

Legal Momentum

Legal Momentum is the nation's oldest legal defense and education fund dedicated to advancing the rights of all women and girls. Over the past forty years, Legal Momentum has made historic contributions through litigation and public policy advocacy to advance economic and personal security for women. Our current programmatic work is focused on five strategic goals: increasing pathways into quality employment opportunities; protecting workplace rights of vulnerable populations; strengthening the safety net; expanding rights, justice, and services for victims of violence; and promoting gender equity.

Love Is Not Abuse

Love Is Not Abuse provides information and resources about teen dating violence.

Love Is Respect—National Teen Dating Helpline

Love Is Respect focuses on teen relationships and can be accessed by phone, text, or live chat. Run by the National Domestic Violence Hotline, it offers real-time, one-on-one support from trained peer advocates who offer support, information, and advocacy to those involved in dating abuse relationships as well as concerned parents, teachers, clergy, law enforcement, and service providers.

Men Can Stop Rape

Men Can Stop Rape provides resources and educational materials to encourage men to get involved in movements against sexual and domestic violence.

Men Stopping Violence

Men Stopping Violence focuses on educating men and encouraging them to take action to stop abuse of women and children.

Mending the Sacred Hoop

Mending the Sacred Hoop is focused on abuse and other social injustices among Native peoples.

MINCAVA (Minnesota Center against Violence and Abuse) Electronic Clearinghouse

The MINCAVA Electronic Clearinghouse contains educational resources about all types of violence, including published research, funding sources, information about upcoming training events, individuals and organizations that can provide technical assistance, and lists of training manuals, videos, and other resources.

Ms. Foundation for Women

Ms. Foundation for Women is a feminist organization that supports domestic violence shelters and sexual assault resources.

National Alliance to End Sexual Violence

The National Alliance to End Sexual Violence educates the policy community about federal laws, legislation, and appropriations impacting the fight to end sexual violence. Its team of experts and advocates, donating time away from their state and local groups, publish written analysis, track legislation, provide media interviews, and advise members of Congress and the executive branch.

National Center for Children Exposed to Violence

The mission of the National Center for Children Exposed to Violence is to increase the capacity of individuals and communities to reduce the incidence and impact of violence on children and families; to train and support the professionals who provide intervention and treatment to children and families affected by violence; and to increase professional and public awareness of the effects of violence on children, families, communities, and society.

National Center for Victims of Crime

The National Center for Victims of Crime provides resources to crime victims and advocates for their rights within the legal system.

National Center on Domestic and Sexual Violence

The mission of the National Center on Domestic and Sexual Violence is to design, provide, and customize training and consultation, influence policy, promote collaboration, and enhance diversity with the goal of ending domestic and sexual violence.

National Center on Domestic Violence, Trauma & Mental Health

The National Center on Domestic Violence, Trauma & Mental Health provides training, support, and consultation to advocates, mental health and substance abuse providers, legal professionals, and policymakers as it works to improve agency- and systems-level responses to survivors and their children. The organization's work is survivor defined and rooted in principles of social justice.

National Center on Elder Abuse

The National Center on Elder Abuse (NCEA) serves as a national resource center dedicated to the prevention of elder mistreatment. Since its inception, the NCEA has operated as a unique, multidisciplinary consortium of equal partners with expertise in elder abuse, neglect, and exploitation. Not only have the NCEA's collaborators come from various professional fields, but also the NCEA has proved a valuable resource to many professionals working in some way with older victims of elder mistreatment, including adult protective services; national, state, and local aging networks; law enforcement; health-care professionals; and domestic violence networks.

National Clearinghouse on Abuse in Later Life

The Wisconsin Coalition against Domestic Violence created the National Clearinghouse on Abuse in Later Life (NCALL) in 1999 with funding from the Department of Justice's Office on Violence Against Women. Since 2002, NCALL has been providing technical assistance to the Department of Justice, Office on Violence Against Women, Enhanced Training and Services to End Violence against and Abuse of Women Later in Life Program. Today, NCALL is a nationally recognized leader on program development, policy, technical assistance, and training that addresses the nexus between domestic violence; sexual assault; and elder abuse, neglect, and exploitation. NCALL's mission is to eliminate abuse in later life. Through advocacy and education, NCALL strives to challenge and change the beliefs, policies, practices, and systems that allow abuse to occur and continue. NCALL also aims to improve victim safety by increasing the quality and availability of victim services and support.

National Clearinghouse for the Defense of Battered Women

The National Clearinghouse for the Defense of Battered Women, a nonprofit organization founded in 1987, is a resource and advocacy center for battered women charged with crimes related to their battering. Through its work, the organization aims to increase justice for—and prevent further victimization of—arrested, convicted, or incarcerated battered women. The National Clearinghouse works with battered women who have been arrested and are facing trial, as well as with those who are serving prison sentences. Its staff provide customized technical assistance to battered women charged with crimes and to members of its defense teams (defense attorneys, advocates, expert witnesses, and others). Staff also conduct training seminars for members of the criminal justice and advocacy communities and for the general public, regarding the unique experiences of battered women defendants.

National Coalition Against Domestic Violence

The mission of the National Coalition Against Domestic Violence (NCADV) is to organize for collective power by advancing transformative work, thinking, and leadership of communities and individuals working to end the violence in our lives. NCADV's work includes coalition building at the local, state, regional, and national levels; support for the provision of community-based, nonviolent alternatives—such as safe home and shelter programs—for battered women and their children; public education and technical assistance; policy development and innovative legislation; focus on the leadership of NCADV's caucuses developed to represent the concerns of organizationally underrepresented groups; and efforts to eradicate social conditions that contribute to violence against women and children.

National Coalition for the Homeless

The National Coalition for the Homeless provides advocacy for the homeless, including those who are so due to domestic violence.

National Coalition of Anti-Violence Programs

The National Coalition of Anti-Violence Programs brings together numerous anti-violence efforts and campaigns.

National Council on Child Abuse and Family Violence

The National Council on Child Abuse and Family Violence provides prevention services by bringing together community and national stakeholders, volunteers, and professionals to prevent intergenerational family violence: child abuse and neglect, spouse/partner abuse, and elder abuse and neglect.

National Domestic Violence Hotline

The National Domestic Violence Hotline creates access by providing twenty-four-hour support through advocacy, safety planning, resources, and hope to everyone affected by domestic violence. You can call the National Domestic Violence Hotline at 1–800–799–SAFE (7233) or TTY 1–800–787–3224.

National Domestic Violence Registry

The registry is an online national database that makes available the convictions of domestic abuse perpetrators and those offenders who have long-term criminal orders of protections placed against them.

National Gay and Lesbian Task Force

The National Gay and Lesbian Task Force provides advocacy and empowerment for GLBT individuals.

National Immigration Forum

The National Immigration Forum promotes immigrants' rights through education and policy advocacy.

National Indigenous Women's Resource Center

The National Indigenous Women's Resource Center (NIWRC) is dedicated to restoring safety to Native women by upholding the sovereignty of Indian and Alaska Native tribes. It is a Native nonprofit organization that was created specifically to serve as the National Indian Resource Center (NIRC) Addressing Domestic Violence and Safety for Indian Women. Under this grant project and in compliance with statutory requirements, the NIWRC seeks to enhance the capacity of American Indian and Alaska Native (Native) tribes, Native

Hawaiians, and Tribal and Native Hawaiian organizations to respond to domestic violence.

National Latino Alliance for the Elimination of Domestic Violence

The National Latino Alliance for the Elimination of Domestic Violence (Alianza) is part of a national effort to address the domestic violence needs and concerns of underserved populations. Alianza's mission is to promote understanding, initiate and sustain dialogue, and generate solutions that move toward the elimination of domestic violence affecting Latino communities, with an understanding of the sacredness of all relations and communities.

National Link Coalition

The National Link Coalition is a multidisciplinary, collaborative initiative to increase awareness and address public policy, programs, and research. Intentional abuse in any form should be taken seriously. This organization serves as the National Resource Center on The Link between Animal Abuse and Human Violence.

National Network to End Domestic Violence

The National Network to End Domestic Violence (NNEDV), a social change organization, is dedicated to creating a social, political, and economic environment in which violence against women no longer exists. It is a membership and advocacy organization of state domestic violence coalitions, allied organizations, and supportive individuals that provides leadership on public policy related to domestic violence.

National Organization for Men Against Sexism

The National Organization for Men Against Sexism (NOMAS) is a male-led feminist organization that promotes gender equality and end to violence against women.

National Organization for Victim Assistance

The National Organization for Victim Assistance promotes dignity and compassion for victims of crime.

National Resource Center on Domestic Violence

The National Resource Center on Domestic Violence (NRCDV) was established to inform, coordinate, and strengthen public and private efforts to end domestic violence. Through technical assistance and training, development of resource materials, and special projects, the NRCDV enhances and expands the domestic violence intervention and prevention efforts of communities and institutions. The Pennsylvania Coalition against Domestic Violence has received core funding to operate the NRCDV since 1993 from the U.S. Department of Health and Human Services, with supplemental funds from the Centers for Disease Control and Prevention to support VAWnet, its national online resource center, and other private and public grants.

National Sexual Violence Resource Center

The National Sexual Violence Resource Center provides information and resources related to sexual assault.

NO MORE

NO MORE was conceived to amplify the power of the domestic violence and sexual assault movement and to drive awareness and break down the barriers of stigma, silence, and shame that keep people from talking about these issues and taking action to prevent them.

No More Tears

This South Florida–based nonprofit organization helps victims of domestic violence and human trafficking in that area and beyond.

The Northwest Network of Bisexual, Transgender, Gay and Lesbian Survivors of Abuse

The NW Network increases communities' ability to support the self-determination and safety of bisexual, transgendered, lesbian, and gay survivors of abuse through education, organizing, and advocacy. It works within a broad liberation movement dedicated to social and economic justice, equality and respect for all people, and the creation of loving, inclusive and accountable communities.

Office for Victims of Crime

The Office for Victims of Crime is the federal government's office for crime victims offering resources and support.

One in Six

Researchers estimate that one in six men have experienced unwanted or abusive sexual experiences before the age of eighteen. This organization offers online individual and group support; information on trauma and healing; and helpful resources for family and friends and professionals through community outreach.

Pathways to Safety International

Pathways to Safety International offers resources for Americans living overseas, including case management, danger-to-safety relocation, legal consultations for mothers seeking divorce and custody, payment of initial legal retainers, housing assistance, and funds to help with emergency needs such as issuing American passports; there is also a twenty-four-hour response to e-mails, as well as international phone options and live chat.

The Pixel Project

The Pixel Project offers people who are first-time supporters of the movement to end violence against entry-level opportunities to contribute their talents to the cause. The Pixel Project also provides online resources for victims to get help and/ or share their stories, including tweeting helplines from over thirty countries daily, resource pages with links to anti-violence against women organizations worldwide, and their annual Survivor Stories campaign.

Planned Parenthood Federation of America

The Planned Parenthood Federation of America provides information, resources, and services related to sexual and reproductive health.

Purple Purse Allstate Foundation

Financial tools, online curriculum, and webinars help domestic violence survivors prepare for the future with a better understanding of and management skills for their personal finances. The organization is operated by the AllState Financial, AllState Foundation, and National Network to End Domestic Violence.

Resource Center on Child Protection and Custody

The Resource Center on Domestic Violence: Child Protection & Custody (CPC) is part of the National Council of Juvenile and Family Court Judges' Family Violence Department and provides information and tangible assistance to those working in the field of domestic violence and child protection and custody. In addition, the CPC identifies and develops model policies, protocols, and programs that are sensitive to the legal, cultural, and psychological dynamics of child protection and custody cases involving family violence.

See the Signs, Speak Out

Three free online video and training courses are provided by Avon Foundation and Ohio Domestic Violence Network: (1) training on how to intervene as a bystander to prevent domestic violence and sexual assault, (2) how to talk to teens about dating abuse, and (3) how to break the cycle of abuse in children of domestic violence. Although developed for employers, this series is useful to a broader audience.

The Sister Fund

The Sister Fund is a private foundation that supports and gives voice to women working for justice from a religious framework.

Soroptimist International of the Americas

Soroptimist International of the Americas is an international organization for business and professional women who work to improve the lives of women and girls.

Southwest Center for Law and Policy

The Southwest Center For Law And Policy provides legal training and technical assistance to tribal communities and to organizations and agencies serving Native people. It is the host of the National Tribal Trial College providing free legal training for attorneys, judges, law enforcement, advocates, and community members on domestic violence, sexual assault, stalking, dating/relationship violence, firearms, violence, abuse of elders, abuse of persons with disabilities, victims' rights, sex offender registration and notification, forensic evidence, tribal court, and trial skills.

Stalking Resource Center

The Stalking Resource Center (SRC) was created in 2000 by the National Center for Victims of Crime in partnership with the U.S. Department of Justice Office on Violence Against Women. The mission of the SRC is to enhance the ability of professionals, organizations, and systems to effectively respond to stalking. The SRC envisions a future in which the criminal justice system and its many allied community partners will have the best tools to effectively collaborate and respond to stalking, improve victim safety and well-being, and hold of-fenders accountable.

Stop Abuse For Everyone

Stop Abuse For Everyone (SAFE) is a human rights organiza-tion providing domestic violence services, publications, and training to marginalized groups, including GLBT victims, teens, and the elderly.

Students Active for Ending Rape

Students Active for Ending Rape (SAFER) is a student-led or-ganization focusing on improving universities' responses to and policies related to sexual violence.

Survivor Project

Survivor Project is a nonprofit organization dedicated to ad-dressing the needs of intersex and transgender survivors of do-mestic and sexual violence through caring action, education, and expanding access to resources and to opportunities for action. Since 1997, it has provided presentations, workshops, consultation, materials, information, and referrals to many anti-violence organizations and universities across the country, as well as gathered information about issues faced by intersex and trans survivors of domestic and sexual violence.

Third Wave Foundation

Third Wave Foundation supports third-wave feminists in their efforts to promote gender equality.

U.S. Department of Justice, Violence Against Women Office

The mission of the Office on Violence Against Women (OVW), a component of the U.S. Department of Justice, is to pro-vide federal leadership in developing the nation's capacity to reduce violence against women and administer justice for and strengthen services to victims of domestic violence, dating violence, sexual assault, and stalking. OVW administers financial and technical assistance to communities across the country that are developing programs, policies, and practices aimed at ending domestic violence, dating violence, sexual assault, and stalking.

Women's Independence Scholarship Program, Inc.

The Women's Independence Scholarship Program (WISP), Inc., is an offshoot of Doris Buffet's The Sunshine Lady Foundation. WISP offers scholarships nationally to women who have left an abusive domestic situation and who are pursuing an education designed to provide economic independence for themselves and their children.

Women's Rural Advocacy Programs

Women's Rural Advocacy Programs is a cooperative of Domestic Violence Community Advocacy programs serving southwestern Minnesota whose mission is to provide supportive services, including crisis intervention, advocacy, and safe housing, for women and their children victimized by domestic violence.

Womenslaw.org

Uniquely, this site is a treasure trove of all sorts of information, though its best attributes are related to legal matters on the topic of domestic violence, including how to stay safe; how to help others in abusive relationships; understanding federal, state, and tribal laws; links to statutes; and preparing for court. Legal questions can also be posed in English or Spanish through the organization's email hotline.

7 Chronology

This chapter offers a comprehensive timeline of important developments related to domestic violence. It focuses largely on the United States but includes some global historical information.

753 BC Romulus, founder of Rome, formalizes the first law of marriage, requiring women to obey their husbands and husbands to rule their wives as possessions.

300 BC Husband's patriarchal authority is affirmed by Roman and Jewish leaders. Constantine the Great, Roman emperor, has his wife burned alive when he decides she is of no use to him. Yet excessive violence is considered grounds for divorce, although women had to prove the charge.

200 BC The end of the Punic Wars results in women being allowed to study philosophy, pursue politics, and join new religious movements. Husbands are prohibited from beating their wives unless they have sufficient evidence for divorce. Men convicted of striking their spouses were required to make monetary compensation.

900–1300 Women in medieval Europe are considered to be subhuman. Men of all social classes routinely beat their wives, and the Church supported their right to castigate or hurt women if they were disobedient or needed correction.

An activist protests domestic violence. (Ammentorp/Dreamstime.com)

1400s Numerous documents advise "chivalrous" men to brutally beat their wives out of concern for their behavior.

1500s Lord Hale, an English Jurist, establishes the basis that marital rape is not prohibited. When women married, Hale wrote, "they gave themselves to their husbands in contract, and could not withdraw that consent until they divorced" (Herstory of domestic violence. 1999). Hale led burnings of so-called witches at the stake.

Late 1500s Ivan the Terrible in Russia oversees widespread oppression of women. The Household Ordinance describes when and how a man can beat his wife, and it is not illegal for a man to kill his wife.

1531 European religious reformer Martin Luther describes women's place as in the home and declared that because men have broader shoulders and more narrow hips than women, they were more intelligent.

1609 King James I of England declares that kings are like fathers and must be obeyed.

1641 Puritans in Massachusetts Bay Colony enact the nation's first laws prohibiting spousal abuse.

1672 Pilgrims in Plymouth, Massachusetts, enact a spousal abuse law.

1736 Posthumous publication of Sir Mathew Hale's *History of the Pleas of the Crown*, which influences the UK and U.S. legal systems in failing to prohibit marital rape.

1760s English jurist William Blackstone's *Commentaries on the Laws of England* declares private acts outside the realm of law. He refers to wife-beating as necessary for chastising women, although he recommends it be done in moderation.

1776 First Lady Abigail Adams tells her husband, John Adams, to "remember the ladies."

1792 In *A Vindication of the Rights of Women*, Mary Wollstonecraft calls for more education for women and improvement in the way men treat their wives.

1800s Beginning of American Temperance Movement, which emphasizes the connection between alcohol and wife-beating.

1824 Mississippi Supreme Court rules in *Bradley v. State* that it is a husband's right to chastise his wife but recommends it be done in moderation and only in cases of "emergency."

1824 Missouri Supreme Court upholds law allowing men to beat their wives with a rod no thicker than their thumbs.

1826 The American Society for the Promotion of Temperance is founded.

1835 The first drawings of wife-beating are published in the *Pennsylvania-New Jersey Almanac*. They depict a drunken husband lifting a chair to beat his wife and children.

1846 Sweden enacts legislation giving men and women equal inheritance rights.

1848 Declaration of Human Sentiments, which lists many grievances including male's oppression of women, is signed in Seneca Falls, New York.

1849 The first temperance journal, *Lily*, is published by Amelia Bloomer and includes many articles about women's rights.

1850 Divorce based on cruelty is allowed in nineteen states, but judges still require women to prove they were submissive and pure.

1852 Susan B. Anthony is booed for speaking out about the exclusion of women in politics at a state temperance meeting. Anthony begins to open her home as a refuge for battered women.

1852 London enacts a law allowing punishment of aggravated assault against women and children below fourteen years with up to six years in prison.

1855 Publisher Horace Greeley, editor of the *New York Tribune*, opposes proposed efforts to permit divorce on the grounds of desertion, drunkenness, or cruelty.

1856 First documented use of the word "wife-beating" during a divorce reform campaign in England.

1857   The Society for the Prevention of Cruelty opens in England and offers help to battered wives.

1860   Susan B. Anthony helps the wife of a Massachusetts's legislator flee from his abuse, and Elizabeth Cady Stanton introduces ten new resolutions at the 1860 New York state convention related to divorce reform.

1864   A court in North Carolina rules that a husband was allowed to choke his wife in order to make her behave because the violence he used was not "excessive" and there was no permanent damage.

1866   The American Society for the Prevention of Cruelty to Animals is formed, predating an organization aimed at preventing cruelty against children or women.

1868   North Carolina Supreme Court rules that a man cannot be prosecuted for assault and battery if his wife's injuries are not permanent.

1870   England passes the Married Women's Property Act, which allows women to keep their property when they divorce.

1871   Alabama Supreme Court is the first appellate court to deny a man the common law right to beat his wife.

1874   North Carolina denies men the right to beat their wives but only when permanent damage has been inflicted.

1876   Lucy Stone, editor of *Woman's Journal*, a newspaper in Boston, begins publishing a list of crimes against women and includes articles denouncing the leniency with which wife-beating was treated.

1878   Suffragist Frances Powell Cobbe graphically depicts wife-beating in her article "Wife Torture in England" and calls for a bill allowing legal separation and child custody for women who have been beaten.

1880s   Delaware, Maryland, and Oregon make wife-beating a crime, punishable by whipping, but the law is rarely enforced.

1885   Chicago's Protective Agency for Women and Children is founded, which provides legal and personal assistance to victims.

1896   The National Association of Colored Women is founded.

1910   Buffalo, New York, establishes the first family court specifically for domestic violence, although judges still focus on keeping families together. Others are established around the country throughout the decade.

1912   The U.S. Children's Bureau is founded.

1919   Women in the United States earn the right to vote with the passage of the Nineteenth Amendment.

1921   Sweden enacts legislation giving women legal independence and equal rights as parents.

1923   England's Matrimonial Causes Act lets women and men use the same grounds for divorce.

1931   Jane Addams, who helped women and children, wins the Nobel Peace Prize.

1945   First Lady Eleanor Roosevelt advocates for women's issues as a delegate to the United Nations.

1946   United Nations establishes the Commission on the Status of Women.

1960s   Publication of "The Battered Child Syndrome" by pediatrician C. Henry Kempe and four colleagues. Although the paper draws needed attention to child abuse, it does not address violence against wives.

1960   A woman is found responsible for involuntary manslaughter because she did not remove her child from the home where her husband was abusing her.

1961   Peter Benenson starts Amnesty International in London.

1961   President John F. Kennedy creates the President's Commission on the Status of Women and appoints Eleanor Roosevelt as chair.

1962   New York State begins transferring domestic violence cases to civil court, where those convicted of abusing their spouse receive lesser sentences than those convicted of assaulting strangers.

1963   May Kay Cosmetics is founded, which goes on to be a corporate leader against domestic violence.

1963   Congress passes the Equal Pay Act.

1964   In "The Wife-Beater's Wife: A Study of Female Interaction," John Snell, Richard Rosenwald, and Ames Robey call women who claim to have been assaulted by their husbands "castrating," "masculine," "frigid," "passive," and "masochistic."

1964   Refuge House, the first battered woman's shelter in the United States, opens in London.

1964   Civil Rights Act prohibits sex discrimination in employment.

1966   National Organization for Women (NOW) is founded.

1967   Affirmative Action programs now include gender.

1971   Erin Pizzey opens the Chiswick Centre for battered women in London.

1971   Publication of the first *Ms.* magazine.

1971   The Red Stockings, a Danish women's liberation organization, opens the first shelter in Copenhagen, Kvindehuset, or The Woman's House.

1972   The first rape crisis center opens in the United States in Berkeley, California.

1972   Title IX, part of the Educational Amendments of 1972, is passed. It mandates gender equality in K-12 public schools and in colleges and universities.

1972   After visiting Chiswick Centre in London, female activists in the United States open Women's Advocates in St. Paul, Minnesota, the first U.S. shelter for battered women.

1973   NOW establishes a task force on battered women. It is led by survivor Nancy Kirk-Gormley.

1973   *Roe v. Wade* ends prohibition on abortions in the United States.

1973–1976   Opening of shelters across the United States, with twenty established by the end of 1976.

1974   The first domestic violence shelter in the Netherlands is opened in Rotterdam.

1974   Elsie, the first battered woman's shelter in Australia, is opened when two women refuse to stop squatting in two abandoned houses.

1974   Erin Pizzey's *Scream Quietly or the Neighbors Will Hear* is the first book about domestic violence.

1974   Despite saying he beats his wife weekly, Japan's Eisaku Satō wins the Nobel Peace Prize.

1975   First National Family Violence Survey.

1975   Publication of Susan Brownmiller's groundbreaking book *Against Our Will*.

1975   New penal code in Brazil prohibits men from selling, renting, or gambling away their wives.

1976   First International Tribunal on Crimes against Women convenes in Brussels and attracts 8,200 women from 33 countries.

1976   Women file lawsuits against police in many cities in the United States, demanding that they get better training on responding to domestic violence.

1976   England's Domestic Violence and Matrimonial Proceedings Act allows women the right to obtain civil protection orders for domestic violence.

1976   Del Martin's Battered Women attributes domestic violence to societal sexism, which is the position held by most in the anti-domestic violence movement.

1976   The first shelter for battered women established by women of color opens in San Francisco, California.

1976   Nebraska becomes the first state to prohibit marital rape.

1977   Francine Hughes sets fire to her home while her abusive husband sleeps. She is found not guilty by reason of insanity, and her story is later made into the film *The Burning Bed*, which aired on national television a decade later.

1977   London opens its first rape crisis center.

1977   Oregon's Family Abuse Prevention Act includes provisions for women obtaining restraining orders and mandates arrest for domestic violence.

1977   England's Homeless Persons Act gives battered women priority in obtaining housing.

1978   Establishment of the National Coalition Against Domestic Violence (NCADV).

1978   Florida becomes the first state to tax marriage licenses to fund battered women's services.

1978   Publication of Lenore Walker's *The Battered Woman*.

1978   Minnesota becomes the first state to use probable cause, or warrantless arrests, in domestic violence cases.

1978   The first domestic violence program at a military facility is established at Fort Campbell, Kentucky.

1978   Women's Aid Federation is established in Northern Ireland.

1978   First trial for marital rape. John Rideout is acquitted of raping his wife, Greta, in Salem, Oregon.

1979   President Jimmy Carter establishes the Office of Domestic Violence with a budget of $90,000 for grants, research, and publications.

1979   First U.S. congressional hearings on domestic violence.

1979   UN General Assembly adopts the Convention on the Elimination of All Forms of Discrimination against Women (CEDAW).

1980   All but six states have laws addressing domestic violence.

1980   NCADV holds its first conference in Washington, D.C.

1980   Establishment of the Duluth Project in Duluth, Minnesota, which becomes the model for batterer intervention programs.

1980   The air force establishes the Office on Family Matters to address domestic violence.

1980   California is the first state to mandate treatment for convicted batterers.

1981   President Ronald Reagan cuts the budget for the Office of Domestic Violence.

1981   Everyone's Shelter, the first domestic violence shelter for Asian women, is established by a Filipina victim, Nilda Rimote, in Los Angeles, California.

1981   NCADV declares October 17 a Day of Unity on behalf of battered women. This eventually is expanded to Domestic Violence Awareness Month.

1981–1982   Minneapolis Domestic Violence Experiment (MDVE) finds that arrest is the best strategy in domestic violence cases, ushering in a period of mandatory arrests.

1982   National Organization for Men Against Sexism (NOMAS) is established.

1982   Child Abuse and Prevention Treatment Act (CAPTA) includes federal funding for domestic violence shelters but only at less than one-quarter the original request.

1984   Florida is the first state to mandate consideration of domestic violence in child custody decisions.

1984   Congress passes the Family Violence Prevention and Services Act and the Victims of Crime Act, the first efforts to provide states with federal funds to support domestic violence shelters.

1985   U.S. surgeon general C. Everett Koop calls domestic violence a public health problem and prompts the Centers for Disease Control to begin conducting research on it.

1985   Tracey Thurman wins a lawsuit against the City of Torrington, Connecticut, after she is left permanently disfigured and partially paralyzed despite repeated calls to the police reporting her ex-husbands abuse.

1985   *Wall Street Journal* publishes a series of articles about the more than nineteen years of abuse Charlotte Fedders endured from her husband John, who was chief of the Enforcement

Division of the Securities and Exchange Commission for the Reagan administration.

1985   Publication of *Chain, Chain, Change* by Evelyn White, the first book about domestic violence and African American women.

1985   First support group for battered lesbians is started in Seattle, Washington.

1986   Indian law includes dowry killings as a form of domestic violence.

1986   Susan Schechter starts the first program in the United States for child witnesses of domestic violence.

1987   Establishment of the National Domestic Violence Hotline.

1987   First book about battering in lesbian relationships, *Naming the Violence*, by Kerry Lobel, is published.

1987   For the first time in *State v. Ciskie*, expert testimony regarding the mental state and behavior of rape victims is allowed to illustrate why a victim did not call the policy immediately. The defendant is convicted on four counts of rape.

1987   Establishment of Global Fund for Women.

1988   Congress amends the Victims of Crime Act to require state victim compensation plans to include domestic violence.

1989   Marc Lepine kills fourteen women at Canada's Ecole Polytechnique.

1990   Domestic violence is first recognized as grounds for asylum by the U.S. Immigration and Naturalization Service (INS).

1990   Ohio's governor Richard F. Celeste (D) grants clemency to twenty-five women who were convicted of assaulting or killing their abusive husbands or boyfriends.

1990   Passage of the Crime Awareness and Campus Security Act of 1990, generally known as the Clery Act, which requires colleges and universities that receive federal funding to report all campus crimes, including rape.

1990   Introduction of the Violence Against Women Act (VAWA) in the 101st Congress. The bill, which did not pass, was championed by Senator Joe Biden (D-Delaware) and Representative Barbara Boxer (D-California).

1990   First Clothesline Project showcasing thirty-one t-shirts painted by survivors in Hyannis, Massachusetts.

1991   The American Medical Association (AMA) begins a public health campaign addressing family violence.

1991   White Ribbon Campaign is founded in Canada focused on getting men to pledge to help prevent domestic violence.

1991   England's Southall Black Sisters help Kiranjit Ahluwalia, who was convicted of setting her abusive husband on fire and received a life sentence. The sentence was changed to manslaughter, and she was released in 1992.

1991   Liz Claiborne, Inc., begins providing funding and support for domestic violence services and prevention.

1991   Israel's Israeli Law for Prevention of Family Violence provides for protection orders for physical, sexual, or psychological abuse. It is the first Middle Eastern country to enact legislation about domestic violence.

1991   Anita Hill testifies before Congress about the sexual harassment she endured by Supreme Court nominee Clarence Thomas. Thomas is sworn into the Court.

1992   First statement by Roman Catholic bishops acknowledging that the Bible does not condone spousal abuse.

1992   First domestic violence law in the Cayman Islands.

1992   Widespread reports that the Bosnian Serbs used rape as a tool of war.

1992   Belize enacts legislation prohibiting domestic violence.

1992   The AMA's Council on Scientific Affairs recommends that physicians routinely screen female patients to identify abuse.

1992   The Campus Sexual Assault Victims' Bill of Rights requires colleges and universities to disclose their policies on sexual assault, including educational programming, victims' rights, and disciplinary procedures.

1993 Oklahoma and North Carolina are the last states to add marital rape laws.

1993 The United Nations issues the Declaration on the Elimination of Violence against Women.

1993 President Bill Clinton signs into law the Family Medical Leave Act (FMLA).

1993 California enacts AB 890, which requires training of health-care professionals about domestic violence after a study by the Family Violence Prevention Fund shows that most emergency department staff are ill-informed about the issue.

1993 Jackson Katz starts Mentors in Violence Prevention (MVP), a domestic violence prevention program focused on empowering bystanders to step up. It initially targets athletes but is later used with military, fraternity, and other populations.

1994 The documentary *Defending Our Lives*, which focuses on women who are in prison for killing their abusers, wins the Academy Award for best documentary.

1994 Murder of Nicole Brown Simpson, ex-wife of NFL star O. J. Simpson, and her friend Ronald Goldman in Brentwood, California. O. J. is arrested and tried for the murders but is acquitted.

1994 England prohibits marital rape.

1994 The United Nations appoints a Special Rapporteur on Violence Against Women.

1994 Rwanda and the former Yugoslavia establish International Criminal Tribunals and include hearings about sexual violence during their civil wars.

1994 Adoption of the Inter-American Convention on the Prevention, Punishment, and Eradication of Violence against Women, known as the Convention of Belem do Para.

1994 Chile and Argentina adopt legislation prohibiting domestic violence.

1994   Passage of the Violence Against Women Act (VAWA), including the establishment of the Office on Violence Against Women in the Department of Justice.

1995   President Bill Clinton opens the Office of Violence Against Women at the U.S. Department of Justice and appoints Bonnie Campbell as its first director.

1995   World Health Organization (WHO) establishes the first working group on female genital mutilation.

1995   Establishment of the National Alliance to End Sexual Violence.

1995   Panama, Ecuador, and Bolivia enact domestic violence legislation.

1995   The United Nations Fourth World Conference on Women is held in Beijing, China, where delegates call for "full and equal participation of women in political, civil, economic, social and cultural life."

1996   Congress passes the Personal Responsibility and Work Reconciliation Act that "reforms" the welfare system. It requires victims to work or go to school but makes special provisions for victims of domestic violence.

1996   Ireland, Costa Rica. El Salvador, and Guatemala pass domestic violence legislation.

1996   Two members of Congress propose legislation requiring professional athletes to lead a campaign against domestic violence, but it is not passed, in part due to opposition from the National Collegiate Athletic Association (NCAA).

1996   Founding of Break the Cycle, a dating violence awareness program, in Los Angeles, California.

1997   Despite having been acquitted in criminal court, O. J. Simpson is found liable for the deaths of Nicole Brown Simpson and Ronald Goldman and ordered to pay their families $33 million.

1997   Belgium, Bermuda, Hong Long, and Honduras all pass laws related to domestic violence.

1997   President Bill Clinton signs into law anti-stalking legislation.

1997   First Lady Hillary Clinton and Secretary of State Madeleine Albright found Vital Voices, a global initiative to help women.

1997   Founding of Prevention Institute.

1998   Jordan becomes the first Arab nation to enact domestic violence legislation.

1998   Taiwan passes domestic violence legislation.

1998   Establishment of the International Criminal Court, which opens in 2000, to prosecute cases of war crimes, crimes against humanity, and genocide. A Gender and Children's Unit is created to prosecute sexual violence and other gender-based crimes that occur within these contexts.

1999   November 25 is established by the United Nations as the International Day for the Elimination of Violence against Women.

1999   Members of the National Task Force on Violence Against Women protest outside of Eric Clapton's concert in Washington, D.C., asserting that his lyrics glorify abuse.

1999   Jessica Gonzales's abusive husband kidnaps and murders her three daughters despite a restraining order. She contacted the Castle Rock, Colorado, police multiple times, but they refused to respond.

1999   Murder of Gladys Ricart by her abusive ex-boyfriend, Agustin Garcia, just moments before she was to marry another man. Garcia was convicted of second-degree murder.

2000   Beijing Plus Five conference in New York addresses multiple forms of gender-based violence, including domestic violence, human trafficking, female genital mutilation, forced marriage, and honor killings.

2000   In *U.S. v. Morrison*, the Supreme Court strikes down a portion of VAWA that gave rape victims the right to sue their attackers.

2000   Founding of INCITE! Women of Color against Violence.

2000   Colombia and the Commonwealth of the North Marianas enact domestic violence laws.

2000   Passage of UN Security Council Resolution 1325 calling for special protection for women and girls during armed conflict.

2000   The Campus Sex Crimes Prevention Act is passed.

2001   China adopts domestic violence legislation.

2001   Germany passes legislation authorizing civil protection orders for domestic violence and harassment.

2002   President Clinton signs the 2000 reauthorization of the Violence Against Women Act.

2002   The Office on Violence Against Women becomes separated from the Department of Justice, which allows it to be more visible and of a higher priority.

2002   CDC issues its first Costs of Intimate Partner Violence against Women in the U.S. report.

2002   A Stop Family Violence stamp is issued by the U.S. Postal Service to raise funds for prevention.

2002   CDC begins its Delta Project, which focuses on primary prevention of domestic violence.

2002   Bangladesh enacts legislation related to acid attacks.

2002   Chad passes a reproductive health law that includes domestic violence.

2003   End Violence Against Women International (EVAW) is founded.

2003   England passes a law prohibiting female genital mutilation.

2003   New legislation in the Dominican Republic establishes shelters for victims of domestic violence.

2003   WHO releases the report *The Economic Dimensions of Interpersonal Violence*, which finds that in some countries,

70 percent of female murder victims were killed by a current or former partner.

2003   The New York Court of Appeals rules that the child welfare system cannot remove a child from a home simply because domestic violence is occurring.

2003   New law in Brazil requires domestic violence hotlines.

2004   Turkey enacts legislation mandating life sentences for persons convicted of honor killings.

2005   CDC report finds that homicide is the second leading cause of traumatic death for pregnant and postpartum women in the United States.

2005   Supreme Court rules that Castle Rock, Colorado, police were not at fault for failing to enforce Jessica Gonzales's restraining order against her ex-husband.

2005   WHO publishes first global comparison of domestic violence, finding it to be widespread.

2005   Mexico passes legislation requiring medical professionals to take measures to detect domestic violence.

2005   Bosnia and Herzegovina enact laws about domestic violence.

2006   President Bush signs into law the 2005 reauthorization of VAWA.

2006   Congress declares the first full week in February to be Teen Dating Violence Awareness Week.

2006   Albania and Greece pass laws related to domestic violence.

2006   The UN secretary-general releases the United Nation's first comprehensive report about domestic violence.

2008   Egypt prohibits female genital mutilation.

2008   Andorra includes domestic violence in its penal code.

2008   The UN secretary-general launches UNiTE to End Domestic Violence against Women, a global campaign.

2009   East Timor and Hungary pass domestic violence legislation.

2009   Obama administration creates new "czar" of Violence against Women.

2009   Supreme Court rules in *United States v. Hayes* that domestic relationship is not necessarily a defining element of the predicate offense to support a conviction for possession of a firearm by a person previously convicted of a misdemeanor crime of domestic violence.

2010   Congress declares February to be Teen Dating Violence Awareness Month.

2010   Obama administration grants asylum to a Mexican woman who was fleeing abuse from her common-law husband.

2010   Tribal Law and Justice Act helps address domestic and sexual violence on tribal lands.

2010   The United Nations launches UN Women.

2010   The UN secretary-general appoints a Special Representative on Sexual Violence in Conflict.

2011   The Inter-American Commission on Human Rights determines that the U.S. Supreme Court erred in stating there is no entitlement to enforcement of restraining orders and calls for dramatic change in the United States.

2011   The Affordable Care Act, often referred to as "Obamacare," prohibits insurance companies from considering domestic violence to be a preexisting condition.

2012   Leaders in the European Union create the Cadiz Declaration, which reiterates the commitment to enforce CEDAW.

2012   The FBI updates its definition of rape to include all genders and forms of sexual assault.

2013   The reauthorization of the Violence Against Women Act includes protections for Native American victims.

2014   The Supreme Court holds in *United States v. Castleman* that Castleman's misdemeanor for domestic assault did not mean he was prohibited by federal law from having firearms.

2014   California enacts legislation requiring affirmative consent in sexual encounters.

2014   Video of NFL player Ray Rice punching his girlfriend is released.

2016   In *Voisine v. United States*, the Supreme Court rules that the federal firearm ban applies to those convicted of reckless domestic violence.

2018   Former attorney general Jeff Sessions announces that domestic violence will no longer be considered an automatic grounds for asylum.

Reference

Herstory of domestic violence. 1999. Minnesota Center Against Violence and Abuse. Retrieved September 5, 2019, from https://people.uvawise.edu/pww8y/Supplement/-ConceptsSup/Gender/HerstoryDomV.html

Glossary

Abuse   Includes but is not limited to physical abuse, emotional abuse, financial abuse, spiritual abuse, and/or verbal abuse.

Abuser   A person who uses abusive tactics and behaviors to exert power and control over another person with whom the abuser is in an intimate, dating, or family relationship.

Advocate   A trained professional or volunteer working for a nonprofit or government-based domestic violence or victim-witness advocate program.

Attorney   A person legally appointed or hired to represent an individual in legal matters.

Batterer   An individual who uses coercive and abusive tactics and behaviors to establish and maintain power and control over another person with whom the batterer is in an intimate, dating, or family relationship.

Burnout   Physical, emotional, and mental exhaustion, often caused by long-term involvement in emotionally demanding situations such as working with victims.

Case management   The coordination of services for a given individual by an advocate at an agency.

Child exposed to domestic violence   A child who lives in a home in which there is domestic violence.

Civil contempt   Situation in which a judge finds the respondent violated a provision of the temporary protection order

(TPO)/civil protection order (CPO) that is civil in nature, including not limited to failure to pay rent to petitioner and/or failure to attend or complete counseling.

Civil protection order (CPO)   A court order that usually requires a respondent to stay away from and have no contact with the petitioner and directs the respondent not to commit any criminal offense against the petitioner. It may also specify terms of custody, require the respondent to vacate the household, and/or order the respondent to relinquish firearms or other property.

Coercion   One person forces or attempts to force another to think or act in a different way.

Compassion fatigue   A state of exhaustion, where one feels depleted, helpless, and hopeless about work, life, and the state of the world; often happens with advocates who work with victims of trauma.

Contempt   Violation of one or more terms of a protection order (TPO/CPO) by the respondent.

Contempt hearing   Hearing to decide a petitioner's motion for civil or criminal contempt. Both sides have the opportunity to present evidence addressing whether the respondent violated the TPO/CPO.

Continuance   Judge reschedules a case to a later hearing date.

Crime Victims Compensation Program (CVC)   A government fund established to assist qualifying victims of violent crime and their families with crime-related expenses, including but not limited to costs related to counseling, funeral and burial, medical and mental health, emergency/temporary shelter, and other costs as permitted by statute.

Criminal contempt   Judge finds the respondent violated a provision of the TPO/CPO that is criminal in nature, including but not limited to failing to stay away from the petitioner or another protected party named in the TPO/CPO, contacting the petitioner or another protected party, committing assault, sexual assault, malicious destruction of property, or harassment.

Cross-petitions   Separate petitions filed by a petitioner and respondent against each other.

Dating violence   The intentional use of tactics by one dating partner to gain, maintain, or regain power and control over the other, including physical violence or threats, verbal abuse, emotional/psychological coercion, sexual abuse, stalking, isolation, or a combination of these strategies.

Domestic violence   A pattern of coercive control that includes the use of physical, sexual, emotional/psychological, verbal, and economic abuse, including manipulation and maltreatment of children by one partner to gain, regain, and maintain power and control over an intimate partner, such as a current spouse, live-in partner, significant other, boyfriend/girlfriend or an ex-spouse, past partner or ex-boyfriend/girlfriend, including someone with whom the victim has a child.

Domestic violence service provider   A nonprofit organization that provides support, counseling, and assistance to victims of domestic violence.

Dual arrest   A police officer arrests both parties in a domestic violence situation because the officer is unable to determine the primary aggressor or believes both parties have committed offenses.

Economic/financial abuse   A batterer uses finances to establish and maintain power and control over a victim, including but not limited to controlling a partner's finances, taking the victim's money without permission, giving the victim an allowance, prohibiting/limiting a victim's access to bank accounts or credit card, denying the victim the right to work, and/or sabotaging a victim's credit.

Emotional/psychological abuse   A batterer uses emotions, self-esteem, and/or a person's mental state to establish and maintain power and control over a victim, including but not limited to putting the victim down or making the victim feel bad about herself/himself; calling the victim names; playing mind games; making the victim think she or he is crazy; making the victim feel guilty; and/or humiliating the victim.

Empathy   One person identifies with or experiences the feelings or thoughts of another.

Guardian Ad Litem (GAL)   A person appointed by the court in a case to represent the best interests of a child in legal proceedings; referred to as court-appointed special advocate (CASA) in some states.

Hotline   A free 24/7 phone number answered by advocates who offer assistance to victims of domestic violence, including access to shelter, legal services, and/or safety planning.

Intimidation   One person uses threats to cause another person fear and/or coerce her or him into doing something, including but not limited to making someone afraid by using looks, actions, gestures, and/or a loud voice; destroying property; abusing pets; and/or displaying weapons.

Isolation   A person uses friends, family, and social networks to establish and maintain power and control over a victim by controlling where a victim goes, who she or he talks to, what she or he wears, and/or who she or he sees, limiting involvement in places of worship, Parent Teacher Association (PTA), and other social networks.

Lethality assessment   An analysis done by an advocate or law enforcement officer to determine the level of risk of homicide for a victim of domestic violence based on recent and changing behaviors of the batterer.

Perpetrator   A person carrying out domestic violence behaviors; also referred to as "abuser" and "batterer."

Petition   An application asking the court to issue a protection order.

Petitioner A person who has filed for a protection order Temporary Protection Order and Civil Protection Order (TPO/CPO) seeking protection from a batterer.

Physical abuse A batterer uses her or his body or other objects to cause harm or injury to establish and maintain power and control over a victim, including but not limited to hitting, kicking, biting, pushing, scratching, slapping, strangling, beating, using a weapon against another person, punching, throwing, burning, poisoning, stabbing, and shooting.

Polyvictimization The incidence of being victim of more than one traumatic event or situation, including child abuse, physical assault, sexual abuse, or bullying.

Post-traumatic stress disorder (PTSD) A psychological disorder that can occur in an individual after she or he has suffered a traumatic event (such as domestic violence) and is characterized by flashbacks, avoidance of things that may trigger a memory of the traumatic event, and a significantly heightened state of alert.

Power and control wheel A tool many advocates use to illustrate abusive tactics and behaviors used by batterers against victims, with emphasis that these behaviors are an attempt to obtain and maintain power and control.

Predominant aggressor The person who poses the most serious ongoing threat in a domestic violence situation.

Pro se A person representing herself or himself in court without an attorney.

Protection order The general term for an order issued by the court mandating a batterer to not contact, harass, or come within a certain distance of the petitioner and/or other persons named in the order; sometimes called a restraining order.

Relationship violence or abuse Often used interchangeably with "teen dating violence," refers to a situation in which one partner uses abusive tactics to control, manipulate, humiliate, and abuse the other partner.

Respondent A person against whom a protection order (ETPO/TPO/CPO) has been filed; the person from whom a petitioner is seeking protection.

Safety plan A verbal or written plan a victim of domestic violence creates with an advocate to ensure his or her safety and the safety of others in an abusive home.

Secondary trauma A situation whereby someone feels deeply the trauma of another; typically occurs with advocates who work with children or victims of domestic violence and sexual assault.

Sexting Sending sexually explicit messages and/or photographs, often used as a control strategy in unhealthy and abusive relationships.

Sexual assault Assault including rape or attempted rape, as well as any unwanted sexual contact or threats.

Spiritual/religious abuse A batterer uses spirituality or religion to establish and maintain power and control over a victim, including but not limited to controlling the partner's ability to practice her or his own religion or attend services; forcing the partner to convert or practice another religion against her or his will; and/or using the spiritual or religious environment, leader, and/or congregation to influence a victim's behavior.

Stalking A pattern of repeated and unwanted attention, harassment, contact, or any other course of conduct directed at a specific person that would cause a reasonable person to feel fear.

Survivor A person who was or is being abused or harmed by another person.

Temporary protection order (TPO) A court order that usually requires a respondent to stay away from and have no contact with the petitioner and directs the respondent not to commit any criminal offenses against the petitioner; the order can also specify issues of custody; require the respondent to vacate the household; and/or relinquish firearms or other property. TPOs are in effect for a period of two weeks, but a judge can extend them. To get a TPO you must show you fear immediate danger from your batterer.

Threats   An expression that demonstrates the intention of one person to inflict pain or injury on another person, for instance, verbal threats, such as threats to leave, harm, or commit suicide, or physical threats, such as a raised hand, fist, or gesture.

Transitional housing   Shelter for victims of domestic violence and their children that typically lasts up to two years, provided during the time between receiving emergency services and finding permanent housing.

Trauma   Experiencing an event that causes injury or stress to a person's physical or psychological well-being.

Trauma bonding   The "strong emotional ties that develop between two persons where one person intermittently harasses, beats, threatens, abuses, or intimidates the other" (Dutton & Painter, 1981).

Trauma-informed services   Integrating a basic understanding of how trauma affects the life of an individual seeking services.

Verbal abuse   When a batterer uses words to establish and maintain power and control over a victim, for instance, the use of language to manipulate, control, ridicule, insult, humiliate, belittle, vilify, and/or show disrespect and disdain to another.

Vicarious trauma   The impact of exposure to extreme events experienced by another person resulting in the listener feeling overwhelmed by the trauma or triggering the listener's own past trauma(s).

Victim   A person who is abused, harmed, or killed by another person.

Index

abusers, 14
  athletes, 15–16, 51–56
  batterer intervention
    programs, 100–104
  brain injuries, 16
  fraternities, 15–16
  military, 16
  risk factors, 14–15
Adverse Child Experiences
  Studies (ACES), 18
Alexander, Marissa, 60
Ali, Somy, 129–139,
  200–201
Amnesty International, 4,
  178–179, 291, 319
Anthony, Susan B., 27, 317,
  318
Ashton, Josie, 83
asylum, 65–69
attitudes towards abuse, 12,
  15, 25, 33, 35, 52, 63,
  91, 167, 262
Avon Foundation, 25, 64,
  151, 183–188

battered woman syndrome,
  98–100, 181–183
Battered Women's Justice
  Project, 9, 292
batterer intervention
  programs, 100–104
Benedict, Jeff, 16, 24, 53–54
Benoit, Christopher, 54
Biden, Joe, 23, 25, 173
Big Little Lies, 158–159,
  185
brain injuries, 16
Break the Cycle, 25, 64, 189,
  292
Briggs, Jimmie, 147–149
Brown, Chris, 34–35
Brown, Cyntoia, 60
Burke, Tarana, 38–39
The Burning Bed, 155, 321
bystander intervention, 35,
  155, 199

Campbell, Jacqueline, 9
Carter, Jimmy, 30, 322

Castle Rock v. Gonzales,
    22–23, 32, 85–86,
    220–226, 328
CDC, 21, 32, 34, 56, 230
child abuse, 11, 27–28,
    69–70, 175, 177–178
Clery Act, 324
Clinton, Bill, 23, 79, 326,
    327, 328, 329
Clinton, Hillary, 25, 36, 328
College Brides Walk, 83,
    140, 295
college students, 11
    athletes, 51–52
Conflict Tactics Scale (CTS),
    179–181
Connell, R.W., 19, 90
Convention on the
    Elimination of
    All Forms of
    Discrimination against
    Women (CEDAW),
    234–247
costs, xv, 20–21
court cases
    Castle Rock v. Gonzales,
        22–23, 32, 85–86,
        220–226, 328
    Scott v. Hart, 29
    United States v. Castleman,
        250–252
    United States v. Hayes,
        247–250
    United States v. Morrison,
        32

Voisine v. United States,
    252–255
criminal justice interventions,
    21–23
    Castle Rock v. Gonzales,
        22–23, 32, 85–86,
        220–226, 328
    mandatory arrest, 21–22,
        30, 86–89
    Minneapolis Domestic
        Violence Experiment
        (MDVE), 21–22, 30,
        86–87, 323
    no drop policies, 88–89
    prosecution, 22, 88
    restraining orders, 22–23,
        83–86, 220–226
criminological theory, 17–19
    choice, 17–18
    feminist, 18–19
    personality, 17
    psychological, 17
    sociological, 18
Cyber Civil Rights Initiative,
    35, 296

dating violence, 11, 24, 25,
    33, 34–35
Declaration of Human
    Sentiments, 317
Deer, Sarah, 149–150
Domestic Violence Counts,
    95, 187, 197
Domestic Violence Month, 31
dowry violence, 5

effect on children, xv, 11–12,
69–72
Child Protective Services
(CPS), 71–72
families, xv, 20
removal from home,
69–72
effects on victims, 19–21
behavioral, 20
physical, 19, 20–21
elder abuse, 11
Eminem, 34–35
explaining abuse, 18
extreme risk protection
orders (ERPOs), 37–38

false accusations, 55
Family Violence Prevention
Fund, 176–177, 189,
297, 326
female abusers, 17, 58
female genital mutilation, 5,
7, 33, 261
feminism, 30–31, 89–92
first wave, 27
liberal feminists, 28–29
radical feminists, 28–29
second wave, xv, 28,
30–31
50 Shades of Grey, 18
Ford, Gerald, 30
forms of abuse, 4
fraternities, 15–16
futures without violence,
189–192

Gelles, Richard, 180
gender quotas, 7
gender-wage gap, 6–7
gendercide, 4–5
guns, 9–10, 37–38, 74–78,
78–80, 247–255
abusers, 78–80
arming victims, 74–78
Lautenberg Amendment,
79
Supreme Court cases,
247–255
Guyland: The Perilous World
Where Boys Become Men,
161

Half the Sky, 5, 165
Hayek, Selma, 150–153
healthcare, 92–95
costs, xv, 20–21
Docs v. Glocks, 94
documentation, 93
HITS scale, 93
preexisting condition,
94–95
screening, 92–93
training requirements, 95
hegemonic masculinity, 19, 90
history of domestic violence
movement, 37, 179, 228
European, 26
first wave feminists, 27–28
human rights, xv, 6, 23,
60, 67, 147, 157, 164,
178, 235

liberal feminists, 28–29
medieval times, 315–316
progressives, 28
Puritans, 26–27, 316
radical feminists, 28–29
homicides, 7, 8, 10, 19, 21,
    36, 38, 78, 83, 100,
    171, 173
  global, 7–8
  guns, 9–10, 74–78
  police officers, xv
  predicting, 8
honor killings, 5
Hughes, Francine, 153–155,
    182, 321

immigrants, 10, 226–234
INCITE!, 24, 33, 61–64, 88,
    97, 192–194
India, 7, 138, 166
International Violence
    against Women Act
    (IVAWA), 33, 157

Johns Hopkins University, 9

Katz, Jackson, 16, 35, 56,
    155–156, 326
Kidman, Nicole, 156–159, 185
Kilbourne, Jean, 18
Kimmel, Michael, 16, 35,
    159–162, 180
Kivel, Paul, 162–164
Kristof, Nicholas and
    WuDunn, Sheryll, 5, 6,
    164–166

laws, 14, 34–35, 37,
    319–330
Lesbian, Gay, Bisexual,
    Transgender and
    Questioning (LGBTQ),
    10, 324
Love Is Respect, 11

male victims, 17, 35, 56–58
Man Box, 169–170
Man Up, 147–149
marital rape, xvi, 5, 316, 321,
    322, 326
mass shootings, xv, 20, 79
media, 18, 35, 39, 63, 80–83,
    97, 143, 157, 159
  advertisements, 18
  books, 5, 8, 16, 22, 161,
    165
  films, 97
  glorification, 80–81
  magazines, 27, 30, 81,
    131, 134, 320
  news, 82–83
  television, 155, 165,
    181–182, 199
#MeToo movement, 7, 36,
    38–39, 40, 152, 155,
    157, 171, 260–261
military, 15–16, 125, 170,
    258, 296, 322, 326
Mentors in Violence
    Prevention (MVP), 25,
    35, 56, 155, 261
Move to End Violence, 173
Ms. Magazine, 30, 320

National Basketball Association (NBA), 54–55, 168

National Coalition against Domestic Violence (NCADV), 3, 56, 304, 322

National Domestic Violence Hotline, 53, 172, 174, 186, 289, 300, 305, 324

National Football League (NFL), 16, 53–54, 168, 196, 332

National Network to End Domestic Violence (NNEDV), 25, 32, 95, 172–173, 187, 194–197, 306, 309

National Organization for Women (NOW), 320

National Rifle Association (NRA), 37–38

Native Americans, 10, 32, 58–59, 149–150, 192–194, 226–234, 289, 331

NO MORE, 197–199, 307

No More Tears, 97, 128–129, 138–139, 200–201, 307

Outside the Lines, 51

Pakistan, 5, 129–137, 166, 200

patriarchy, 4, 28–29, 96, 104, 166–167
    politics, 7, 38, 315, 317

perspectives, 117–144
    Caribbean, 118–120
    counselor, 117, 140
    dating violence, 120–123, 123–125
    male victim, 125–128
    Pakistan, 129–137
    volunteer, 128–129

pet abuse, 15, 72–74, 290
    American Humane Society, 73–74
    Animal Welfare Institute, 72–73
    felony animal cruelty statutes, 73

Pizzey, Erin, 166–169, 320, 321

Pleck, Elizabeth, 26, 28

politicians, 25, 40, 80

Porter, Tony, 168–172

post-traumatic stress disorder (PTSD), 16, 92, 99, 125, 179, 182, 337

poverty, 7, 15, 33, 34, 165, 236

pregnancy, 11, 92, 242, 243, 258

prevention programs, 25–26, 36, 104, 226, 261
    CDC, 21, 32, 34, 56, 230, 329, 330
    coordinated community responses, 34, 204
    Domestic Violence Prevention Enhancement and

Leadership Through
Alliances Program, 34
Safe Dates, 25–26
profiles, 147–205
Puritans, xv, 26, 27, 316

rape, 6, 33
war, 6, 325
Rape, Abuse and Incest
National Network
(RAINN), 201–203
Reagan, Ronald, 30, 323, 324
refugees, 65–69, 130, 152
reproductive coercion, 11
revenge porn, 35
Ricart, Gladys, 83, 152, 295,
328
Rice, Ray, 16, 53, 332
Rihanna, 34
risk factors, 10–12
gender, 4
immigrants, 10
LGBTQ, 10
patriarchy, 4
pregnancy, 11
Roosevelt, Eleanor, 319
Rosenthal, Lynn, 172–174

Schechter, Susan, 174–177,
324
Scott v. Hart, 29
self-defense, 60, 63–64, 76,
100, 154, 161, 180
classes, 97–98
homicide, 171, 173

Sessions, Jeff, 67–69
sex trafficking, 5, 40, 165,
233–234
sexual violence, 201–203,
215–217
Simpson, O.J., 16, 31–32,
53, 81, 82
Smith, Andrea, 192–193
Society for the Prevention of
Cruelty, 28, 72, 318
stalking, 23, 24, 31, 32,
37, 56, 80, 203–204,
215–216
Stewart, Sir Patrick, 177–179
Straus, Murray, 179–181

Temperance Movement, 19,
27, 317
A Terrorist within the Family,
167
Thurman, Tracey, 30, 323
Title IX, 52, 199, 320
Tough Guise, 156
Trafficking Victims
Protection Act (TVPA),
32
Tribal Law and Justice Act,
32
Trump, Donald, 36–37
asylum and refugee status,
65–69
global gag rule, 36
government shutdown, 59
Kavanaugh, Brett, 36
Moore, Roy, 37

Porter, Rob, 36
sexual assault allegations,
    54, 152

UN Commission on the
    Status of Women, 319
UN Women, 33, 157
U.S. Department of Justice
    Office on Violence
    Against Women, 3,
    203–205
United States v. Castleman,
    250–252
United States v. Hayes, 247–250
United States v. Morrison, 32,
    328

victim services, 23–25
    against Women Act, 23–24
    shelters, 24, 95–97
Violence against Women Act
    (VAWA), xvi, 23–24,
    31–33, 37, 58–59, 192,
    226–234

violent crime, xv, 38, 58, 66,
    80, 90, 227, 229–230,
    233
Voisine v. United States,
    252–255

Walker, Lenore, 24, 98–100,
    181–183, 322
Weinstein, Harvey, 39–40,
    152, 157, 185
White House Council on
    Women and Girls, 173
Witherspoon, Reese, 64,
    183–186
women of color, 10, 29, 31,
    34, 60, 88, 162–163,
    176, 192–194, 219,
    298–299, 321
World Health Organization
    (WHO), 4, 11, 262,
    327
World Wrestling
    Entertainment (WWE),
    54

About the Author

Laura L. Finley, PhD, is professor of sociology and criminology at Barry University in Miami Shores, Florida. She earned her PhD from Western Michigan University in 2002. Dr. Finley is the author, editor, or coauthor of twenty-seven books and numerous journal articles and book chapters as well as coeditor of two book series. She is also involved with a number of organizations promoting peace, justice, and human rights. Dr. Finley serves as cochair of the board of directors of the Peace and Justice Studies Association and is a board member for No More Tears, a domestic violence organization; The Humanity Project, an anti-bullying group; and Floridians for Alternatives to the Death Penalty.